The Official
THEORY TEST
for Learner Drivers
in all Licence Categories

Questions and Answers

Fourth Edition

Written and compiled by the Road Safety Authority.

Acknowledgements

The Road Safety Authority would like to thank the following for their assistance:

National Roads Authority

An Garda Síochána

The Department of Transport

The Association for Children and Adults with Learning Disabilities

The National Adult Literacy Agency

Staff of the Road Safety Authority

Contents

Chapter 1 – see explanation on page vi

Chapter 2 – see explanation on page vi

Foreword

It is important that learner drivers have knowledge of the principles of safe driving as well as the practical ability to drive competently and responsibly.

The driver theory test is designed to help you to be a safe, courteous and informed driver. It is relevant to your preparation as a driver whether you are a young learner driver being tested on road signs, good judgement and perception, and allowing for vulnerable road users; or an aspiring professional truck or bus driver being tested on such matters as braking systems, use of the tachograph, or load distribution.

This book, along with the Rules of the Road will help you prepare for your theory test and ultimately for your driving career. The questions are set out in an easy to read style with the correct answers identified.

Introduction

Driver Theory Test

The driving theory test is designed to examine the driving knowledge of novice drivers. There are four separate theory tests dependent on the vehicle categories, which the person wishes to have on their Learner Permit *(formerly the provisional licence)* or driving licence. These are set out in the following table:

Theory Test Certificate Categories	Driving Licence/ *Learner Permit (*formerly the provisional licence) Categories
AM	A, A1 and M
BW	B, EB and W
C	C, C1, EC and EC1
D	D, D1, ED and ED1

This book contains the theory test question bank for each licence category.

The table overleaf provides details of the vehicles covered by each driving licence category:

Licence Categories

A   motorcycles

A1   motorcycles with an engine capacity not exceeding 125 cubic centimetres and with a power rating not exceeding 11 kilowatts

B   cars (and other vehicles) having a design gross weight not exceeding 3,500 kg. and having passenger accommodation for 8 (or fewer) persons. (Motorcycles, mopeds, work vehicles and land tractors are not included)

C   trucks (or other vehicles) having a design gross weight exceeding 3,500 kg. and having passenger accommodation for 8 (or fewer) persons. (Work vehicles and land tractors are not included)

C1   (trucks or other vehicles) in C having a design gross weight not exceeding 7,500 kg.

D   buses having passenger accommodation for more than 8 persons

D1   buses in D having accommodation for not more than 16 persons

M   mopeds

W   work vehicles and land tractors

The tests for categories B, C, C1, D, D1 and W also cover Learner Permits *(formerly provisional licences)* for these categories with a drawing vehicle without having to undergo a separate theory test.

Preparation

Make sure you are well prepared before applying for your test. Study carefully the material in this book in conjunction with the Rules of the Road booklet.

You can apply for a theory test to the Driver Theory Testing Service in one of the following ways:

Online at: **www.theorytest.ie**

By telephone:
For an **English language** test call: **1890 606 106**
For an **Irish language** test call: **1890 606 806**
Text phone call: **1890 616 216**

This is a LoCall service.

Please have to hand credit/debit card details and your PPS number (formally RSI number).

By post:
An application form may be obtained from any Motor Taxation office or **online** from: **www.theorytest.ie** and posted to:

The Driver Theory Testing Service,
PO Box 788
Togher,
Cork.

Further information including where and when theory tests are held can be obtained by contacting any of the above.

If you have any special needs or language requirements **please state this when applying in order that appropriate arrangements may be made.**

About this Book

Chapter I has three parts.

Part I

Covers questions which relate to the categories A, B, M and W.

These are questions common to motorcycles, cars, mopeds, tractors and work vehicles.

Part II

Covers questions which relate to the theory test category BW, i.e cars, tractors and work vehicles.

Part III

Covers questions which relate to the theory test category AM, i.e motorcycles and mopeds.

Chapter 2 contains three parts, this covers the progressive licence categories i.e. heavy goods vehicles and buses.

Part I

Covers questions common to both categories C and D, i.e heavy goods vehicles and buses.

Part II

Covers further questions solely for category C, i.e heavy goods vehicles.

Part III

Covers further questions solely for category D, i.e buses.

Please Note: *The theory test for categories C and D will also include questions from Chapter I.*

There are between three and six possible answers listed with each question.

The correct or **_most_** correct answer for each question is marked with an asterisk.

Some questions have multiple answers. Each correct answer is marked with an asterisk. If more than one answer is required, this will be indicated, e.g., Select 3 answers.

Different types of questions are used.

Questions may show a graphic of a road sign, road markings, traffic lights, hand signals or a particular driving situation, which require interpretation.

For Example:

Q.   **What does this sign mean?**

Ans.   (a) Give way to traffic coming from your right.
    (b) Other traffic must give way to you.
* (c) Stop your vehicle.
    (d) Stop, for school crossing ahead.

Q.   **Select 2 correct answers. There is a signed cycle track accompanied by a continuous white line, on your left-hand side.**

Ans. * (a) Only a cyclist may use it.
   * (b) Cyclists must use it.
    (c) You may drive in it to overtake a vehicle turning right.
    (d) You may drive in it provided you are not towing a trailer.
    (e) You may drive in it provided it is not being used by a cyclist.

Q. There are road works up ahead and earth-moving machinery is moving about. Which of the following should you avoid doing .....

Ans. * (a) switch on the headlights as a warning and carry on as heretofore.
    (b) be aware that there may be loose gravel on the road.
    (c) engage a lower gear.
    (d) be aware that the road surface may be uneven.
    (e) be aware that oncoming traffic may have to follow diversions at the scene.

Q. Select 3 answers. What dangers must you reckon with at tram stops like this?

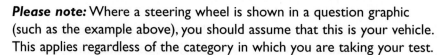

Ans. * (a) Pedestrians occasionally leave the traffic island without paying attention.
    * (b) Pedestrians may dash across the roadway to catch the tram.
    * (c) Motorists ahead may be forced to brake sharply owing to careless pedestrians.
    (d) Children will always be controlled by an adult.

Please note: Where a steering wheel is shown in a question graphic (such as the example above), you should assume that this is your vehicle. This applies regardless of the category in which you are taking your test.

Number of questions per test

Each test will contain 40 questions.

Providing you have spent sufficient time and effort in preparing for your test you should not find it difficult and you should pass.

The knowledge you have gained in passing this test should contribute to your safer driving throughout your driving career.

Summary of Chapter 1

PART II
CATEGORY BW

PART III
CATEGORY AM

Summary of Chapter 2

PART III
CATEGORY D

CHAPTER I

PART I

CATEGORIES A, B, M and W

ROAD SIGNS, MARKINGS AND TRAFFIC REGULATIONS

REGULATORY SIGNS

Q. **What does this sign mean?**

ABMW0001

Ans.   (a) Give way to traffic coming from your right.

      (b) Other traffic must give way to you.

  * (c) Stop your vehicle.

      (d) Stop, for school crossing ahead.

Q. **What should you do when this sign is accompanied by a white stop line on the road. You should stop .....**

ABMW0002

Ans.   (a) when you have passed the line.

  * (b) at the line.

      (c) only if there is traffic on the major road.

      (d) no more than one car length past the line.

Q. Where this sign is not
ABMW0003 accompanied by a white line on
the road, you should stop .....

Ans. (a) only when having passed the
sign.
* (b) at the sign.
(c) only if there is traffic at the
junction.
(d) no more than one car length
past the sign.

Q. What does this sign mean?
ABMW0004

Ans. (a) Slow down and stop for
pedestrians.
(b) Yield to all heavy goods
vehicles.
(c) Yield to traffic coming from
your right.
* (d) Yield to traffic on the major
road.

Q. What does this sign mean?
ABMW0005

Ans. (a) Yield to trucks and buses only.
(b) Yield to traffic coming from the
right.
* (c) Yield to traffic on the major
road.
(d) All vehicles, except
motorcycles, must yield.

Q. **What does this sign mean?**

ABMW0006

Ans.
    (a) One way street ahead.
    (b) Parking permitted from this point on.
* (c) Straight ahead only.
    (d) Overtaking lane ahead.

Q. **What does this sign mean?**

ABMW0007

Ans. * (a) Turn left only.
       (b) Motorway to the left.
       (c) Traffic from the right has priority.
       (d) Diversion ahead to the left.

Q. **What does this sign mean?**

ABMW0008

Ans.
    (a) Overtake only on the right.
* (b) Turn right only.
    (c) Major road joining from the left.
    (d) Diversion ahead to the right.

Q. **What does this sign mean?**

ABMW0009

Ans.
    (a) Diversion to the left ahead.
    (b) Parking area to the left ahead.
* (c) Turn left ahead.
    (d) One-way traffic to the left ahead.

Q. **What does this sign mean?**

ABMW0010

Ans.
    (a) Diversion to the right ahead.
* (b) Turn right ahead.
    (c) Sharp bend ahead.
    (d) One-way traffic to the right ahead.

Q. What does this sign mean?

ABMW0011

Ans. * (a) Keep left.
  (b) Roundabout ahead.
  (c) Sharp bend to the left ahead.
  (d) Steep decline ahead to the left.

Q. What does this sign mean?

ABMW0012

Ans. * (a) Keep right.
  (b) Turn back.
  (c) Traffic crossing from the left.
  (d) Steep decline ahead to the right.

Q. What does this sign mean?

ABMW0013

Ans. (a) One-way street.
  (b) Dual-carriageway ahead.
  * (c) Pass either side.
  (d) Two way traffic ahead.

Q. What does this sign mean?

ABMW0014

Ans. (a) Cul-de-sac ahead.
  (b) Parking not allowed ahead.
  * (c) No entry.
  (d) No hard shoulder ahead.

Q. What does this sign mean?

ABMW0015

Ans. * (a) No right turn.
  (b) Turn right if there is no oncoming traffic.
  (c) Yield to other traffic when turning right.
  (d) No hard shoulder to the right.

Q. What does this sign mean?

Ans. * (a) No right turn.
(b) Turn right.
(c) Dangerous bend to the right ahead.
(d) No hard shoulder to the right.

Q. What does this sign mean?

Ans. (a) Cul-de-sac to the left.
(b) Roundabout ahead with no left exit.
* (c) No left turn.
(d) No hard shoulder to the left.

Q. What does this sign mean?

Ans. (a) Slippery road ahead.
* (b) 'U'-turn not permitted.
(c) Reversing not permitted.
(d) Two-way traffic prohibited.

Q. What does this sign mean?

Ans. (a) Motorway continues for 30 kilometres.
(b) Distance to junction is 30 metres.
(c) Parking not allowed for more than 30 minutes.
* (d) Maximum speed is 30 km/h.

Q. What does this sign mean?

ABMW0020

Ans. (a) Motorway continues for 50 kilometres.
* (b) Maximum speed is 50 km/h.
(c) Minimum speed is 50 km/h.
(d) Minimum distance between vehicles is 50 metres.

Q. What does this sign mean?

ABMW0021

Ans. * (a) Maximum speed is 60 km/h.
(b) Height restriction is 60 metres.
(c) Distance to junction is 60 metres.
(d) Parking not allowed for more than 60 minutes.

Q. What does this sign mean?

ABMW0022

Ans. (a) 80 metres to end of motorway.
(b) 80 metres to start of motorway.
* (c) Maximum speed is 80 km/h.
(d) Maximum permitted weight is 80 tonnes.

Q. What does this sign mean?

ABMW0023

Ans. (a) Motorway continues for 100 kilometres.
(b) Clearway ahead at 100 metres.
(c) Minimum speed is 100 km/h.
* (d) Maximum speed is 100 km/h.

Q. What does this sign mean?

ABMW0024

Ans.
   (a) Motorway continues for 120 kilometres.
   (b) Motorway exit ahead at 120 metres.
   (c) Traffic merging at 120 metres ahead.
 * (d) Maximum speed is 120 km/h.

Q. What do these signs together mean?

ABMW0025

Ans. * (a) Parking permitted at times shown.
   (b) Parking prohibited at times shown.
   (c) Parking reserved for people with disabilities.
   (d) Maximum parking for 1 hour during times shown.

Q. What does this sign mean?

ABMW0026

Ans.
   (a) Parking permitted.
 * (b) Parking prohibited.
   (c) Private vehicles prohibited.
   (d) Public service vehicles prohibited.

Q. What do these signs together mean?

ABMW0027

Ans.

(a) Crossroads ahead with roads of equal importance.

(b) Pedestrianised street - no access for vehicles.

* (c) Clearway - no stopping or parking during the times shown.

(d) Road closed during the times shown.

Luan - Aoine
0700 - 0930
MON. - FRI.

Q. What does this sign mean?

ABMW0028

Ans. * (a) Disc parking operates during the times shown.

(b) Parking is allowed during the hours shown.

(c) Parking is prohibited during the hours shown.

(d) Disc parking operates except during the hours shown.

Diosca-Pháirceail
1 uair
DISC PARKING
1 hour
Luan - Sath.
08.30
TO
18.30
MON.- SAT.

Q. What does this sign mean?

ABMW0029

Ans.

(a) You may park when the rank is empty.

(b) You may pick up or set down passengers.

* (c) Appointed stand for taxis.

(d) Only taxis may turn right or left ahead.

Q. What do these signs together mean?

ABMW0030

Ans.
    (a) Bicycle race track.
* (b) Start of cycle track.
    (c) Track reserved for motorcyclists.
    (d) Cyclists must dismount ahead.

Q. What does this sign mean?

ABMW0031

Ans.
    (a) Area reserved for children learning to ride bicycles.
    (b) Cyclists must dismount and walk.
* (c) Shared cycle/pedestrian track.
    (d) Parking area for cyclists ahead.

Q. What does this sign mean?

ABMW0032

Ans.
    (a) No access. Pedestrianised street ahead.
* (b) Stop, for school warden.
    (c) Pedestrian crossing ahead.
    (d) No access area for children.

Q. What do these signs together mean?

ABMW0033

Ans.
    (a) Parking not allowed during times shown.
    (b) Access for buses and taxis only during times shown.
* (c) Pedestrianised street ahead - traffic not allowed except during times shown.
    (d) Roundabout ahead - no stopping or parking during times shown.

Q. **What does this sign mean?**

Ans. * (a) Maximum permitted weight is 3 tonnes.
    (b) 3 axled vehicles not permitted.
    (c) Minimum permitted weight is 3 tonnes.
    (d) Only 3 axled vehicles are permitted.

Q. **What does this sign mean?**

Ans. (a) Vehicles weighing more than 10 tonnes per axle not permitted.
    (b) Minimum permitted weight is 10 tonnes.
    (c) Vehicles exceeding 10 metres in length are not permitted.
* (d) Vehicles weight restriction is 10 tonnes.

Q. **What does this sign mean?**

Ans. (a) Racing track ahead.
    (b) Car transporter unloading area.
* (c) Axle weight restriction of 4 tonnes.
    (d) Minimum permitted weight is 4 tonnes.

Q. **What does this sign mean?**

ABMW0037

Ans.   (a) Maximum permitted weight of vehicle is figure indicated.

      (b) Maximum permitted length of vehicle is figure indicated.

* (c) Maximum permitted height of vehicle is figure indicated.

      (d) Vehicles exceeding length measurements must have reflective strips.

Q. **What does this sign mean?**

ABMW0038

Ans. * (a) Parking of vehicles exceeding the weight shown is not allowed.

      (b) Passing other traffic that exceeds the weight shown is prohibited.

      (c) Parking in loading area is not allowed.

      (d) Parking of vehicles under the weight shown is not allowed.

Q. **What does this sign mean?**

ABMW0039

Ans.   (a) End of dual carriageway.

* (b) No overtaking.

      (c) Double parking not allowed.

      (d) No stopping/parking on the right.

Q. What do these signs together mean?

ABMW0040

Ans.

(a) Outside the times indicated, only buses and, cyclists may use the lane.

(b) Only cyclists and buses are allowed to use the lane during the hours indicated.

(c) Only buses and cyclists may park during the times indicated.

* (d) Only buses, cyclists and taxis are allowed to use the lane during the hours indicated.

Q. What does this sign mean?

ABMW0041

Ans.

(a) Only buses and cyclists may park.

(b) Only buses and cyclists may use the lane.

* (c) 'With-flow' bus lane ahead on your left.

(d) Cyclists and buses must turn left.

Q. What does this sign mean?

ABMW0042

Ans. * (a) 'With-flow' bus lane ahead.

(b) Parking for buses and cyclists on the left.

(c) Cycle-track ahead may be crossed by buses only.

(d) Cyclists and buses not allowed ahead.

Q. ABMW0043 **What does this sign mean?**

Ans. * (a) Bus lane ahead on the right.
(b) Cyclists must give way to buses ahead.
(c) Buses must give way to cyclists ahead.
(d) Buses must give way to other traffic ahead.

Q. ABMW0044 **What does this sign mean?**

Ans. (a) Buses may block cyclists from your view.
(b) Bus and cycle parking ahead.
* (c) With-flow bus lane on the right.
(d) Contra flow bus lane ahead.

Q. ABMW0045 **What does this sign mean?**

Ans. (a) Cycle track may be crossed by buses.
(b) 'With-flow' bus lane on the right.
* (c) Contra-flow bus lane ahead.
(d) Bus and cycle parking ahead.

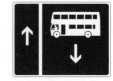

Q. ABMW0046 **What does this sign mean?**

Ans. (a) Double deck buses only.
* (b) Contra-flow bus lane ahead.
(c) Two-way traffic system ahead.
(d) 'With-flow' bus lane ahead.

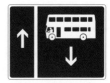

Q. **What does this sign mean?**

ABMW0047

Ans. * (a) Buses will approach from the right.
(b) Buses will proceed to the right.
(c) Passengers will queue to the right.
(d) Bus station is ahead on the right side.

Q. **What does this sign mean?**

ABMW0048

Ans. * (a) Buses will approach from the left.
(b) Buses will proceed to the left.
(c) Passengers will queue to the left.
(d) Bus station is ahead on the left side.

Q. **What does this sign mean?**

ABMW0049

Ans. (a) Bus lane ahead offside.
(b) With-flow bus lane ahead.
(c) Access for buses only.
* (d) Tram lane ahead.

Q. **What does this sign mean?**

ABMW0050

Ans. (a) Parking only inside the white line.
(b) 'With-flow' bus lane ahead.
(c) Fire station ahead.
* (d) Tram lane, be aware of approaching trams.

WARNING SIGNS

Q.

ABMW0051

What does this sign mean?

Ans. * (a) Junction ahead with roads of
lesser importance.
(b) Junction ahead with roads of
greater importance.
(c) Junction ahead with roads of
equal importance.
(d) Series of dangerous corners
ahead.

Q.

ABMW0052

What does this sign mean?

Ans. (a) You must stop at the junction
ahead.
* (b) Main road bears to the left.
(c) Main road bears to the right.
(d) Heavy vehicles must go left.

Q.

ABMW0053

What does this sign mean?

Ans. (a) Traffic-calming ramps ahead.
(b) Cul-de-sacs to both left and
right.
* (c) Staggered crossroads ahead.
(d) Roads closed ahead to both left
and right.

Q. **What does this sign mean?**

ABMW0054

Ans.
    (a) Clearway - no stopping or parking.
* (b) Crossroads ahead with roads of equal importance.
    (c) Pedestrianised street - no vehicles allowed.
    (d) Crossroads ahead with roads of lesser importance.

Q. **What does this sign mean?**

ABMW0055

Ans.
    (a) No entry.
    (b) Overhead electric cables ahead.
* (c) Junction ahead with roads of equal importance.
    (d) Flyover ahead.

Q. **What does this sign mean?**

ABMW0056

Ans.
    (a) Major road ahead.
    (b) Railway crossing ahead.
* (c) Junction ahead with roads of equal importance.
    (d) End of dual-carriageway.

Q. **What does this sign mean?**

ABMW0057

Ans. * (a) Junction ahead with roads of equal importance.
    (b) Stop and yield to traffic ahead.
    (c) Traffic island ahead, pass either side.
    (d) Stay to the left ahead - oncoming traffic from the right.

Q. **What does this sign mean?**

ABMW0058

Ans. * (a) Major road ahead.
  (b) T-junction ahead with road of greater importance.
  (c) Road passing under a bridge ahead.
  (d) Flyover ahead.

Q. **What does this sign mean?**

ABMW0059

Ans. (a) Cul-de-sac to the right.
  * (b) Junction ahead with a road of major importance.
  (c) Junction ahead with a road of minor importance.
  (d) Toll-roads ahead.

Q. **What does this sign mean?**

ABMW0060

Ans. (a) Level crossing ahead guarded by gates.
  * (b) Dual-carriageway ahead.
  (c) Two-way traffic ahead.
  (d) Unguarded level crossing ahead.

Q. **What does this sign mean?**

ABMW0061

Ans. (a) Low bridge ahead.
  (b) Speed ramps ahead.
  * (c) T-junction with dual-carriage way ahead.
  (d) Cul-de-sac ahead.

Q. What does this sign mean?

Ans. * (a) Traffic merging from the left.
(b) Traffic from the left has priority.
(c) Road fencing in progress ahead.
(d) Junction ahead with road of minor importance.

Q. What does this sign mean?

Ans. (a) Road narrows briefly.
* (b) Traffic merging/diverging ahead.
(c) Clearway at junction ahead.
(d) Yield to merging/diverging traffic.

Q. What does this sign mean?

Ans. (a) One-way street ahead.
(b) 'U'-turn prohibited ahead.
** (c) Roundabout ahead.
(d) 'U'-turn permitted ahead.

Q. What does this sign mean?

Ans. * (a) Mini-roundabout ahead.
(b) 'U'-turn permitted ahead.
(c) Roadworks ahead, diversion in operation.
(d) 'U'-turn prohibited ahead.

Q. What does this sign mean?

Ans. (a) Dangerous bend ahead.
(b) One-way street ahead.
* (c) Dangerous corner ahead.
(d) Junction to the left ahead.

Q. **What does this sign mean?**

ABMW0067

Ans. (a) Turn left.
   (b) No left turn.
   (c) Dangerous corner ahead.
* (d) Dangerous bend ahead.

Q. **What does this sign mean?**

ABMW0068

Ans. (a) Overhead electric cables.
   (b) Temporary surface ahead, keep left.
* (c) Series of dangerous corners ahead.
   (d) Slippery road ahead.

Q. **What does this sign mean?**

ABMW0069

Ans. (a) Slippery road ahead.
   (b) Diversion ahead.
* (c) Series of dangerous bends ahead.
   (d) Steep climb ahead.

Q. **What does this sign mean?**

ABMW0070

Ans. (a) Traffic from the left has priority.
* (b) Sharp change of direction ahead.
   (c) Road closed - you must turn back.
   (d) Series of speed ramps ahead.

Q. **What does this sign mean?**

ABMW0071

Ans.
    (a) You must overtake on the right only.
    (b) Left-hand lane has an uneven surface.
  * (c) Road narrows on one side.
    (d) Merging traffic from the left.

Q. **What does this sign mean?**

ABMW0072

Ans.
    (a) Dual-carriageway ahead.
    (b) Railway crossing ahead.
  * (c) Road narrows on both sides.
    (d) Tunnel ahead.

Q. **What does this sign mean?**

ABMW0073

Ans. * (a) Road divides ahead.
    (b) Two lanes of oncoming traffic merge ahead.
    (c) Lay-by ahead.
    (d) Roundabout ahead.

Q. **What does this sign mean?**

ABMW0074

Ans.
    (a) Tunnel ahead.
    (b) Oncoming traffic has priority.
  * (c) Dual-carriageway ends.
    (d) Road narrows ahead.

Q. **What does this sign mean?**

ABMW0075

Ans.
    (a) One-way street.
    (b) Dual-carriageway ahead.
  * (c) Two-way traffic ahead.
    (d) Traffic may not stop.

Q. What does this sign mean?

ABMW0076

Ans.
    (a) River or unprotected quay ahead.
  * (b) Steep descent ahead.
    (c) Sharp climb ahead.
    (d) Uneven road surface to the right.

Q. What does this sign mean?

ABMW0077

Ans. * (a) Steep ascent ahead.
    (b) Hump-backed bridge ahead.
    (c) Only ascending traffic ahead.
    (d) Uneven road surface to the left.

Q. What does this sign mean?

ABMW0078

Ans.
    (a) Restricted weight limit for road segment indicated.
  * (b) Restricted headroom up ahead.
    (c) Restricted road width ahead.
    (d) Road narrows ahead, maximum length of vehicle is as indicated.

Q. What does this sign mean?

ABMW0079

Ans. * (a) Overhead electric cables.
    (b) Sharp corners ahead.
    (c) Radio transmission mast ahead.
    (d) Crosswinds ahead.

Q. What does this sign mean?

ABMW0080

Ans.
    (a) Major roadworks ahead.
* (b) Level crossing ahead unguarded by gates or barriers.
    (c) Machinery crossing ahead.
    (d) End of major roadworks.

Q. What does this sign mean?

ABMW0081

Ans.
* (a) Level crossing ahead guarded by gates or barriers.
    (b) Farm machinery crossing ahead.
    (c) Private grounds - no entry.
    (d) Road fencing ahead.

Q. What does this sign mean?

ABMW0082

Ans.
    (a) Railway station ahead.
* (b) Level crossing ahead with lights and barriers.
    (c) Railway bridge ahead.
    (d) Do not stop on railway crossing.

Q. What does this sign mean?

ABMW0083

Ans.
    (a) You must stop when you see brake-lights ahead.
    (b) Emerging vehicles have priority. You must stop if necessary.
* (c) You must stop when red lights show.
    (d) Stop, and wait for green light before proceeding.

STOP
When
Red Lights
Show

STOP
nuair a lasann na soilse dearga

Q. What does this sign mean?

ABMW0084

Ans. * (a) Automatic level crossing ahead.
       (b) Bridge may be raised ahead.
       (c) Traffic lights may be activated by passing traffic.
       (d) Pelican crossing ahead.

Q. What does this sign mean?

ABMW0085

Ans. (a) Road reflective studs ahead.
      (b) Series of bumps or hollows ahead.
  * (c) Sharp rise in the road ahead (e.g. hump-back bridge).
      (d) Road falls from centre to left and right.

Q. What does this sign mean?

ABMW0086

Ans. (a) Low bridge ahead.
  * (b) Sharp depression ahead.
      (c) Road divides ahead - pass left or right.
      (d) Road damage ahead.

Q. What does this sign mean?

ABMW0087

Ans. (a) Steep hills ahead.
  * (b) Series of bumps or hollows ahead.
      (c) Industrial estate ahead.
      (d) Rumble strips ahead.

Q. **What does this sign mean?**

ABMW0088

Ans.
    (a) Series of bends ahead.
* (b) Slippery stretch of road ahead.
    (c) Steep hill ahead.
    (d) Crosswinds ahead.

Q. **What does this sign mean?**

ABMW0089

Ans. * (a) Quay, canal, or river ahead
       without barrier.
    (b) Steep descent ahead.
    (c) Slippery road ahead.
    (d) Road liable to flooding.

Q. **What does this sign mean?**

ABMW0090

Ans.
    (a) Railway level crossing ahead.
* (b) Traffic signals ahead.
    (c) Advance warning for school
       children crossing ahead.
    (d) Stop at pedestrian crossing.

Q. **What does this sign mean?**

ABMW0091

Ans. * (a) School ahead.
    (b) Children's play area ahead.
    (c) Pedestrian crossing ahead -
       prepare to stop.
    (d) Recreation area ahead.

Q.
ABMW0092

What does this sign mean?

Ans.
    (a) Picnic area ahead.
    (b) Level crossing ahead with pedestrian walkway.
* (c) School children crossing ahead.
    (d) Playground ahead.

Q.
ABMW0093

What does this sign mean?

Ans.
    (a) School playground ahead.
    (b) Children's play area ahead.
* (c) School children crossing ahead.
    (d) Railway crossing ahead.

Q.
ABMW0094

What do these signs together mean?

Ans. * (a) Beware of children crossing.
    (b) People jogging have right of way.
    (c) Loose chippings ahead on the road.
    (d) Slippery road, children may fall.

Q.
ABMW0095

What does this sign mean?

Ans. * (a) Possibility of riders on horseback ahead.
    (b) Entrance to horse riding school.
    (c) Riding path - no vehicles allowed.
    (d) Racecourse ahead.

Q. **What does this sign mean?**

ABMW0096

Ans. * (a) Possibility of cattle or farm
             animals ahead.
         (b) Livestock mart ahead.
         (c) Veterinary station ahead.
         (d) Cattle grid ahead.

Q. **What does this sign mean?**

ABMW0097

Ans. (a) Abattoir ahead.
     * (b) Possibility of sheep ahead.
         (c) Sheep market ahead.
         (d) No animals permitted ahead.

Q. **What does this sign mean?**

ABMW0098

Ans. (a) Stag-hunting ahead.
         (b) Wildlife reserve - no stopping.
     * (c) Possibility of deer or wild
             animals up ahead.
         (d) No hunting ahead.

Q. **What does this sign mean?**

ABMW0099

Ans. (a) Airport ahead.
     * (b) Crosswinds.
         (c) Nature reserve. Do not litter.
         (d) Golf course ahead.

Q. **What does this sign mean?**

ABMW0100

Ans. * (a) Pedestrian crossing ahead.
         (b) Lane reserved for pedestrians.
         (c) Beware of pedestrians at night.
         (d) Jogging lane ahead.

Q. What does this sign mean?

ABMW0101

Ans.
    (a) Cathedral or church ahead.
    (b) Historic site ahead.
* (c) Tunnel ahead.
    (d) Turning bay for heavy goods vehicles ahead.

Q. What does this sign mean?

ABMW0102

Ans. * (a) Danger of falling rocks ahead.
    (b) Rugged coast ahead.
    (c) Possibility of falling leaves.
    (d) Road uneven, beware of unsecured loads on high-sided vehicles.

Q. What does this sign mean?

ABMW0103

Ans.
    (a) Airport ahead.
* (b) Possibility of low flying aircraft.
    (c) Direction of prevailing wind.
    (d) Traffic merging/diverging ahead.

Q. What does this sign mean?

ABMW0104

Ans.
    (a) You may not overtake.
    (b) You may not park.
* (c) You must drive on the left-hand side.
    (d) You must maintain sufficient distance from the vehicle ahead of you.

Q. What does this sign mean?

ABMW0105

Ans.
   (a) Level crossing ahead.
   (b) Railway station.
* (c) Tramway crossing ahead.
   (d) Overhead electric cables.

Q. What does this sign mean?
Look both ways because of .....

ABMW0106

Ans.
   (a) railway station ahead.
* (b) tramway crossing ahead.
   (c) unguarded level crossing ahead.
   (d) guarded level crossing ahead.

Féach gach treo
LOOK BOTH WAYS

Q. What does this sign mean?

ABMW0107

Ans.
* (a) Tram track, cyclists beware.
   (b) Cyclists and trams only ahead.
   (c) Trams may block cyclists from your view.
   (d) Cycle track ahead.

Tramrian
TRAM TRACK

MOTORWAY SIGNS

Q. Where you see this sign which of the following is permitted on the road?

ABMW0108

Ans.
   (a) Learner drivers.
* (b) Motorhomes.
   (c) Slow vehicles.
   (d) Pedestrians, animals, or cyclists allowed.

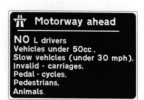

Motorway ahead

NO L drivers
Vehicles under 50cc.,
Slow vehicles (under 30 mph).
Invalid - carriages,
Pedal - cycles,
Pedestrians,
Animals.

Q.
ABMW0109

What does this sign mean?

Ans.
    (a) Toll-bridge ahead.
* (b) Entry to motorway.
    (c) Low bridge ahead.
    (d) End to motorway.

Q.
ABMW0110

What does this sign mean?

Ans.
    (a) No overtaking for 500 metres.
* (b) Motorway ends 500 metres ahead.
    (c) Low bridge 500 metres ahead.
    (d) Bridge repair 500 metres ahead.

Q.
ABMW0111

What does this sign mean?

Ans.
    (a) Crossing onto the opposite carriageway is not allowed.
    (b) No overtaking.
* (c) End of motorway.
    (d) Stopping under bridge is not allowed.

Q.
ABMW0112

What does this sign mean?

Ans.
    (a) Three lanes ahead.
    (b) Crossing traffic ahead.
* (c) Three hundred metres to the next exit.
    (d) Steep climb up ahead for 3 kilometres.

Q. **What does this sign mean?**

ABMW0113

Ans. (a) Dual-carriageway crossing ahead.

* (b) Two hundred metres to the next exit.

(c) Steep climb ahead for 2 kilometres.

(d) Sharp corner to left.

Q. **What does this sign mean?**

ABMW0114

Ans. * (a) One hundred metres to the next exit.

(b) Single carriageway ahead.

(c) Low bridge ahead.

(d) Steep climb ahead for 1 kilometre.

ROAD SIGNS

Q. **What does this sign mean?**

ABMW0115

Ans. (a) Tree planting ahead.

* (b) Roadworks ahead.

(c) Building site ahead.

(d) Mud slide ahead.

Q. **What does this sign mean?**

ABMW0116

Ans. (a) Series of steep hills ahead.

* (b) Uneven surface ahead.

(c) Industrial estate ahead.

(d) Pipe laying ahead.

Q.

ABMW0117

What does this sign mean?

Ans.

    (a) Series of bends ahead.

* (b) Slippery stretch of road ahead.

    (c) Steep hill ahead.

    (d) Crosswinds ahead.

Q.

ABMW0118

What does this sign mean?

Ans.

    (a) You must overtake on the right only.

    (b) Left-hand lane has an uneven surface.

* (c) Road narrows from left-hand side.

    (d) Slow lane ends ahead.

Q.

ABMW0119

What does this sign mean?

Ans.

    (a) You must overtake on the right only.

    (b) Right-hand lane has an uneven surface.

* (c) Road narrows from right-hand side.

    (d) Overtaking lane ends ahead.

Q.

ABMW0120

What does this sign mean?

Ans.

    (a) Dual-carriageway ahead.

    (b) Railway crossing ahead.

* (c) Road narrows ahead.

    (d) Tunnel ahead.

Q. **What does this sign mean?**
ABMW0121

Ans.
    (a) Football stadium ahead.
    (b) Litter is not allowed.
   * (c) Manual traffic control ahead.
    (d) Hitch-hiking permitted.

Q. **What does this sign mean?**
ABMW0122

Ans.
    (a) Railway crossing ahead.
   * (b) Traffic lights ahead.
    (c) School children crossing ahead.
    (d) Roundabout with traffic lights ahead.

Q. **What does this sign mean?**
ABMW0123

Ans.
    (a) One-way street.
    (b) Dual-carriageway ahead.
   * (c) Two-way traffic.
    (d) Traffic may not stop.

Q. **What does this sign mean?**
ABMW0124

Ans.
    (a) No overtaking.
   * (b) Left-hand lane closed ahead.
    (c) Stop sign ahead.
    (d) Overtaking permitted on right only.

Q. **What does this sign mean?**
ABMW0125

Ans.
    (a) No left turn ahead.
    (b) Do not drive on the hard shoulder.
   * (c) Left-hand lane closed ahead.
    (d) Overtaking permitted, except in left lane.

Q. What does this sign mean?

Ans.   (a) Dual-carriageway ahead.
    * (b) Middle lane closed ahead.
        (c) 'T'-junction ahead.
        (d) No stopping, except in middle lane.

Q. What does this sign mean?

Ans.   (a) Corner ahead on right-hand lane.
    * (b) Right-hand lane closed ahead.
        (c) End of dual-carriageway ahead.
        (d) No stopping, except in right-hand lane.

Q. What does this sign mean?

Ans.   (a) Faster traffic should use the right-hand lanes.
        (b) Overtake only on the right.
    * (c) Left-hand lane closed ahead.
        (d) Dangerous bends in the right-hand lane.

Q. What does this sign mean?

Ans.   (a) Dual-carriageway slip lane ahead.
    * (b) Middle lane closed ahead.
        (c) Uneven surface ahead in middle lane.
        (d) Dangerous bend in the far right-hand lanes.

Q. What does this sign mean?

ABMW0130

Ans.
    (a) 'T'-junction ahead.
    (b) Major road ahead.
   * (c) No through road.
    (d) Minor road ahead.

Q. What does this sign mean?

ABMW0131

Ans. * (a) Pedestrians keep right.
    (b) Do not drive on the footpath.
    (c) Shopping mall on the right.
    (d) Pedestrianised street to the right.

Q. At road works, when a flagman displays this sign, you should .....

ABMW0132

Ans.
    (a) proceed with hazard warning lights on.
    (b) only proceed when flagman beckons you on.
   * (c) proceed with caution.
    (d) proceed using hand signals only.

Q. At road works, when a flagman displays this sign, you should .....

ABMW0133

Ans.
    (a) make a detour.
   * (b) stop.
    (c) only proceed if road is clear ahead.
    (d) stop only if faced by oncoming traffic.

Q. ABMW0134 **What do these signs together mean?**

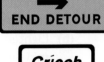

Ans.   (a) End of road.
        (b) End of speed limit.
  *   (c) End of detour.
        (d) End of road works.

Q. ABMW0135 **What does this sign mean?**

Ans. *   (a) Crossover to left-hand side.
        (b) Slow lane ahead for heavy traffic.
        (c) Lay-by ahead.
        (d) Bend in the road to the left ahead.

Q. ABMW0136 **What does this sign mean?**

Ans.   (a) End of "no overtaking" zone.
        (b) Traffic calming measures ahead.
  *   (c) Traffic crossover ahead due to roadworks.
        (d) Bend in the road to the right ahead.

Q. ABMW0137 **What does this sign mean?**

Ans. *   (a) Traffic flow divides at road works.
        (b) Heavy vehicles have priority.
        (c) Lay-by ahead.
        (d) Dual-carriageway ahead.

Q. **What does this sign mean?**

ABMW0138

Ans. * (a) End of traffic separation at roadworks.
(b) Lighter vehicles should use the middle lane.
(c) Beware of vehicles with a wide load.
(d) Dual-carriageway ends ahead.

Q. **This sign means that work is taking place at tram lines so .....**

ABMW0139

Ans. (a) entry is controlled by lights.
(b) entry is controlled by a flagman.
* (c) proceed with caution.
(d) be aware of raised tram tracks ahead.

HAND SIGNALS

Q. **What does this hand signal mean?**

ABMW0140

Ans. (a) The cyclist intends to slow down.
(b) The cyclist intends to turn left.
* (c) The cyclist intends to move out or to turn right.
(d) The cyclist intends to stop.

Q.

ABMW0141

What does this hand signal mean?

Ans.

    (a) The cyclist intends to move out or to turn right.

*   (b) The cyclist intends to slow down or stop.

    (c) The cyclist is signalling following traffic to overtake.

    (d) The cyclist intends to turn left.

Q.

ABMW0142

What does this hand signal mean?

Ans. * (a) The cyclist intends to go straight on.

    (b) The cyclist is turning to her left.

    (c) The cyclist is yielding right of way to you.

    (d) The cyclist is preparing to stop.

Q.

ABMW0143

What does this hand signal mean?

Ans. * (a) The cyclist intends to turn left.

    (b) The cyclist intends to overtake.

    (c) The cyclist intends to dismount.

    (d) The cyclist intends to stop.

Q.
ABMW0144
What does this hand signal mean?

Ans. * (a) The cyclist intends to turn right.
  (b) The cyclist intends to slow down.
  (c) The cyclist intends to stop for pedestrians.
  (d) The cyclist intends to turn to her left.

Q.
ABMW0145
What does this hand signal mean?

Ans. (a) The cyclist intends to stop.
  (b) The cyclist intends to cross the road.
 * (c) The cyclist intends to turn left.
  (d) The cyclist is signalling you to stop.

Q.
ABMW0146
What does this hand signal mean?

Ans. * (a) The driver intends to turn left.
  (b) The driver intends to turn right.
  (c) The driver intends to slow down or stop.
  (d) The driver intends to yield to oncoming traffic.

Q.
ABMW0147

What does this hand signal mean?

Ans.
    (a) The driver intends to turn left.
    (b) The driver intends to do a 'U'-turn.
* (c) The driver intends to move out or turn right.
    (d) The driver intends to stop.

Q.
ABMW0148

What does this hand signal mean?

Ans.
    (a) The driver intends to turn left.
* (b) The driver intends to slow down or stop.
    (c) The driver intends to turn right.
    (d) The driver intends to begin a 'U'-turn.

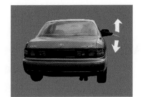

Q.
ABMW0149

What does this hand signal mean?

Ans.
    (a) The driver intends to perform a reverse manoeuvre.
    (b) The driver is telling you to turn right.
* (c) The driver intends to turn left.
    (d) The driver is indicating an emergency situation.

Q. ABMW0150 **What does this hand signal mean?**

Ans.

    (a) The driver is telling other drivers to slow down.

  * (b) The driver intends to turn right.

    (c) The driver intends to slow down or stop.

    (d) The driver intends to perform a reverse manoeuvre.

Q. ABMW0151 **What does this hand signal mean?**

Ans. * (a) The driver intends to move straight ahead.

    (b) The driver intends to reverse.

    (c) The driver is signalling you to proceed.

    (d) The driver intends to stop.

GARDA SIGNALS

Q. ABMW0152 **What does this Garda signal mean?**

Ans. * (a) Halt if approaching from the front.

    (b) Proceed if approaching from the front.

    (c) Halt if approaching from behind.

    (d) Proceed if approaching from behind.

Q. ABMW0153 **What does this Garda signal mean?**

Ans.   (a) Turn left.
    * (b) Halt if approaching from behind.
    (c) Halt if approaching from front.
    (d) Turn right.

Q. ABMW0154 **What does this Garda signal mean?**

Ans. * (a) Halt if approaching from either front or rear.
    (b) Proceed if approaching from the front.
    (c) Turn left.
    (d) Turn right.

Q. ABMW0155 **What does this Garda signal mean?**

Ans.   (a) You must not proceed to the left.
    (b) He is beckoning on traffic approaching from the front.
   * (c) He is beckoning on traffic approaching from either side.
    (d) You must not proceed to the right.

Q.
ABMW0156
This Garda signal means beckon on traffic approaching from the .....

Ans. * (a) front.
(b) right.
(c) behind and halts from the front.
(d) left.

ROAD MARKINGS

Q.
ABMW0157
What does this road marking mean?

Ans. (a) Cycle lane ahead.
(b) Traffic-calming ahead.
* (c) Stop and give way to pedestrians.
(d) Pedestrian island ahead.

Q.
ABMW0158
What does this road marking mean?

Ans. (a) Speed control ramp ahead.
* (b) Stop and give way to pedestrians.
(c) Entering a built-up area.
(d) Traffic calming ahead.

Q. ABMW0159 **What does this road marking mean?**

Ans. * (a) Pedestrian crossing is nearby.
(b) Road surface is uneven.
(c) You may park for a maximum of one hour only.
(d) You may overtake if the road is clear ahead.

Q. ABMW0160 **What does this road marking mean?**

Ans. * (a) You must not enter unless your exit is clear or unless you are turning right.
(b) Traffic from right and left have the right-of-way.
(c) You have right-of-way over traffic from both right and left.
(d) Taxi pick-up area.

Q. ABMW0161 **What does this road marking mean?**

Ans. (a) You may overtake.
(b) You are approaching a stop sign.
* (c) You must not cross the line.
(d) Road narrows ahead.

Q.
ABMW0162

White arrows painted on the road indicate .....

Ans. * (a) the lane you should use for the direction which you intend to take.
(b) heavy vehicles should separate from lighter traffic.
(c) left and right-hand lanes are for buses only.
(d) traffic flow divides at roadworks ahead.

Q.
ABMW0163

What does this road marking and sign together mean?

Ans. (a) Taxi parking only outside the times shown.
(b) Parking only at times shown.
* (c) Parking not allowed at the times shown.
(d) Taxi parking only at the times shown.

Luan - Aoine
0700 - 0930
MON. - FRI.

Q.
ABMW0164

What does this road marking and information plate together mean?

Ans. (a) Taxi rank.
* (b) Parking not allowed at the times shown.
(c) No parking at any time.
(d) Parking only allowed at the times shown.

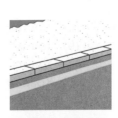

Luan - Aoine
0700 - 0930
MON. - FRI.

Q. What does this road marking
ABMW0165 mean?

Ans. (a) You may overtake provided you
do not cross the broken white
line.
(b) You may not overtake.
* (c) You may not cross the broken
white line unless it is safe to do so.
(d) You may not perform a reverse
manoeuvre.

Q. What does this road marking
ABMW0166 mean?

Ans. (a) You are approaching a stop sign.
* (b) A continuous white line lies ahead.
(c) All traffic must keep to the left of
the broken white lines.
(d) Dual-carriageway ahead.

Q. If driving from A to B, what do
ABMW0167 these road markings mean?

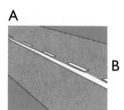

Ans. (a) You may cross the continuous
white line only when performing
a 'U'-turn.
(b) You may not overtake by crossing
the continuous white line.
(c) You may not overtake, only
motorcyclists may cross the
continuous white line.
* (d) You may overtake by crossing the
continuous white line.

Q. ABMW0168 **If driving from A to B, what do these road markings mean?**

Ans. (a) You may overtake by crossing the continuous white line.
* (b) You may overtake provided you don't cross the continuous white line.
(c) Only motorcyclists may overtake crossing the continuous white line.
(d) You may not overtake.

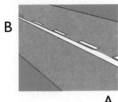

Q. ABMW0169 **What does this road marking mean?**

Ans. (a) Pedestrian crossing.
(b) The road ahead is a cul-de-sac.
* (c) No entry.
(d) Private vehicles not allowed.

Q. ABMW0170 **What does this road marking mean?**

Ans. (a) Keep outside the yellow lines.
* (b) Parking prohibited at all times.
(c) Parking prohibited during business hours.
(d) Taxi parking only.

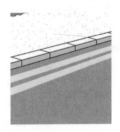

Q.
ABMW0171
What does this road marking mean?

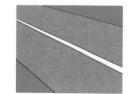

Ans. * (a) You must keep left of the continuous white line.
(b) You may overtake provided there is no oncoming traffic.
(c) Traffic on either side of the continuous white line can overtake provided it is safe to do so.
(d) Road narrows ahead.

Q.
ABMW0172
What does the broken yellow line road marking mean?

Ans. (a) No stopping for any reason except in an emergency.
(b) Slow lane for heavy vehicles only.
* (c) The edge of the carriageway/hard shoulder.
(d) Lay-by ahead.

TRAFFIC LIGHTS

Q.
ABMW0173
What does this traffic light mean?

Ans. (a) Proceed if the way is clear.
* (b) Stop, unless it would be unsafe to do so.
(c) Stop.
(d) Prepare to move off.

Q.
ABMW0174
What does this traffic light mean?

Ans.
    (a) You must stop and wait until the full green light appears.
    (b) All traffic must turn right.
* (c) You may proceed in the direction of the green arrow if the way is clear.
    (d) Traffic is not allowed to turn right.

Q.
ABMW0175
What does this traffic light mean?

Ans.
    (a) All traffic must turn left only.
* (b) Left turning traffic may proceed if the way is clear.
    (c) Traffic is not allowed to turn left.
    (d) Traffic turning left should prepare for full green to move off.

Q.
ABMW0176
What does this traffic light mean?

Ans. * (a) You must stop.
    (b) You may proceed.
    (c) You may stop if you can do so safely.
    (d) You may proceed if you can do so safely.

Q.
ABMW0177

What does this traffic light mean?

Ans.   (a) You must stop.
*   (b) You may proceed if the way is clear.
       (c) You must give way to any oncoming traffic turning right.
       (d) You may proceed but not turn right.

Q.
ABMW0178

What colour traffic light comes on after the green?

Ans.   (a) Red only.
*   (b) Amber only.
       (c) Flashing amber.
       (d) Green arrow.

Q.
ABMW0179

When traffic lights are green you should not proceed when .....

Ans. * (a) by doing so, your vehicle blocks the junction.
       (b) buses are stopped waiting to turn from the road on your right.
       (c) buses are stopped waiting to turn from the road on your left.
       (d) oncoming traffic is waiting to make a left turn.

Q.
ABMW0180

What colour traffic light comes on after a flashing amber light?

Ans.   (a) Red only.
*   (b) Green only.
       (c) Red or green.
       (d) Flashing green light.

Q.
ABMW0181

What traffic light comes on after a non-flashing amber light?

Ans. * (a) Red only.
     (b) Green only.
     (c) Red or Green.
     (d) Flashing blue light.

Q.
ABMW0182

What do flashing amber lights at a Pelican Crossing mean?

Ans. (a) Danger ahead - you must stop and wait until they stop flashing.
     (b) You are entering a special speed limit area.
* (c) Stop and give way to pedestrians, but proceed if the way is clear.
     (d) Drivers have right-of-way.

SPEED LIMITS

Q.
ABMW0183

The maximum permissible speed for cars or motorcycles on motorways is?

Ans. (a) 60 km/h.
     (b) 80 km/h.
     (c) 100 km/h.
* (d) 120 km/h.

Q.
ABMW0184

The maximum permissible speed for cars or motorcycles on national primary roads is?

Ans. (a) 60 km/h.
     (b) 80 km/h.
* (c) 100 km/h.
     (d) 120 km/h.

Q.
ABMW0185

What is the maximum permissible speed of a car towing a caravan on national primary roads?

Ans.   (a)   60 km/h.
     *   (b)   80 km/h.
       (c)   100 km/h.
       (d)   120 km/h.

Q.
ABMW0186

What is the maximum permissible speed of a car towing a caravan on a motorway?

Ans. *   (a)   80 km/h.
       (b)   90 km/h.
       (c)   100 km/h.
       (d)   120 km/h.

Q.
ABMW0187

What is the maximum permissible speed of a car towing a trailer on national primary roads?

Ans.   (a)   60 km/h.
     *   (b)   80 km/h.
       (c)   100 km/h.
       (d)   120 km/h.

Q.
ABMW0188

What is the maximum permissible speed of a car towing a trailer on a motorway?

Ans.   (a)   60 km/h.
     *   (b)   80 km/h.
       (c)   100 km/h.
       (d)   120 km/h.

PARKING

Q.
ABMW0189

You may not park .....

Ans. * (a) at or near a bend.
(b) where there is a broken white line along the centre of the road.
(c) where there are two broken white lines along the centre of the road.
(d) on a single yellow line outside the times indicated.

Q.
ABMW0190

You may not park within what distance of a zebra crossing?

Ans. * (a) 15 metres.
(b) 10 metres.
(c) 5 metres.
(d) 20 metres.

Q.
ABMW0191

You may not park your vehicle within what distance of a junction?

Ans. (a) 15 metres.
* (b) 5 metres.
(c) 3 metres.
(d) 8 metres.

Q.
ABMW0192

You wish to park your vehicle and the only available space is at a bus stop. You may .....

Ans. (a) park for a maximum of 10 minutes.
(b) park for a maximum of 30 minutes.
* (c) never park at a bus stop.
(d) park for a maximum of 5 minutes.

Q.
ABMW0193

When may you park your vehicle at an entrance to a property?

Ans.   (a) For a maximum of 5 minutes at any one time.
    *   (b) Never, except with the property owner's consent.
         (c) For a maximum of 10 minutes at any one time.
         (d) For a maximum of 15 minutes at any one time.

Q.
ABMW0194

When may you park your vehicle on a footpath?

Ans. * (a) Never.
         (b) When no more than half your vehicle is on the footpath.
         (c) When at least half the footpath remains free for pedestrians.
         (d) When cars are parked both sides of the road.

Q.
ABMW0195

When may you double-park your vehicle?

Ans.   (a) When there are double yellow lines.
         (b) When there is a hard shoulder.
    *   (c) Never.
         (d) When there are double white lines.

Q.
ABMW0196

When may you park your vehicle at a taxi rank?

Ans. * (a) Never.
         (b) When parking for less than 15 minutes.
         (c) When the rank is unoccupied.
         (d) When waiting to collect passengers from a taxi.

Q.
ABMW0197

When may you park your vehicle at a sharp bend?

Ans.   (a) When drivers coming from behind can see your vehicle.
    *   (b) Never.
         (c) When you put on your hazard warning lights.
         (d) Provided you park no more than 45 centimetres from the kerb or edge of the road.

Q. When may you park your vehicle on the brow of a hill?

ABMW0198

Ans. (a) When it has an efficient handbrake.
(b) When you angle the wheels towards the kerb.
* (c) Never.
(d) Only when there is no traffic on the road.

PEDESTRIANS

Q. If there is no footpath you must walk as near as possible to the .....

ABMW0199

Ans. (a) left-hand side of the road.
* (b) right-hand side of the road.
(c) I metre from the edge.
(d) there is no regulation.

Q. Where a party or group consists of 20 or more they must walk as near as possible to the .....

ABMW0200

Ans. (a) right-hand side of the road.
* (b) left-hand side of the road.
(c) I metre from the edge.
(d) there is no regulation.

Q. A group of 20 or more walking at night should arrange to have a member bringing up the rear carry a .....

ABMW0201

Ans. * (a) red light.
(b) green light.
(c) yellow light.
(d) flashing blue light.

Q.
ABMW0202

A group of 20 or more walking at night should arrange to have a member at the front carry a .....

Ans.
    (a) red light.
    (b) green light.
    (c) flashing yellow light.
  * (d) yellow or white light.

Q.
ABMW0203

Where a road is narrow or carries heavy traffic you should walk .....

Ans.
    (a) two abreast.
    (b) not more than two abreast.
  * (c) in single file.
    (d) three abreast.

Q.
ABMW0204

Select 2 answers. Light coloured outer clothing and a reflective armband should be worn at night?

Ans.
    (a) Inside urban areas.
  * (b) Outside urban areas.
    (c) Where street lighting is provided.
  * (d) Where no street lighting is provided.

Q.
ABMW0205

Pedestrian lights comprise a set of traffic lights for .....

Ans.
    (a) drivers only.
  * (b) drivers and a set of light signals for pedestrians.
    (c) pedestrians only.
    (d) school children only.

OTHER REGULATORY MATTERS

Q.
ABMW0206
What does this marker board on a large vehicle indicate?

Ans.   (a) Slow vehicle.
      (b) Hazardous goods carried.
      (c) Livestock.
   * (d) Wide load.

Q.
ABMW0207
When are 'lighting up hours' .....

Ans. * (a) from half an hour after sunset to half an hour before sunrise.
      (b) when visibility is less than 300 metres.
      (c) from mid-night until 6 a.m.
      (d) when visibility is less than 200 metres.

Q.
ABMW0208
What lights should your vehicle show at dusk?

Ans. * (a) Side lamps or dipped headlights.
      (b) Full headlamps.
      (c) No lights.
      (d) Fog lamps.

Q.
ABMW0209
The purpose of 'rumble' strips is to warn drivers .....

Ans. * (a) to reduce speed if necessary.
      (b) that there is a stop sign ahead.
      (c) that they are entering a speed limit area.
      (d) that there is a railway level crossing ahead.

Q. Traffic calming measures are intended to .....

ABMW0210

Ans.   (a) prioritise heavy goods traffic.
    * (b) slow down traffic in the vicinity.
    (c) alert the driver to road flooding ahead.
    (d) reduce tyre wear.

Q. When may a trailer be towed on a public road

ABMW0211 without a rear number plate?

Ans.   (a) When being pulled by an agricultural tractor.
    * (b) Never.
    (c) When carrying a load that overhangs the rear of the trailer.
    (d) When the tailboard is removed.

Q. When may you pass another vehicle on the left-hand

ABMW0212 side?

Ans.   (a) Never.
    (b) When there is sufficient space to do so.
    * (c) When the vehicle in front is signalling to turn right, or in slow-moving lanes of traffic.
    (d) When the car in front of you is moving too slowly and you cannot pass on the right-hand side because of oncoming traffic.

Q. Select 2 correct answers. There is a signed cycle

ABMW0213 track accompanied by a continuous white line, on your left-hand side?

Ans. * (a) Only a cyclist may use it.
    * (b) Cyclists must use it.
    (c) You may drive in it to overtake a vehicle turning right.
    (d) You may drive in it provided you are not towing a trailer.
    (e) You may drive in it provided it is not being used by a cyclist.

Q. ABMW0214

What traffic may drive along on a cycle lane accompanied by a continuous white line?

Ans.

   (a) A vehicle in which driving instruction is being given.
   (b) Cyclists and taxis.
   (c) Buses, taxis and cyclists.
   (d) Cyclists and motorcyclists.
* (e) Cyclists.

Q. ABMW0215

What traffic may drive along on a cycle lane accompanied by a broken white line?

Ans.

   (a) Buses, taxis and cyclists.
   (b) Buses on a scheduled service and cyclists.
   (c) Cyclists and mopeds.
* (d) Cyclists.
   (e) Cyclists and taxis.

Q. ABMW0216

Select 2 correct answers. At a railway level crossing controlled by lights and barriers, you must stop .....

Ans.

   (a) when the lights stop flashing.
* (b) when the lights start to flash.
* (c) when the barrier has started to lower.
   (d) when the barrier is fully up.

Q. ABMW0217

At a level crossing with unattended gates, you should .....

Ans.

   (a) drive half-way across and close the first gate before opening the second.
   (b) open both gates and after passing the first stop and close it.
* (c) open both gates before proceeding to cross.
   (d) telephone the nearest railway station before opening a gate.

Q.
ABMW0218

A Zebra crossing is indicated by .....

Ans.
    (a) flashing red beacons.
    (b) continuously lit amber beacons.
* (c) flashing amber beacons.
    (d) continuously lit red beacons.

Q.
ABMW0219

Flashing amber arrows at a junction mean .....

Ans. * (a) you may proceed in the direction indicated provided the way is clear.
    (b) the direction indicated is a cul-de-sac.
    (c) it is prohibited to proceed in the direction indicated.
    (d) there is a weight restriction in the direction indicated.

Q.
ABMW0220

Temporary traffic lights at road works .....

Ans.
    (a) need only be obeyed while road workers are on site.
* (b) must be obeyed at all times.
    (c) need not be obeyed if there is no oncoming traffic.
    (d) need not be obeyed if a convoy of traffic is going the same direction as you.

Q.
ABMW0221

Temporary speed limit signs at road works .....

Ans.
    (a) only apply when the road workers are on site.
    (b) need not be obeyed if there is no oncoming traffic.
* (c) apply at all times.
    (d) do not apply to earth moving vehicles being used on the road work site.

ALERT DRIVING, AND CONSIDERATION FOR ROAD USERS

ILLUSTRATED TRAFFIC SITUATIONS

Q. **What must you do in this situation?**

ABMW0222

Ans.   (a) Drive closer to the left-hand kerb.

   * (b) Keep a close eye on the children, if necessary give a warning signal and be prepared to brake in good time.

     (c) Continue to drive at a fast speed.

     (d) Speed up to pass the children quickly.

Q. **Select 2 answers. The boy on the children's bicycle has said goodbye to his friend. You must .....**

ABMW0223

Ans. * (a) be prepared for the boy setting off at any moment without paying attention to your vehicle.

   * (b) be prepared for the boy setting off even if he has looked left and you have sounded your horn.

     (c) stop the car until the boy has moved off.

     (d) proceed as if the boy was not there.

Q. ABMW0224   **You are the driver of the car. Which conduct is correct?**

Ans.   *   (a) You may proceed.

           (b) You must wait.
           (c) You must drive on the right-hand side to allow clearance to the motorcyclist.
           (d) The motorcyclist has right of way.

Q. ABMW0225   **You are the driver of the car. Which conduct is correct?**

Ans.   *   (a) You must allow the cyclist to proceed.

           (b) You must allow the motorcyclist to proceed.
           (c) You may drive around the corner before the cyclist.
           (d) You must stop and yield right of way to the other road users.

Q. ABMW0226   **Select 2 answers. You are driving the car. For which of the following must you be prepared?**

Ans.   (a) The ball may burst after you have passed.

     *   (b) One of the children could turn back to collect the ball from the roadway.
     *   (c) The child running to the right could turn and run back to join the group.
           (d) The ball could damage your vehicle.

Q.
ABMW0227

You are approaching the pedestrian crossing. What do you do in this situation?

Ans.

(a) Maintain your speed because the pedestrians have not stepped on to the crossing.

(b) Continue to drive on fast because the pedestrians have to wait.

* (c) Slow down in good time and be prepared to stop.

(d) Sound the horn to draw attention to your vehicle and continue to drive at the same speed.

Q.
ABMW0228

Select 2 answers. Which conduct is correct?

Ans. * (a) I must wait.

(b) The yellow car must wait.

* (c) The yellow vehicle on the roundabout has right of way.

(d) Treat the roundabout as a junction with roads of equal importance.

Q.
ABMW0229

Which conduct is correct?

Ans. * (a) I must allow the motorcycle to proceed.

(b) I must allow the bus to proceed.

(c) I proceed first.

(d) I am not allowed to turn right.

Q.
ABMW0230

Which conduct is correct?

Ans.

(a) I must allow the blue car to proceed.

* (b) I may turn in front of the other two cars.

(c) I must allow the red car to proceed.

(d) I must stop and allow all other traffic to proceed.

Q.
ABMW0231

Select 3 answers. Why must you pay special attention to pedestrians here?

Ans. * (a) Pedestrians frequently switch from one side of the street to the other.

* (b) Parked vehicles restrict the view of motorists and pedestrians.

* (c) Pedestrians frequently step on to the road way without paying attention.

(d) Pedestrians are only allowed to cross the road at pedestrian crossings.

Q.
ABMW0232

There are children playing at the edge of the roadway. What should you do?

Ans.

(a) Give a warning signal and drive past at the same speed.

* (b) Reduce speed, drive cautiously and remain ready to brake.

(c) Maintain the same speed because the children can see an oncoming vehicle quite clearly at this point.

(d) Stop and separate the children.

Q.
ABMW0233

Which conduct is correct?

Ans. (a) I have to let the van cross the junction.
* (b) I may cross first.
    (c) The cyclist must proceed first.
    (d) The cyclist must allow the other vehicles to proceed.

Q.
ABMW0234

Which conduct is correct?

Ans. * (a) I may proceed first.
    (b) I must let the orange car cross.
    (c) I am not allowed to turn right.
    (d) I am not allowed to turn left.

Q.
ABMW0235

Select 2 answers. Which conduct is correct?

Ans. * (a) I allow the blue truck to proceed.
    * (b) I have the right of way before the red car.
    (c) I allow the red car to proceed.
    (d) I am not allowed to turn right.

Q.
ABMW0236

Select 2 answers. What must you be conscious of in this situation?

Ans. * (a) People crossing the street at the rear of the bus.
    * (b) People crossing the street from the left to catch the bus.
    (c) Caution and proper road conduct on the part of all road users.
    (d) The bus driver will always signal before moving off.

Q.

ABMW0237

Select 2 answers. You are overtaking a parked car, what do you do?

Ans.

    (a) Drive on at the same speed.

    (b) Drive on if you don't hit the ball.

    * (c) Reduce speed considerably at once and remain ready to brake.

    * (d) Allow extra clearance to the parked car.

Q.

ABMW0238

Select 3 answers. What dangers must you reckon with at tram stops like this?

Ans. * (a) Pedestrians occasionally leave the traffic island without paying attention.

    * (b) Pedestrians may dash across the roadway to catch the tram.

    * (c) Motorists ahead may be forced to brake sharply owing to careless pedestrians.

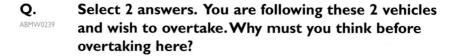

    (d) Children will always be controlled by an adult.

Q.

ABMW0239

Select 2 answers. You are following these 2 vehicles and wish to overtake. Why must you think before overtaking here?

Ans.

    (a) The roadway marking forbids overtaking here.

    * (b) You cannot see far enough ahead for oncoming traffic.

    * (c) It is possible that the vehicle directly in front will overtake first.

    (d) You should overtake both vehicles together.

Q.
ABMW0240

Select 2 answers. A car is reversing into a parking space. The red car immediately in front of you is moving into the right-hand lane. What should you do?

Ans. * (a) If the traffic behind permits, move into the right-hand lane.

(b) Give warning signal and drive on quickly.

* (c) If vehicles behind you are over-taking stay in the left-hand lane, drive slowly, and if necessary, stop.

(d) Drive close to the car without crossing the broken line.

Q.
ABMW0241

Select 2 answers. What must you be prepared for in icy conditions?

Ans. (a) Expect the bus driver to wait until you have overtaken him.

* (b) A longer braking distance.

* (c) The bus may move off immediately.

(d) Pedestrians will not dash across the road.

Q.
ABMW0242

You want to turn left. What can you do?

Ans. (a) Turn the corner before the cyclist.

(b) Increase speed to be able to turn the corner before the cyclist.

* (c) Allow the cyclist heading straight on to pass.

(d) Beckon to the cyclist that you intend to turn left.

Q.
ABMW0246

Select 2 answers. What adversely affects road safety in this situation?

Ans.
    (a) The headlights of the oncoming traffic.
* (b) Poor visibility.
* (c) Reduced grip of the tyres on wet roadway.
    (d) The presence of high trees on each side of the road.

Q.
ABMW0247

Select 3 answers. What dangers could arise if you want to turn left here?

Ans. * (a) You might not be able to stop in time if a pedestrian crosses the side street.
* (b) Vehicles coming out of the side street might go into a skid on braking.
* (c) Your vehicle could go into a skid if you turn too quickly.
    (d) Your vehicle will not skid provided your tyres have good tread.

Q.
ABMW0248

Select 2 answers. What do you reckon with in this situation?

Ans.
    (a) You should allow more clearance than usual and drive on.
    (b) The pedestrians will first allow the vehicle to drive past before crossing the road.
* (c) The pedestrian will cross the roadway in front of your vehicle.
* (d) Children may suddenly appear from behind the parked vehicles.

Q.

Select 2 answers. What do you do when approaching this situation?

Ans.   (a)   Be prepared for the vehicle in front to increase speed.

  * (b)   Be prepared for the vehicle in front to stop, to allow the girl to cross the roadway.

  * (c)   Reduce speed and remain ready to brake since the girl on foot could suddenly cross the roadway.

  (d)   Increase speed so as to be clear of the girl.

Q.

Which conduct is correct?

Ans.   (a)   I may cross the junction first.

  (b)   I must allow the cyclist to turn.

  * (c)   I must allow the yellow car to proceed.

  (d)   I do not need to signal.

Q.

Which car, if any, is parked incorrectly?

Ans. * (a)   Both cars.

  (b)   The red car.

  (c)   The green car.

  (d)   Neither car.

Q.   **What must you reckon with in this situation?**

ABMW0252

Ans.   *   (a) The cyclist will switch to the roadway without paying attention to moving traffic.

(b) The cyclist will stop at the end of the cycle path and allow the traffic to pass by.

(c) The cyclist will stay on the cycle path.

(d) You should drive on the right-hand side in case the cyclist switches on to the road.

Q.   **You want to pull out of a driveway and turn right on to the road. At the same time a cyclist is approaching from the right and a pedestrian wants to cross. Who must wait?**

ABMW0253

Ans.   *   (a) You must wait.

(b) The pedestrian must wait.

(c) The cyclist must wait.

(d) The pedestrian and cyclist must wait.

Q.   **Which conduct is correct?**

ABMW0254

Ans.   *   (a) You must first halt at the stop line.

(b) The cyclist must allow bus to proceed.

(c) The cyclist must allow both you and the bus to proceed.

(d) You may turn off before the cyclist when the bus has passed.

Q.
ABMW0255

Select 2 answers. You are following this vehicle. What must you do?

Ans. * (a) Maintain a greater distance than normal from the vehicle in front.

　　 * (b) Avoid overtaking.

　　 (c) Drive up as close as possible to the vehicle ahead in order not to lose it out of your sight.

　　 (d) Switch on full headlights before overtaking.

Q.
ABMW0256

Select 2 answers. What may you not do on this road?

Ans. (a) Reverse the vehicle.

　　 * (b) Perform a 'U'-turn.

　　 (c) Pick up a passenger.

　　 * (d) Park on the left-hand side.

Q.
ABMW0257

You wish to overtake the cyclist. You may .....

Ans. * (a) cross the broken line.

　　 (b) overtake only if you do not cross any of the lines.

　　 (c) straddle both lines provided it is safe to do so.

　　 (d) not overtake here.

Q.
ABMW0258

Select 2 answers. You wish to overtake the cyclist. You may .....

Ans.
    (a) straddle both lines provided it is safe to do so.
* (b) overtake only if you do not cross any of the lines.
    (c) cross the continuous white line.
* (d) not cross the continuous white line.

Q.
ABMW0259

A white line in the centre of the road indicates that .....

Ans. * (a) vehicles may not cross or straddle the line.
    (b) only motorcycles may cross or straddle the line.
    (c) the line may only be crossed during daylight hours.
    (d) you may only park during day light hours.

Q.
ABMW0260

This road marking indicates that .....

Ans.
    (a) only oncoming traffic towards you may cross the line.
* (b) you may straddle or cross the broken line in order to avoid an obstruction or to overtake.
    (c) oncoming traffic other than slow earth moving vehicles may overtake.
    (d) no traffic may cross the line.

Q. Which behaviour is correct? You should .....

ABMW0261

Ans.
     (a) yield right of way to the van.
* (b) allow the cyclist to continue before you proceed.
     (c) allow the truck and the cyclist to proceed.
     (d) sound the horn to alert the cyclist before you proceed.

Q. What are the dangers in driving here in the unevenly lit street?

ABMW0262

Ans.
     (a) Traffic lights will not be working.
     (b) Only following traffic will see you.
     (c) Only oncoming traffic will see you.
* (d) Pedestrians crossing in a dark area may not be seen.

Q. What are the dangers in driving here in the unevenly lit street?

ABMW0263

Ans.
     (a) Traffic lights will not be working.
     (b) Only following traffic will see you.
     (c) Only oncoming traffic will see you.
* (d) It may be difficult to make out poorly lit vehicles in the dark areas.

Q.
ABMW0264

Select 2 answers. You should .....

Ans.

(a) proceed before the motorcycle.
* (b) allow the motorcycle to proceed.
(c) proceed before the bus.
* (d) proceed after the bus.

Q.
ABMW0265

You should .....

Ans.

(a) proceed to your right as you have right of way.
(b) allow the cyclist to proceed.
(c) proceed after the bus.
* (d) stop at the line.

Q.
ABMW0266

Select 2 answers. What must you do if you are dazzled by the full beam of oncoming traffic?

Ans.

(a) Accelerate to get out of the range of the dazzle as quickly as possible.
* (b) Direct your gaze to the left-hand edge of the roadway.
* (c) If necessary, reduce your speed.
(d) Switch on full headlights.

Q.
ABMW0267

Select 2 answers. A strong side wind is blowing from the left. You want to overtake the truck. You are most exposed to danger .....

Ans.
   (a) prior to entering the slipstream of the truck.
* (b) on leaving the slipstream of the truck.
* (c) when you enter the slipstream of the truck.
   (d) if you apply the brakes while in the slipstream of the truck.

Q.
ABMW0268

You are 25 metres from traffic lights which change to amber. You intend to turn right. You should .....

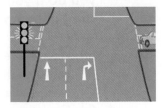

Ans. * (a) stop, unless it is not safe.
   (b) accelerate and complete the turn.
   (c) proceed, as the green light is about to come on.
   (d) continue with care being ready to stop if the light turns to red.

Q.
ABMW0270

You are turning right at the junction. Which behaviour is correct?

Ans. * (a) You should wait, and allow the oncoming vehicle to pass.
(b) You should wait; the truck may proceed first.
(c) You should continue with care.
(d) You should wait; the truck and the oncoming vehicle may proceed first.

Q.
ABMW0271

You are turning right at the junction. Which behaviour is correct?

Ans. (a) You should wait; the truck may proceed first.
(b) The oncoming vehicle should wait.
* (c) You may proceed before the truck.
(d) You may proceed before both vehicles.

Q.
ABMW0272

Your driving should allow for which danger over the brow of this hill?

Ans. (a) Traffic calming measures may apply.
(b) There may be a bus stop.
* (c) There may be a slow-moving vehicle in your lane.
(d) You may have to reduce speed at a Pelican-Crossing.

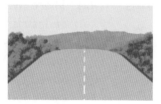

Q. **Your driving should allow for which danger over the brow of this hill?**

ABMW0273

Ans.
    (a) Traffic calming measures may apply.
    (b) There may be a bus stop.
    (c) You may have to reduce speed at a Pelican-Crossing.
* (d) A vehicle may have broken down.

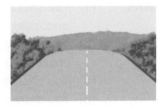

Q. **Your driving should allow for which danger over the brow of this hill?**

ABMW0274

Ans. * (a) An oncoming vehicle may be straddling part of your lane.
    (b) There may be no road markings.
    (c) Speed cameras may be in operation.
    (d) A high-sided vehicle may be oncoming.

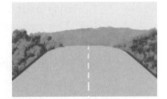

Q. **Your driving should allow for which danger over the brow of this hill?**

ABMW0275

Ans. * (a) There may be oncoming pedestrians.
    (b) There may be no road markings.
    (c) Speed cameras may be in operation.
    (d) A high-sided vehicle may be oncoming.

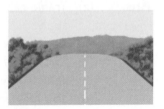

Q.

ABMW0276

Your driving should allow for which danger over the brow of this hill?

Ans.   (a) An oncoming vehicle may not have a catalytic converter.
  (b) An oncoming vehicle may have low oil pressure.
  (c) An oncoming vehicle may not have power steering.
* (d) There may be livestock on the road.

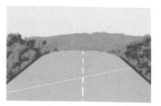

Q.

ABMW0277

Your driving should allow for which danger over the brow of this hill?

Ans.   (a) An oncoming vehicle may not have a catalytic converter.
  (b) An oncoming vehicle may have low oil pressure.
  (c) An oncoming vehicle may not have power steering.
* (d) There may be hedge-cutting taking place.

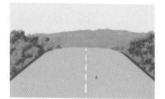

Q.

ABMW0278

What should you be aware of in this situation?

Ans.   (a) A car oncoming towards you will not overtake the bus.
  (b) Only buses may use the road.
  (c) The bus may be towing a trailer.
* (d) There may be a car in front of the bus, which is hidden from view.

Q.
ABMW0279

You are following in the middle lane. You wish to continue straight ahead. You should .....

Ans.

(a) take position in the right-hand lane even if proceeding straight ahead.

(b) take any lane as convenient.

* (c) slow down and allow the driver in front to change lanes.

(d) overtake the other vehicles quickly on the right-hand side.

Q.
ABMW0280

The traffic light is on amber. You should .....

Ans.

(a) ensure you pass the lights before they turn red.

(b) continue as there is no traffic at the junction.

(c) continue only if you can see that the junction is clear of pedestrians.

* (d) stop at the line unless it is not safe to do so.

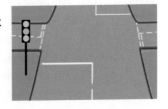

Q.
ABMW0281

You are following the motorcyclist. The white car is reversing onto the road. What should you be aware of?

Ans.

(a) The motorcyclist may beckon the reversing driver to stop.

* (b) The motorcyclist may suddenly brake.

(c) The reversing driver will stop when he sees the motorcyclist.

(d) The brake-lights may go off and the car continue reversing.

Q.
ABMW0282

You are following the motorcyclist. The white car is reversing onto the road. What should you beware of?

Ans.

(a) The motorcyclist may beckon the reversing driver to stop.

(b) The reversing driver will stop when he sees the motorcyclist.

* (c) You may need a longer braking distance than normal.

(d) The brake-lights may go off and the car continue reversing.

Q.
ABMW0283

You are approaching this narrow bridge against the oncoming white car. You should .....

Ans.

(a) drive on because the oncoming traffic must wait.

* (b) reduce speed and, if necessary, stop.

(c) increase speed in order to clear the bridge in advance of the oncoming vehicle.

(d) give way only if you are towing a trailer or caravan.

Q.
ABMW0284

Select 2 answers. You are turning right. Which behaviour is correct? You .....

Ans.

(a) may proceed before the motor-cycle.

* (b) must allow the motorcycle to proceed.

* (c) must allow the tram to proceed.

(d) may proceed before the tram.

Q.
ABMW0285

Select 2 answers. You are driving on the cobble stone road where there is a tram line. What might require you to take extra care?

Ans.

(a) The road surface is particularly even and tyre grip is improved.

* (b) The road surface is uneven and road grip varies.

* (c) Driving on the tracks can reduce tyre grip.

(d) Driving on the tracks can improve tyre grip.

Q.
ABMW0286

Select 2 answers. After a heavy downpour why should you keep a greater distance from vehicles in front? Because .....

Ans. * (a) wheel-spray may impair visibility.

(b) wheels rotate at slower speed after rain.

(c) wheels rotate at greater speed after rain.

* (d) stopping distances are greater.

Q.
ABMW0287

Select 2 answers. When driving on this one way street with vehicles parked on both sides, you should be prepared for?

Ans.

(a) The truck may not have proper markings.

* (b) The truck driver suddenly jumping down into the roadway.

* (c) Traffic signs that may be concealed by the truck.

(d) The truck may be a left-hand drive vehicle.

Q. Select 2 answers. When driving on this one way
ABMW0288 street with vehicles parked on both sides, you should
be prepared for?

Ans.   (a) The truck may not have proper
markings.

  * (b) Pedestrians crossing between
vehicles.

  * (c) A passenger door opening.

   (d) The truck may be a left-hand
drive vehicle.

Q. **Why must you be particularly careful here?**
ABMW0289

Ans.   (a) The vehicle coming from the
right has right of way.

   (b) Because a vehicle could come
from the left.

  * (c) Because there is an increased
danger of skidding.

   (d) The vehicle coming from the
right is not required to signal.

Q. **What should you do?**
ABMW0290

Ans. * (a) Wait and allow both pedestrians
to cross.

   (b) Proceed between both
pedestrians.

   (c) Sound the horn, and accelerate
to proceed promptly.

   (d) Allow one pedestrian to cross,
and then proceed as there
should be room to clear the junction.

Q. You are turning right at the junction. What should you do?

ABMW0291

Ans.
    (a) Proceed.
    (b) Stop, oncoming traffic has right of way.
  * (c) Allow the red car to proceed from your left.
    (d) Allow the blue car to proceed from your right.

Q. Select 2 answers. What should the car driver be aware of here?

ABMW0292

Ans.
  * (a) Oncoming traffic may cut the corner.
    (b) Following traffic may cut the corner.
    (c) The road ahead will be a dual-carriageway.
  * (d) A vehicle may have broken down beyond the bend.

Q. Select 2 answers. What should the car driver be aware of here?

ABMW0293

Ans.
    (a) Road marking is taking place ahead.
  * (b) There could be a pedestrian oncoming around the bend.
    (c) The road ahead is solely for cars and other light vehicles.
  * (d) Animals could suddenly appear on the road ahead.

Q.
ABMW0294

Select 3 answers. You are driving along a shopping street with many different light sources. What dangers must you reckon with?

Ans. * (a) Traffic lights may be difficult to distinguish because of the neon coloured lighting.

(b) Parking spaces may be full.

* (c) Other persons may not notice your vehicle in good time.

* (d) You may not be aware of oncoming vehicles until they are very close.

Q.
ABMW0295

Select 2 answers. You are driving along this street. What should you do?

Ans. (a) Drive at the full speed limit.

* (b) Drive much slower than the speed limit because children might run out from between the parked vehicles at any time.

(c) Drive quickly to clear the area.

* (d) Drive much slower than the speed limit because a car door might be suddenly opened.

Q.
ABMW0296

You are driving along this street. What should you do?

Ans. * (a) Reduce your speed at once and be prepared to brake because other children could follow.

(b) Sound the horn as a warning and proceed.

(c) Maintain your speed. You need not expect other children.

(d) Drive on quickly in order not to delay following traffic.

Q. **Who should wait?**

ABMW0297

Ans. (a) Whichever driver is furthest away from the van.
(b) The oncoming traffic must wait.
* (c) You should wait.

Q. **Who should wait?**

ABMW0298

Ans. * (a) The driver in the red car.
(b) You should wait.
(c) Either driver should wait.

Q. **You are following the cyclist who is approaching a parked car. What should you be aware of?**

ABMW0299

Ans. (a) You have enough space to pass the cyclist and car together safely.

* (b) The cyclist may overtake the parked car on the right.
(c) The cyclist must allow you to pass first.
(d) The cyclist will take proper observations before proceeding.

Q. **Should you overtake the cyclists?**

ABMW0300

Ans. (a) Yes, provided the broken line does not become continuous.

* (b) No, you cannot see clearly ahead.
(c) Yes, the cyclists will hear your vehicle and thus will get out of the way.
(d) Yes, any oncoming traffic can observe the situation and will get out of the way.

Q.
ABMW0301

Select 2 answers. What should you be prepared for in this situation?

Ans.
    (a) The cyclist will take up position further to the left.

    (b) The cyclist further ahead may sway to the left.

* (c) The heavy loaded carrier may cause the near cyclist to weave from side to side.

* (d) The cyclist farther ahead may move to the right.

Q.
ABMW0302

What should you do in this situation?

Ans.
    (a) Sound your horn and drive on.

    (b) Wait at the zebra crossing until the van has turned off.

* (c) Allow the pedestrian to cross the road.

    (d) Accelerate quickly to clear the crossing.

Q.
ABMW0303

You are driving the silver car. What should you do if the black overtaking car has underestimated your speed?

Ans.
    (a) Accelerate so that the other driver cannot overtake you.

    (b) Drive on and sound your horn.

    (c) Beckon to the overtaking driver to stay back.

* (d) Reduce speed and, if necessary, brake gently.

Q.

ABMW0304

What should you be aware of?

Ans.
   (a) A dangerous depression.
  * (b) A dangerous right-hand bend.
   (c) A minor road to the left.
   (d) A minor road to the right.

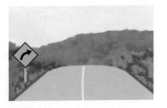

Q.

ABMW0305

Select 2 answers. What must you be prepared for in this situation?

Ans.
   (a) An area where there is cattle on the road.
   (b) An area where signals are not given.
  * (c) The road ahead may be uneven and dirty.
  * (d) Road workers and construction vehicles.

Q.

ABMW0306

You are in the left-hand lane although you want to turn right. What do you do?

Ans. * (a) Proceed straight ahead or turn left.
   (b) Proceed straight ahead and take a wide turn to the right.
   (c) Carefully turn off to the left after sounding horn.
   (d) Reverse and get into right lane.

Q.
ABMW0307

Select 3 answers. You wish to make a right turn at the junction up ahead. Which of the following positions are incorrect?

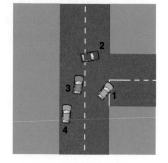

Ans.
* (a) 2.
* (b) 4.
  (c) 3.
* (d) 1.

Q.
ABMW0308

Select 3 answers. You wish to make a left turn up ahead. Which of the following positions are incorrect?

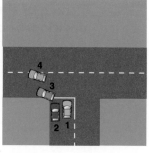

Ans.
* (a) 1.
  (b) 2.
* (c) 3.
* (d) 4.

Q.
ABMW0309

Select 2 answers. You are approaching from the direction of the arrow and wish to take the 3rd exit at the roundabout. Which of the following positions are correct?

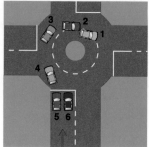

Ans.
* (a) 1.
  (b) 2.
  (c) 3.
* (d) 6.

Q.
ABMW0310

Select 2 answers. You are approaching from the direction of the arrow and wish to take the 3rd exit at the roundabout. Which of the following positions are incorrect?

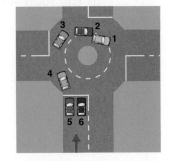

Ans.
　　(a) 1.
*　(b) 4.
*　(c) 5.
　　(d) 6.

Q.
ABMW0311

You wish to turn right onto a main road. Which of the following positions is correct?

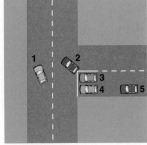

Ans.
　　(a) 2.
　　(b) 4.
　　(c) 5.
*　(d) 3.

Q.
ABMW0312

You wish to turn right onto a main road. Which of the following positions are correct?

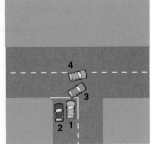

Ans.
　　(a) 2.
　　(b) 3.
*　(c) 1.
　　(d) 4.

Q.
ABMW0313

You wish to turn left onto a main road. Which of the following positions is correct?

Ans. * (a) 2.
(b) 1.
(c) 3.
(d) 4.

ANTICIPATION

Q.
ABMW0314

What should you do when there is a sharp dip in the road ahead?

Ans. * (a) Reduce your speed, keep to the left and be alert for parked vehicles.
(b) Increase your speed.
(c) Move to the centre of the road in order to avoid a vehicle that may be parked on the left.
(d) Flash your lights to warn oncoming drivers of your presence.

Q.
ABMW0315

When you see a red warning triangle on the road up ahead, you should .....

Ans. (a) avoid it, maintain speed and carry on.
(b) stop and await instructions.
* (c) slow down and watch for a hazard up ahead.
(d) stop at the triangle before proceeding.

Q.
ABMW0316

You are approaching traffic lights that you know have been green for some time. What should you do?

Ans.
(a) Maintain your speed.
(b) Accelerate to clear them before they change.
* (c) Prepare to stop in case they may change before you reach them.
(d) Maintain your speed and sound your horn as you approach.

Q.
ABMW0317

You are approaching a junction that is controlled by traffic lights. They are temporarily not lighting. What should you do?

Ans.
(a) Drive smartly through the junction to avoid delay.
(b) Stop at the junction and give way to traffic on your left.
* (c) Drive cautiously while watching out for other traffic.
(d) Switch on your hazard warning lights and drive on.

Q.
ABMW0318

You are driving along and see cattle on the road up ahead. What should you do?

Ans.
(a) Sound the horn to try to get the cattle to move aside.
(b) Switch on your headlights and try to pass as quickly as possible.
* (c) Reduce speed and overtake with care.
(d) Sound the horn and overtake with care.

Q. ABMW0319 **You see horse riders on the road up ahead. You should .....**

Ans.
    (a) turn on your hazard warning lights and continue at normal speed.
* (b) reduce your speed and allow extra clearance.
    (c) maintain your speed while taking extra observation of the horses and how they are controlled by the riders.
    (d) sound your horn and allow extra clearance.
    (e) sound the horn and reduce your speed.

Q. ABMW0320 **Select 2 answers. If you meet horses with riders on the road, you should be aware that ......**

Ans.
* (a) loud noise from your vehicle may frighten the horses.
    (b) all horse riders are experienced at handling horses.
    (c) any loud noise from your vehicle will not frighten the horses.
* (d) the horses may bolt.
    (e) they may only pass in single file.

Q. ABMW0321 **What should you do when you approach a hump-backed hill?**

Ans.
* (a) Reduce speed, keep to the left and be alert for any parked vehicle which may be hidden from your view.
    (b) Press the clutch pedal and sound the horn as a warning.
    (c) Maintain normal speed and road position.
    (d) Stop at the crest of the hill.

Q. You notice a large oil-spill on the road as you drive
ABMW0322 along. You should .....

Ans. (a) maintain normal speeds in a lower gear and apply the
        hazard warning lights.
   * (b) reduce speed by gently applying the brakes and apply the
        hazard warning lights.
      (c) depress the clutch and brake sharply and apply the
        hazard warning lights.
      (d) try to straddle it with your wheels while maintaining
        normal speed.

Q. Select 3 answers. Which of the following statements
ABMW0323 are true. When meeting an oncoming vehicle with
        flashing amber beacons, the vehicle .....

Ans. * (a) may be extra wide.
       * (b) may be extra high.
          (c) is an emergency vehicle.
       * (d) is slow moving.
          (e) is broken down.
          (f) is fast moving.

Q. If you meet a vehicle with flashing amber beacons,
ABMW0324 you should .....

Ans. (a) flash your headlights to acknowledge the beacons.
      (b) stop because it is an emergency vehicle.
   * (c) slow down and prepare to stop.
      (d) maintain your speed while keeping left.

Q.
ABMW0325

Select 3 answers. When approaching railway lines or tram lines, you should be aware that .....

Ans.
    (a) the wheels may become caught in the rails.
* (b) the rails may be lower than the road surface.
* (c) the rails might be higher than the road surface.
    (d) tyre grip may be improved crossing the rails.
* (e) tyre grip may be reduced crossing the rails.

Q.
ABMW0326

When crossing road markings such as lines and directional arrows, you should be aware that .....

Ans.
    (a) tyre grip is improved.
* (b) stopping distance is increased due to reduced tyre grip.
    (c) braking is improved.
    (d) stopping distance is reduced due to improved tyre grip.
    (e) steering control is improved.

CONSIDERATION

Q.
ABMW0327

There are pedestrians on the footpath ahead and there are pools of water on the road. What should you do?

Ans.
    (a) Brake suddenly as you approach the pools of water.
    (b) Sound the horn as a warning to the pedestrians and continue on.
* (c) Reduce speed and try to avoid the pools of water so as not to splash the pedestrians.
    (d) Flash the lights as a warning to the pedestrians.

Q.   You are about to stop and notice that the vehicle

ABMW0328   behind you is towing a trailer. What should you do?

Ans.   (a) Stop quickly keeping a close eye on the rear-view mirror.

         (b) Use the hand brake to stop.

    * (c) Indicate in good time and pull up gradually to allow the vehicle behind you extra stopping distance.

         (d) Speed up temporarily to put more distance between your vehicle and the vehicle behind you.

Q.   A bus ahead is moving away from a bus stop. What

ABMW0329   should you do?

Ans.   (a) Try to get past it to avoid being delayed.

    * (b) Slow down and allow it to move out.

         (c) Drive alongside it because you have right-of-way.

         (d) Signal to the bus driver to let you pass.

Q.   What should you do on a narrow road when another

ABMW0330   vehicle is coming in the opposite direction?

Ans.   (a) Maintain your position and expect the other vehicle to move over if necessary.

    * (b) Reduce speed and allow reasonable clearance between your vehicle and the oncoming one, before proceeding.

         (c) Drive along the middle of the road to encourage the other driver to pull in.

         (d) Expect the other driver to pull off the road and allow you to pass.

Q.   **You are driving along and wish to call into a shop on**
ABMW0331   **the side of the street in order to make a purchase.**
    What should you do?

Ans.   (a)   Park on the footpath so as not to impede the free flow
        of traffic on the road.
      (b)   Switch on your hazard warning lights and park slightly up
        on the footpath.
   *   (c)   Continue on until you find a proper parking space.
      (d)   Continue to a point where a 'U'-turn can be made safely
        and return to park on the footpath in the proper
        direction.

Q.   **You are driving behind another vehicle that you do**
ABMW0332   **not intend to overtake. What should you do?**

Ans.   (a)   Drive close behind it in order to let following traffic
        overtake both vehicles.
      (b)   Signal to following traffic to overtake both vehicles.
   *   (c)   Keep well back to allow following traffic to overtake you.
      (d)   Keep well back and to the centre of the road.

Q.   **You are driving in a line of traffic and do not intend**
ABMW0333   **to overtake. What should you do?**

Ans.   (a)   Drive close to the vehicle in front.
      (b)   Beckon to following traffic to overtake.
   *   (c)   Stay back and leave a gap for other drivers who may
        want to overtake you.
      (d)   Indicate left as a signal to following traffic to overtake.

Q.
ABMW0334

Select 3 answers. If you do not stay well back from a vehicle which you do not intend to overtake .....

Ans. * (a) other drivers may attempt to overtake both vehicles thereby reducing the clearance for oncoming drivers.
  * (b) air turbulence from a large vehicle in front could blow your vehicle off course.
  (c) there will always be sufficient clearance for following drivers to overtake you and the vehicle in front.
  (d) it may be easier for following traffic to overtake you.
  * (e) it may be more difficult for following traffic to overtake you.

Q.
ABMW0335

Select 2 answers. You are behind another vehicle which you do not intend to overtake. If you do not stay well back .....

Ans. (a) it would be easier for following traffic to overtake you.
  * (b) following drivers may attempt to overtake both vehicles reducing the clearance for oncoming drivers.
  (c) following traffic will always see the vehicle in front of your vehicle.
  * (d) you may collide with the vehicle if it brakes suddenly.
  (e) fuel efficiency for both vehicles is improved.

Q.
ABMW0336

You are driving along behind another vehicle that you do not intend to overtake. What should you do?

Ans. * (a) Stay well back to allow following traffic to overtake you.
  (b) Drive close behind the vehicle in front so as to reduce the space required for any overtaking vehicle.
  (c) Beckon to following drivers when it is safe for them to overtake you.
  (d) Maintain your position and do not ease back.

Q.
ABMW0337
Why is tailgating (driving too close behind the vehicle in front) dangerous?

Ans.
   (a) You prevent other vehicles from overtaking both vehicles safely.

   (b) Your braking system is less efficient.

* (c) There is not sufficient space to allow you to stop in an emergency without colliding with the vehicle in front.

   (d) You exceed the speed limit when tailgating.

Q.
ABMW0338
Tailgating on a motorway or dual-carriageway is .....

Ans.
   (a) safe, because traffic will not have to stop suddenly.

   (b) safe when all traffic moves in the one direction at the same speed.

* (c) not safe because of the possibility of the vehicle in front stopping suddenly.

   (d) safe, because there will be no oncoming traffic.

ALERTNESS

Q.
ABMW0339
Select 2 answers. What danger can arise during daylight when you are driving into an area which is heavily shaded by overhanging trees?

Ans.
   (a) Your vehicle's engine could suddenly run cold.

* (b) Your visibility could be seriously reduced.

   (c) Your vehicle's windscreen could fog up.

* (d) Your vehicle could be damaged by low-hanging branches.

Q. What should you do when you are being overtaken by another vehicle?

ABMW0340

Ans.   (a) Increase your speed.
        (b) Move to the right.
    * (c) Maintain your course and reduce speed if necessary.
        (d) Move to the left.

Q. Signals should be given to other road users .....

ABMW0341

Ans. * (a) clearly and in good time to warn all other traffic.
        (b) only when it is necessary to warn oncoming traffic.
        (c) only when it is necessary to warn following traffic.
        (d) except where road markings indicate your direction.

Q. You are facing into a narrow gap between oncoming traffic and vehicles parked on your left. You should .....

ABMW0342

Ans.   (a) signal to oncoming traffic to halt and move to the right and drive as normal.
        (b) indicate and drive on enforcing your priority.
        (c) edge your way forward around the parked vehicles.
    * (d) indicate right, stopping if necessary, until the oncoming traffic has passed by.

Q. If you give a late signal, other road users .....

ABMW0343

Ans.   (a) are not affected.
    * (b) may not have sufficient time in which to react.
        (c) always have sufficient time in which to react.
        (d) if oncoming only are not affected.

OBSERVATION/FIELD OF VIEW

VISIBILITY

Q. **Select 2 answers. The rain in this situation .....**

ABMW0344

Ans. * (a) reduces your visibility.
(b) increases your visibility.
* (c) increases the danger of skidding.
(d) reduces the danger of skidding.

Q. **You are at a junction where visibility is extremely limited. What should you do?**

ABMW0345

Ans. (a) Drive the front of your vehicle out onto the other road to enable other drivers to see you.
(b) Seek help from a passer-by.
* (c) Move out with extreme care, watching carefully to the left and the right.
(d) Sound your horn and quickly proceed.

Q. **When should you use your vehicle's rear view mirrors? Before .....**

ABMW0346

Ans. (a) reversing only.
* (b) moving off or changing lanes.
(c) changing gears.
(d) moving off only.

Q.   How do you proceed if your view is obstructed at a
ABMW0347 **junction?**

Ans. * (a) Move out slowly onto the road while watching carefully
            for other traffic.
         (b) Sound the horn several times and proceed.
         (c) Ask a passer-by to guide you out onto the other road.
         (d) Flash lights on and off quickly before moving out.

Q.   **What should you do when approaching traffic lights**
ABMW0348 **stuck on red?**

Ans.   (a) Check that there are no oncoming vehicles, and increase
            your speed.
         (b) Sound your horn.
       * (c) Stop and proceed with great caution.
         (d) Indicate and increase your speed.

Q.   **In daytime when there are dark clouds and visibility**
ABMW0349 **is reduced, you should .....**

Ans. * (a) drive with your side-lights or dipped headlights switched
            on.
         (b) drive with your full headlights switched on.
         (c) not switch on your lights until 'lighting-up hours'.
         (d) keep close to any vehicle in front with your headlights
            off.

BLINDSPOTS

Q.
ABMW0350
You are driving behind a heavy goods vehicle that is signalling to make a right-hand turn. What should you do?

Ans.
   (a) See if the vehicle can complete the turn without stopping, and if not, overtake it yourself.
   (b) Overtake it slowly on the inside by driving partly on the footpath if necessary.
* (c) Stay behind until there is sufficient space to overtake it on the inside or until it has completed the turn.
   (d) Tap your brakes to signal other vehicles to slow down.

Q.
ABMW0351
You are driving behind a bus which is signalling to make a left-hand turn. There is oncoming traffic. What should you do?

Ans.
   (a) Overtake it on the right-hand side.
   (b) Overtake it on the left-hand side.
* (c) Stay back and allow it to complete the turn.
   (d) Tap your brakes to signal other vehicles to slow down.

Q.
ABMW0352
What might be described as a bus driver's 'blind' spots?

Ans. * (a) The areas to the front, sides and rear of the bus which the driver cannot see.
   (b) The seats at the rear of the bus.
   (c) The windscreen area covered by the sun-visor.
   (d) The sunscreens or blinds covering individual seats when pulled down.

Q.
ABMW0353
You are driving behind a heavy goods vehicle. What are its driver's 'blind spots'?

Ans. * (a) The areas to the front, sides and rear which the driver cannot see.
(b) Parts of the road ahead which are obscured by other large vehicles.
(c) The portion of the windscreen covered by the sun-visor.
(d) The area directly behind the vehicle.

Q.
ABMW0354
What are a driver's 'blind spots' when towing a loaded trailer?

Ans. * (a) The areas to the side and rear of the vehicle and of the trailer that cannot be seen.
(b) The view to the front hidden by the sun visor.
(c) The number plate and lights on the rear of the vehicle and of the trailer.
(d) The area directly behind the vehicle.

Q.
ABMW0355
You are driving on a wide road behind a vehicle that has signalled to turn right ahead. What should you do?

Ans. (a) Stay behind until it has completed the turn.
* (b) Overtake on the left-hand side and carry on.
(c) Overtake on the left but only if you are turning left a short distance ahead.
(d) Stay behind and tap brakes to signal other drivers.

OVERTAKING

Q. When is it permissible to overtake another vehicle
ABMW0356 on the left-hand side?

Ans.　(a) Never.
　　　　(b) When there is sufficient space to do so.
　* (c) When the vehicle in front is signalling to turn right, or in slow-moving lanes of traffic.
　　　　(d) When there are three lanes available.

'U'-TURN

Q. You wish to perform a 'U'-turn. You should .....
ABMW0357

Ans. * (a) check ahead and behind for approaching traffic.
　　　　(b) check ahead for approaching traffic and signal them to stop.
　　　　(c) check behind for approaching traffic and signal them to stop.
　　　　(d) only perform a 'U'-turn outside the urban speed limit area.

Q. You want to turn your vehicle around on the road.
ABMW0358 You should .....

Ans.　(a) reverse into somebody's driveway and drive onto the road.
　* (b) check ahead and behind for oncoming traffic and turn briskly while still keeping a look-out.
　　　　(c) drive onto a footpath, if necessary, in order to ensure that you have sufficient room to turn.
　　　　(d) drive into somebody's driveway and reverse back onto the road.

GOOD JUDGEMENT AND PERCEPTION

FATIGUE

Q.
ABMW0359

What should you do if you become drowsy while driving?

Ans.
    (a) Turn up the heating.
* (b) Stop, take a break, including a short walk if possible.
    (c) Stretch your arms and close your eyes for short periods.
    (d) Open a window or turn on the air conditioning to let cool air into the vehicle.

Q.
ABMW0360

What should you do if you are driving and you feel tired?

Ans.
    (a) Increase your speed to shorten the journey time.
    (b) Drive along the centre of the road.
* (c) Stop and take a break.
    (d) Eat something.

AWARENESS

Q.
ABMW0361

You are behind schedule in arriving at a destination at an appointed time. What should you do?

Ans.
    (a) Exceed the speed limit, if necessary, to make up the time.
    (b) Drive aggressively.
* (c) Be patient and drive so as to arrive safely.
    (d) Drive on the hard shoulder where available.

Q.
ABMW0362

You are driving along in traffic and you do not want to travel as fast as the vehicles in front of you. What should you do?

Ans.

    (a) Keep your position and allow following vehicles to overtake you if they wish.

    (b) Indicate left and keep to the left.

 * (c) Keep to the left and allow following vehicles to overtake you if they wish.

    (d) Give a hand signal to following traffic to overtake you.

Q.
ABMW0364

You wish to turn right onto a busy road with a continuous flow of traffic, and the traffic lights which control the junction are temporarily out of action. You should .....

Ans.

    (a) turn right initially, and rejoin your intended route as the road system allows.

    (b) sound the horn and proceed slowly to cross the road.

 * (c) turn left initially, and rejoin your intended route as the road system allows.

    (d) proceed slowly with hazard warning lights on.

Q.
ABMW0365

You wish to drive across a busy road and the traffic lights which control the junction are temporarily out of action. You should .....

Ans.

    (a) sound the horn and proceed slowly to cross the road.

    (b) slowly force your way across, using hazard warning lights if necessary.

 * (c) take good observations, wait for a clear break in the traffic and proceed to cross the road.

    (d) beckon to other drivers your intention to cross, and proceed.

Q.
ABMW0366

You see a school bus stopped on your side of the road up ahead. What is the most correct action for you to take?

Ans.
(a) Sound the horn as a warning and continue on.
(b) Carry on regardless.
* (c) Reduce speed and overtake with caution.
(d) Signal and maintain current speed.

Q.
ABMW0367

You come up behind a vehicle that is going from side to side on the road in an unsafe manner. What should you do?

Ans. * (a) Stay well back until the road widens sufficiently to allow you overtake safely.
(b) Flash your lights and gesture aggressively at the other driver.
(c) Drive close behind with a view to overtaking.
(d) Signal and go around to the left of the vehicle.

Q.
ABMW0368

A heavy goods vehicle has moved out in order to make a left turn up ahead. What should you do?

Ans.
(a) Drive into the space on its left-hand side.
* (b) Stay behind it and allow it to finish the turn.
(c) Move out immediately and overtake as quickly as possible.
(d) Move to the right, but do not overtake.

Q. ABMW0369

A bus up ahead is signalling to make a left-hand turn and has moved out to make the turn. There is oncoming traffic. What should you do?

Ans.
    (a) Overtake on the left-hand-side.
    (b) Overtake on the right-hand-side.
* (c) Stay back and allow the bus to complete the turn.
    (d) Maintain your speed until you are close behind the bus.

Q. ABMW0370

You see a truck reversing into a side entrance on the left-hand side up ahead. What should you do?

Ans.
    (a) Try to drive past it.
    (b) Sound your horn to indicate to the driver of the truck that you wish to overtake.
* (c) Stop and wait until your way is clear.
    (d) Drive up close to the truck and stop.

Q. ABMW0371

You want to turn right at traffic lights and the green light is on. There is oncoming traffic. What should you do?

Ans. * (a) Go forward towards the centre of the junction and wait for a suitable gap to appear in the oncoming traffic before making the turn.
    (b) Remain at the stop line until a suitable gap in the oncoming traffic appears before making the turn.
    (c) Wait until a green arrow comes on.
    (d) Wait for the light to turn amber and then make the turn.

Q.
ABMW0372

When should you overtake a vehicle where you are likely to force oncoming traffic onto the hard shoulder on the opposite side of the road?

Ans.

   (a) When the shoulder is wide enough.

   (b) When none of the oncoming traffic is overtaking.

* (c) Never.

   (d) When the vehicle you are overtaking moves over and slows down.

Q.
ABMW0373

Forcing oncoming traffic on to the hard shoulder on the opposite side of the road is considered to be .....

Ans.

   (a) safe driving.

* (b) dangerous driving.

   (c) dangerous driving only at night.

   (d) acceptable when the oncoming traffic is slow moving.

Q.
ABMW0374

Other than on a motorway, can you move into the hard shoulder if there is oncoming traffic, to allow following traffic to overtake you?

Ans.

   (a) Never.

* (b) When the shoulder is clear, and it is safe to drive there.

   (c) Yes, when a truck or bus is oncoming.

   (d) Yes, when there is a junction up ahead on the left.

Q.
ABMW0375

Other than on a motorway, can you drive on the hard shoulder in order to let faster moving traffic overtake you?

Ans. * (a) Yes, temporarily, when the shoulder is clear, and it is safe to drive there while the traffic overtakes you.
(b) Only when driving on a dual-carriageway.
(c) Only when a truck or bus wishes to overtake you.
(d) Never.

Q.
ABMW0376

In a queue of traffic which is being controlled by traffic lights, you should .....

Ans. (a) overtake on the right and move to the head of the queue.
* (b) maintain your position in the queue.
(c) overtake on the left and move to the head of the queue.
(d) watch only for any vehicle overtaking on your right side.

Q.
ABMW0377

You are driving a vehicle which you are not familiar with. You should .....

Ans. * (a) drive initially with extra care and at lower speed than normal.
(b) drive at your normal speed and become accustomed to its features over time.
(c) avoid any long journeys until you are more familiar with the vehicle.
(d) drive faster than normal in order to assess its capability.

Q.
ABMW0378

There are road works up ahead and earth-moving machinery is moving about. Which of the following should you avoid doing .....

Ans. * (a) switch on the headlights as a warning and carry on as heretofore.
(b) be aware that there may be loose gravel on the road.
(c) engage a lower gear.
(d) be aware that the road surface may be uneven.
(e) be aware that oncoming traffic may have to follow diversions at the scene.

REACTION TIME

Q.
ABMW0379

Subject to the speed limit, what is the 'safest' speed to drive?

Ans. * (a) The speed which enables you to stop within the distance ahead that you can see to be clear.
(b) At the speed limit.
(c) The speed of other road users.
(d) The speed of the slowest vehicle on the road.

ATTENTION

Q.
ABMW0380
You are driving along and wish to use a hand held mobile phone. What should you do?

Ans.
    (a) Steer with one hand.
* (b) Stop at a safe location before using the phone.
    (c) Secure the phone between your shoulder and the side of your head while steering with both hands.
    (d) Move the phone as needed and keep the call to just a few minutes.

Q.
ABMW0381
You are stopped at traffic lights and the green light comes on. What should you do?

Ans.
    (a) Accelerate quickly so as not to delay the traffic.
    (b) Check your mirrors and move off quickly.
* (c) Check that other road users have cleared the junction, and move off with care.
    (d) Accelerate at the same rate as other drivers.

PATIENCE

Q.
ABMW0382
What should you do if another vehicle denies your right-of-way at a junction?

Ans. * (a) Be patient.
    (b) Flash your lights to express your displeasure.
    (c) Go after the vehicle with the intention of complaining to the driver.
    (d) Sound your horn.

Q. You are about to undertake a journey and are upset
ABMW0383 or angry. You should .....

Ans. * (a) not drive until you are calm.
    (b) try to relax as you drive along.
    (c) drive faster than normal for a distance.
    (d) only drive in a low gear for a period.
    (e) drive slower than normal for a distance.

Q. You are driving along and another vehicle is
ABMW0384 overtaking you. There is oncoming traffic. What
should you do?

Ans. * (a) Reduce speed and allow the other vehicle to move in
      front of you.
    (b) Maintain your position because the other driver should
      not have attempted to overtake you.
    (c) Maintain your position and flash your lights to warn the
      oncoming traffic.
    (d) Speed up so they cannot overtake you.

Q. When in a hurry and another vehicle cuts into your
ABMW0385 path, you should .....

Ans. * (a) be patient and not retaliate.
    (b) flash your lights to express your annoyance.
    (c) drive faster to make up for lost time.
    (d) pull up closely behind them so that other vehicles cannot
      cut into your path.

Q.
ABMW0386

One of your tyres goes flat as you are driving along. What should you do?

Ans. * (a) Stop at a safe place and change the tyre.
(b) Stop immediately and change the tyre.
(c) Stop immediately, unless on a motorway, and change the tyre.
(d) Drive to the closest repair shop and have them change the tyre.

Q.
ABMW0387

You wish to change to the traffic lane on your right in which there is other traffic driving along. What should you do?

Ans. * (a) Use your mirror, signal, and move into the right-hand lane when a suitable gap appears in the traffic in that lane.
(b) Indicate and move gradually into the right-hand lane.
(c) Pull in and stop, wait until a suitable gap appears and then move out to the right-hand lane.
(d) Increase your speed until you are travelling at the same speed as the traffic in the right lane, then move over.

ALCOHOL

Q.   **Select 2 answers. What effect can alcohol have on**
ABMW0388 **driving behaviour?**

Ans.   (a) It can increase perception and awareness.
   *   (b) It can contribute to a false sense of security and
          alertness.
        (c) It does not affect driving behaviour.
        (d) It can reduce your confidence.
   *   (e) It slows down your reactions.

Q.   **Select 2 answers. What effect does drinking alcohol**
ABMW0389 **have on a driver?**

Ans.   (a) It increases awareness.
   *   (b) It slows down the driver's ability to react.
        (c) It increases your concentration.
   *   (d) It makes the driver drowsy.
        (e) It improves co-ordination.

MEDICATION

Q.   **You are taking medication which may affect your**
ABMW0390 **driving. You should .....**

Ans. *   (a) ask your doctor if you may drive.
        (b) drink plenty of water while driving.
        (c) drive for short distances only.
        (d) make sure that the medication is recorded on your
          licence record.

Q.
ABMW0391
Which 2 of the following are correct?

Ans. * (a) Medication issued with or without a medical prescription may cause drowsiness.
   (b) Use of soft drugs prior to driving will not affect your driving.
 * (c) Driving without breaks may cause tiredness.
   (d) Use of soft drugs would never cause you to take risks while driving.
   (e) Only medication issued under prescription may cause drowsiness.

OBSERVANCE OF SAFE DISTANCE AND DRIVING IN VARIOUS WEATHER/ROAD CONDITIONS

SAFE DISTANCE/CLEARANCE

Q.
ABMW0392
What effect does a wet road surface have on your vehicle's braking ability?

Ans. * (a) Generally, it doubles the normal braking distance which is required on a dry surface.
(b) It makes no difference.
(c) It reduces the braking distance required.
(d) It increases the braking distance for vehicles without A.B.S.

Q.
ABMW0393
When driving uphill behind a slow-moving vehicle, you should .....

Ans. (a) drive close behind it while keeping well to the left.
(b) drive close behind it while keeping to the centre of the road.
* (c) stay well behind until you can safely overtake it.
(d) drive alongside of it until you can overtake it.

Q.
ABMW0394
After overtaking another vehicle, you should .....

Ans. (a) cut into the left as soon as you have passed it.
* (b) check that you are well past the other vehicle before gradually moving into the left.
(c) continue to signal right for a distance.
(d) continue to travel in the right-hand lane until an oncoming vehicle is within sight, then cut into the left lane as soon as you can.

Q. **What is the possible effect of cutting in too soon**
ABMW0395 **when overtaking another vehicle?**

Ans. * (a) Both vehicles could collide.
(b) The steering could lock.
(c) Your engine could lose power.
(d) Your engine could increase power.

Q. **When you are overtaking parked vehicles, you**
ABMW0396 **should .....**

Ans. * (a) allow sufficient clearance as you pass.
(b) watch in your right-hand mirror.
(c) keep close to the vehicles and watch out for pedestrians.
(d) move as far to the right as possible.

Q. **What stopping distance should you allow when you**
ABMW0397 **suspect that the road may be icy?**

Ans. * (a) Up to 4 times the normal.
(b) Up to half the normal.
(c) Twice the normal distance.
(d) The normal distance.

Q. **What clearance should drivers normally allow for**
ABMW0398 **parked vehicles?**

Ans. * (a) A door-width.
(b) The width of a mirror.
(c) The width of an average person.
(d) Six metres.

ROADHOLDING

Q.
ABMW0399
Why does it take longer to stop the vehicle after heavy rain?

Ans.   (a) The brake fluid is less effective in wet weather.
   *   (b) The tyres have less road grip than in dry weather.
       (c) The suspension of the vehicle is lighter in wet weather.
       (d) The suspension of the vehicle is heavier in wet weather.

Q.
ABMW0400
Where there is a film of water between your vehicle's tyres and the road surface, the vehicle's .....

Ans.   (a) steering and braking will be more effective.
       (b) braking will be more effective.
   *   (c) steering and braking will be less effective.
       (d) steering is more effective.

Q.
ABMW0401
What should you do if you encounter loose chippings on a road?

Ans.   (a) Press your hand against the windscreen or motorcycle faring.
       (b) Increase speed so as to avoid causing damage to the vehicle.
   *   (c) Slow down and allow extra clearance to all traffic until you have cleared the chippings.
       (d) Stop your vehicle until the loose chippings can be removed.

Q. **Spilled diesel on the road would .....**

ABMW0402

Ans. * (a) make the road more slippery.
   (b) increase tyre noise.
   (c) improve tyre grip on bends.
   (d) improve the vehicles braking ability.

Q. **What should you do when driving in slippery road conditions?**

ABMW0403

Ans. * (a) Drive at lower speeds and use gentle acceleration and braking.
   (b) Apply the brakes sharply from time to time to test the road surface.
   (c) Drive at normal speed but allow extra stopping distance.
   (d) Drive at faster speeds to maintain tyre grip.

Q. **What should you do when driving downhill on snow or ice?**

ABMW0404

Ans. (a) Use a higher gear than normal in order to avoid wheel spin.
   (b) Keep close to the left and brake sharply to keep the speed down.
   * (c) Use a lower gear and brake gently to keep the speed down.
   (d) Avoid using the brake and use a high gear.

Q.
ABMW0405

How does driving at high speed affect your vehicle's road holding?

Ans.
   (a) The wheel alignment keeps the tyres in full contact with the road.
   (b) The suspension compensates for any unevenness in the road surface.
* (c) The road holding ability of the vehicle is reduced.
   (d) The road holding ability of the vehicle is increased.

STOPPING DISTANCE AND BRAKING ABILITY

Q.
ABMW0406

The normal stopping distance of a car or motorcycle travelling at 50 km/h on a dry road is .....

Ans.
   (a) 5 metres.
   (b) 15 metres.
* (c) 25 metres.
   (d) 50 metres.

Q.
ABMW0407

The normal stopping distance of a car or motorcycle travelling at 50 km/h on a wet road is .....

Ans.
   (a) 5 metres.
   (b) 15 metres.
   (c) 20 metres.
* (d) 35 metres.

Q.
ABMW0408

The normal stopping distance of a car or motorcycle travelling at 100 km/h on a dry road is approximately .....

Ans.
   (a) 66 metres
* (b) 77 metres
   (c) 88 metres
   (d) 99 metres

Q.
ABMW0409

The normal stopping distance of a car or motorcycle travelling at 100 km/h on a wet road is approximately .....

Ans.
    (a) 102 metres
    (b) 112 metres
* (c) 122 metres
    (d) 132 metres

Q.
ABMW0411

If two vehicles each travelling at 60 km/h collide head-on, the speed on impact is .....

Ans.
    (a) 30 km/h.
    (b) 60 km/h.
* (c) 120 km/h.
    (d) 240 km/h.

Q.
ABMW0412

If two vehicles each travelling at 100 km/h collide head-on, the speed on impact is .....

Ans.
    (a) 50 km/h.
    (b) 100 km/h.
    (c) 150 km/h.
* (d) 200 km/h.

Q.
ABMW0420

If two vehicles each travelling at 80 km/h collide head-on, the speed on impact is .....

Ans.
    (a) 40 km/h.
    (b) 80 km/h.
    (c) 120 km/h.
* (d) 160 km/h.

Q.
ABMW0413

The recommended minimum gap per km/h which should be left between vehicles travelling on dry roads is .....

Ans.
    (a) I car length for each km/h.
    (b) 10 metres for each km/h.
    (c) 15 metres for each km/h.
  * (d) I metre for each km/h.

Q.
ABMW0425

If you have to brake suddenly .....

Ans. * (a) the vehicle behind might run into the back of your vehicle.
    (b) your vehicle's braking system could lose a lot of air.
    (c) your vehicle's braking system could overheat.
    (d) your vehicle's braking system could lose a lot of fluid.

Q.
ABMW0426

Which of the following does not affect braking distance?

Ans.
    (a) The speed and weight of the vehicle.
    (b) Road conditions and the tyres on the vehicle.
  * (c) The power of the engine.
    (d) The number of passengers carried.

Q.
ABMW0427

In dry weather, in order to judge a safe distance to drive behind the vehicle in front, you should .....

Ans. * (a) allow at least 2 seconds to elapse between the vehicle in front and your vehicle passing a fixed point.
    (b) allow at least 2 vehicle lengths between the vehicles.
    (c) allow at least 2 vehicle lengths for each kilometre per hour.
    (d) drive at the same speed as the vehicle in front.

Q.
ABMW0428

In wet weather, in order to judge a safe distance to drive behind the vehicle in front, you should .....

Ans. * (a) allow at least 4 seconds to elapse between the vehicle in front and your vehicle passing a fixed point.
(b) allow 2 seconds to elapse between the vehicle in front and your vehicle passing a fixed point.
(c) allow 4 vehicle lengths between the vehicles.
(d) drive at the same speed as the vehicle in front.

Q.
ABMW0429

You are following another vehicle in dry weather. In order to judge that you are not too close to it at any given point, you might say which of the following within the time it takes you to reach the same point?

Ans. (a) Two seconds.
(b) Only a fool.
* (c) Only a fool breaks the two second rule.
(d) Too near.

Q.
ABMW0430

What effect does carrying a load have on your vehicle's braking ability?

Ans. * (a) It increases the distance required to stop.
(b) It reduces the distance required to stop.
(c) It has no effect provided the brakes are in good condition.
(d) It increases the efficiency of the brakes.

Q.
ABMW0434

What effect does towing a loaded trailer have on stopping ability?

Ans. (a) It significantly reduces stopping distance.
* (b) It significantly increases stopping distance.
(c) It has no effect.
(d) It increases the efficiency of the brakes.

DRIVING RISK FACTORS RELATED TO VARIOUS ROAD CONDITIONS, IN PARTICULAR AS THEY CHANGE WITH THE WEATHER AND THE TIME OF DAY OR NIGHT

DRIVING IN FOG

Q. What should you do when you are driving in dense fog?

ABMW0435

Ans. * (a) Drive slowly on dipped headlights.
(b) Drive on sidelights only.
(c) Drive on sidelights and hazard warning lights.
(d) Drive on high beam headlights only.

Q. What should you do when driving in dense fog?

ABMW0436

Ans. (a) Drive along the central dividing line and watch for the reflective studs.
(b) Switch on your full headlights and drive slowly.
* (c) Drive slowly on your dipped headlights.
(d) Drive along the shoulder and watch for reflective markers.

DRIVING AT NIGHT

Q.
ABMW0437
When driving at night time your headlights should enable you to see for a distance of how many metres?

Ans.
  (a) 50.
* (b) 100.
  (c) 150.
  (d) 200.
  (e) 250.

Q.
ABMW0438
When driving at night time your dipped headlights should enable you to see for a distance of how many metres?

Ans.
  (a) 10.
  (b) 20.
* (c) 30.
  (d) 50.
  (e) 60.

Q.
ABMW0439
Incorrectly aimed headlights could .....

Ans.
  (a) cause the headlights to overheat.
  (b) reduce the wattage of the headlights.
* (c) dazzle oncoming road users and reduce their visibility.
  (d) increase the stopping distance.

Q.
ABMW0440
Driving at night, you should dip your headlights when .....

Ans.
  (a) approaching a bend or the brow of a hill.
  (b) driving at less than 50 km/h.
* (c) meeting or driving behind other traffic, or in a lit-up area.
  (d) entering a motorway.

Q. If you are blinded by the lights of an oncoming
ABMW0441 vehicle, you should .....

Ans. (a) reduce speed and switch on your full headlights.
    (b) drive well to the left and maintain your speed.
* (c) slow down and stop if necessary.
    (d) repeatedly flash your headlights until the oncoming
        vehicle's lights are dipped.

Q. You have been driving regularly in daylight and must
ABMW0442 now undertake a journey at night. You should drive
at .....

Ans. (a) a higher speed than during the day as traffic is lighter at
        night.
    (b) the same speed as during the day.
* (c) a slower speed than in the day as visibility is reduced at
        night.
    (d) a higher speed than during the day to minimise chances
        of falling asleep.

Q. What should you do when driving at night?
ABMW0443

Ans. (a) Increase your speed as traffic is lighter at night.
    (b) Turn up the radio volume to help maintain your
        concentration.
* (c) Drive at a speed that enables you to stop within the
        distance which you can see to be clear.
    (d) Drive at a higher speed than during the day to minimise
        chances of falling asleep.

Q.
ABMW0444
When driving at night, what is the safest approach to adopt?

Ans.
    (a) Drive with full headlights at all times.
* (b) Drive at a speed which allows you to stop within the distance which you can see to be clear.
    (c) Drive with dipped headlights at all times.
    (d) Drive with full headlights and spotlights.

Q.
ABMW0445
When meeting an oncoming vehicle at night, you should .....

Ans.
    (a) focus your eyes directly on its lights.
* (b) not look directly at its lights.
    (c) look down at the dash until it has passed so as not to be dazzled by its lights.
    (d) focus your eyes toward the passenger's window.

Q.
ABMW0446
When may you drive with full headlights in a built-up area at night?

Ans. * (a) This practice is not permitted.
    (b) When there is no oncoming traffic.
    (c) Between the hours of 11.30 p.m. and 7.00 a.m.
    (d) Between the hours of 1.00 a.m. and 6.00 a.m.

Q.
ABMW0447
What lights should you have on when driving close behind other traffic at night?

Ans. * (a) Dipped headlights.
    (b) Full headlights.
    (c) Sidelights.
    (d) Fog lights.

Q. ABMW0448   **When must you dip your headlights?**

Ans. * (a) When meeting or driving behind other vehicles or in lit-up areas.
(b) When driving at less than 50 km/h.
(c) When approaching a bend or the brow of a hill.
(d) When approaching roadworks.

Q. ABMW0449   **When driving late at night what should you be aware of .....**

Ans. (a) that reflectorised studs will warn you of bends ahead.
* (b) of the danger of falling asleep.
(c) that speed limits do not apply between midnight and 6 a.m.
(d) trucks may drive in the outer lane of a motorway.

Q. ABMW0450   **What should you do if you are dazzled by the lights of an oncoming vehicle at night?**

Ans. (a) Turn your head to one side.
(b) Shield your eyes with your hand.
* (c) Slow down and do not look directly at the lights of the oncoming vehicle.
(d) Look directly at the lights of the oncoming vehicle.

Q. ABMW0451   **When driving at night you see a single headlight approaching from ahead. What should you do?**

Ans. (a) Carry on because it can only be a motorcycle.
(b) Switch on your high beams as a warning.
* (c) Keep well to the left in case it is a four wheeled-vehicle.
(d) Move to the centre of the road to improve your visibility of the oncoming vehicle.

DRIVING ON SLIPPERY SURFACES

Q.
ABMW0452

Select 2 answers. How might you know if there is black ice on the road?

Ans.
(a) Steering will be heavy.
* (b) You will not be able to hear the noise of the tyre on the road.
(c) Tyre pressure will seem heavier.
(d) There will be louder tyre noise on the road.
(e) Tyre pressure will seem lighter.
* (f) Steering will seem lighter.

Q.
ABMW0453

Select 2 answers. If there is black ice on the road, you should ......

Ans.
(a) use a low gear.
* (b) avoid harsh braking, steering and acceleration.
(c) increase tyre pressure to improve stability.
* (d) use a high gear.
(e) drive with the choke on until you have cleared the area.

Q.
ABMW0454

You are likely to have black ice on the road .....

Ans.
(a) after wet and windy weather.
(b) after rain in darkness.
* (c) in cold weather after rain.
(d) in mild weather after rain.

Q.
ABMW0455

What should you do when driving on an icy road?

Ans.
    (a) Drive in a low gear at all times.

    (b) Drive at normal speed but apply the brakes from time to time to check for grip.

* (c) Drive at a slower speed than usual using gentle acceleration and braking.

    (d) Do not use the brakes.

Q.
ABMW0456

When driving a vehicle, what effect could icy roads have?

Ans. * (a) The vehicle could skid more easily than normal.

    (b) Tyre grip could improve.

    (c) Rear tyre treads could wear out more rapidly.

    (d) Front tyre treads could wear out more rapidly.

Q.
ABMW0457

What should you do when driving in slippery road conditions?

Ans.
    (a) Accelerate harder using the lower gears.

    (b) Apply the brakes regularly in order to improve tyre grip.

* (c) Use gentle acceleration and braking.

    (d) Drive slower than normal and do not use the brakes.

Q.
ABMW0458

How should you negotiate a bend when the road is slippery?

Ans.
    (a) Press the clutch and brake together.

    (b) Press the clutch only.

* (c) Drive slowly and smoothly.

    (d) Engage neutral gear position.

Q. Apart from the risk of skidding, what danger may
ABMW0459 arise when driving in snow?

Ans. * (a) You may not be able to see road signs and markings
clearly.
(b) The vehicle's exhaust may rapidly cool.
(c) The air in the tyres may freeze causing them to blow.
(d) The air blower may freeze.

Q. What should you do when driving in heavy rain?
ABMW0460

Ans. * (a) Beware of aquaplaning.
(b) Maintain normal speeds as on a dry road.
(c) Weave the vehicle slightly from side to side in order to
improve tyre grip.
(d) Speed up so that the vehicle will glide over any standing
water.

Q. What is the danger in driving with badly worn tyres
ABMW0461 at high speed on wet roads?

Ans. * (a) You have less control over your vehicle because it is
gliding on a film of water.
(b) Air pressure in the tyres is reduced.
(c) There is no danger provided the tyres are at the correct
pressure.
(d) There is no danger provided the tyre pressure has been
reduced to account for the worn tread.

Q. What should you do when you encounter mud on the
ABMW0462 road?

Ans.　(a)　Apply the brakes immediately.

　　　　(b)　Change to a lower gear and carry on.

　*　(c)　Reduce speed gradually while keeping a look out for
　　　　　tractors or earthmoving machines.

　　　　(d)　Gently increase speed to prevent mud from sticking to
　　　　　tyres.

Q. When crossing tram lines at an angle, you should .....
ABMW0463

Ans.　(a)　be aware that tyre grip is improved on the lines.

　　　　(b)　be aware that the wheels could get caught in the lines.

　　　　(c)　reduce speed to first gear.

　　　　(d)　depress the clutch pedal and 'coast' across.

　*　(e)　be aware that tyre grip is reduced on the lines.

Q. When driving over road markings such as lines, or
ABMW0464 arrows .....

Ans.　*　(a)　tyre grip is reduced.

　　　　(b)　tyre grip is improved.

　　　　(c)　A.B.S. will prevent the vehicle from skidding.

　　　　(d)　tyre grip is not affected.

　　　　(e)　steering control is improved.

DRIVING ON A FLOODED ROAD

Q.
ABMW0465

You have just driven through a flooded part of the road. What should you do?

Ans.

(a) Drive faster for a time in order to dry out your brakes.

(b) Apply the brakes firmly to check if they are still effective.

* (c) Press the brake pedal lightly at slow speed for a short distance in order to dry your brakes.

(d) Do nothing.

Q.
ABMW0466

How does wet weather affect your vehicle's engine performance?

Ans.

(a) It reduces the power output.

(b) It causes it to run at higher temperatures.

* (c) It has no effect.

(d) It causes it to run at lower temperatures.

Q.
ABMW0467

What should you do when you come to a part of the road that is flooded?

Ans.

(a) Increase speed in order to get through it quickly.

* (b) Reduce speed, and use a lower gear.

(c) Use a high gear and maintain your speed.

(d) Use a low gear and maintain your speed.

ROADWORKS

Q.
ABMW0468
What should you do when you are driving along and see road-works up ahead?

Ans. * (a) Reduce speed and be prepared to stop for earthmoving machinery or a flagman.
(b) Engage a lower gear to improve grip and maintain your speed.
(c) Increase speed in order to avoid getting stuck in soft ground.
(d) Maintain your speed until signalled to do otherwise by flagman.

Q.
ABMW0469
When you see road works up ahead, you should be aware that .....

Ans. * (a) there may be mud or chippings on the road.
(b) traffic is likely to travel much faster.
(c) you have right of way over earthmoving machinery.
(d) the area will be cleared for you and you should not delay.

CHARACTERISTICS OF VARIOUS TYPES OF ROAD

ONE-WAY STREET

Q.
ABMW0470
You are driving in a one-way street and you wish to turn right. You should drive close to the .....

Ans.
    (a) centre line of the road.
    (b) left-hand-side of the road.
  * (c) right-hand-side of the road.
    (d) centre line of the road while indicating right.

Q.
ABMW0471
When you are on a one-way street and wish to turn right up ahead, you should .....

Ans.
    (a) drive on the left until you are close to the turn before taking up position on the right.
  * (b) move to the right-hand side in good time.
    (c) drive close to the centre of the road.
    (d) continue in the lane you are in.

BUS LANE

Q.
ABMW0472
You wish to turn left into your driveway and there is a bus lane on your left. What should you do?

Ans.
    (a) Use a 'slowing down' hand signal in addition to your left turn indicator.
  * (b) Watch out for cyclists, taxis and buses which may be using the lane.
    (c) Watch out for buses only.
    (d) Not turn left across a bus lane.

Q. When may you drive in a 'contra-flow' bus lane?

ABMW0473

Ans.
      (a) After lighting-up time.
* (b) Never.
      (c) When the regular bus service is finished.
      (d) When there are more than two passengers in the vehicle.

Q. What traffic may use a 'contra-flow' bus lane?

ABMW0474

Ans.
      (a) Buses, taxis and cyclists.
* (b) Buses on a scheduled service.
      (c) Buses and taxis.
      (d) Buses, taxis and motorcycles.

Q. What traffic may use a 'with-flow' bus lane during the specified times?

ABMW0475

Ans.
      (a) Buses only.
      (b) All traffic.
* (c) Buses on a scheduled service, taxis and cyclists.
      (d) Vehicles with more than one passenger.

Q. When may you drive in a 'with-flow' bus lane?

ABMW0476

Ans.
      (a) During the hours specified on the bus lane information plate.
* (b) Outside the hours specified on the bus lane information plate.
      (c) After a bus has gone through on it.
      (d) After 9 p.m.

DUAL-CARRIAGEWAY

Q.
ABMW0477
When you are driving along on a dual-carriageway, you should normally drive .....

Ans.
    (a) on the right-hand lane.
    (b) on either lane of your choice.
* (c) on the left-hand lane unless you wish to overtake, or turn right.
    (d) on the right-hand lane, except when driving a tractor or works vehicle.

Q.
ABMW0478
When you wish to turn right from a minor road onto a dual-carriageway which has a wide median strip, you should .....

Ans.
    (a) not drive onto the dual-carriageway until there is a suitable gap in the traffic from both directions.
* (b) drive onto the median strip when the nearest carriageway is clear and then wait for a gap in traffic from the left, before proceeding.
    (c) not turn right onto a dual-carriageway.
    (d) not halt on the median strip.

Q.
ABMW0479
When you wish to turn right on to a dual-carriageway which has a narrow median strip, what should you do?

Ans. * (a) Wait on the side road until there is a suitable gap in the traffic from both directions.
    (b) When the nearest carriageway is clear, drive on to the median strip and wait.
    (c) You should not turn right onto a dual-carriageway.
    (d) Stop on the narrow median strip before proceeding.

2 PLUS 1 ROAD

Q.
ABMW0480

On a 2 plus 1 road, there are .....

Ans.

    (a) two motorway lanes and one non-motorway lane, in two directions.

    (b) two non-motorway lanes and one motorway lane, in two directions.

    (c) two motorway lanes in one direction and one non-motorway lane in the opposite direction.

* (d) two non-motorway lanes in one direction and one non-motorway lane in the opposite direction.

Q.
ABMW0481

On a 2 plus 1 road, you may turn right only .....

Ans.

    (a) when in the one-lane stretch.

    (b) when in the two-lane stretch.

* (c) at controlled junctions.

    (d) when directed by a pointsman.

Q.
ABMW0482

A 2 plus 1 road .....

Ans. * (a) separates opposing traffic streams.

    (b) has barriers between lanes of traffic going in the same direction.

    (c) has barriers between the hard shoulder and the verge.

    (d) has two lanes for cars and one lane for trucks and buses.

Q.
ABMW0483

Where may you overtake on a 2 plus 1 road?

Ans.

    (a) In the one-lane stretch.

* (b) In the two-lane stretch.

    (c) In the one-lane stretch if there is no oncoming traffic, and in the two-lane stretch.

    (d) In either the one-lane stretch or the two-lane stretch.

Q.
ABMW0484

What should you do when driving on a motorway or dual-carriageway?

Ans.

    (a) Relax because there will be no oncoming or crossing traffic.

* (b) Be alert for other drivers who may suddenly change lanes or reduce speed.

    (c) Match your speed to that of the vehicle in front.

    (d) Match your speed to that of the vehicle in the adjoining lane.

Q.
ABMW0485

When driving on a motorway, you should .....

Ans. * (a) drive in the left-hand lane unless you intend to overtake.

    (b) drive on whichever lane has the least volume of traffic.

    (c) not drive on the left-hand lane as it is reserved for heavy goods vehicles and coaches.

    (d) drive in the right-hand lane unless you intend to take a left exit.

Q.
ABMW0486

When driving on a motorway, you should .....

Ans.

    (a) relax because there will be no oncoming or crossing traffic.

    (b) match your speed to that of the vehicle in front.

* (c) be alert for other drivers who may suddenly change lanes or reduce speed.

    (d) drive at the maximum permitted speed.

Q. ABMW0487

Which statement is true about tyre pressure and driving on a motorway?

Ans.   (a) You should increase tyre pressure in order to cope with sustained high speeds.
             (b) You should reduce tyre pressure because high speeds will cause them to heat up.
       * (c) You should ensure tyre pressure is normal.
             (d) You should increase the front tyre pressure.

Q. ABMW0488

What should you do when you wish to join a motorway from a slip road?

Ans. * (a) Try to match your speed to that of traffic already on the motorway and merge into it in a suitable gap.
             (b) Drive directly onto the motorway.
             (c) Drive along the hard shoulder if necessary until a suitable gap appears in the motorway traffic to allow you to merge with it.
             (d) Always stop and give a hand signal.

Q. ABMW0489

When may you pick up or set down a passenger on a motorway?

Ans.   (a) When you stop on the hard-shoulder.
       * (b) Never.
             (c) When you are within 200 metres of a slip-road.
             (d) Only during daylight hours.

Q.
ABMW0490
You are driving on a motorway and you wish to turn back. What should you do?

Ans.
   (a) Cross to the opposite side of the motorway when there is a suitable gap in the oncoming traffic.
   (b) Wait on the hard shoulder until a suitable gap appears in traffic from both directions and then cross to the opposite side of the motorway.
* (c) Carry on to the next available slip road and cross the motorway by means of the fly over.
   (d) Wait on the right-hand side shoulder until a suitable gap appears in oncoming traffic.

Q.
ABMW0491
You are driving on a motorway and wish to take a break. You should .....

Ans. * (a) leave by the next exit and find a lay-by or suitable place to stop.
   (b) stop on the hard shoulder and use the roadside phone to inform the authorities.
   (c) only stop for 15 minutes or less.
   (d) pull well in on the left of the hard shoulder and switch on the hazard warning lights.

Q.
ABMW0492
On leaving a motorway, you should .....

Ans.
   (a) reduce speed gradually for a few kilometres.
   (b) maintain your speed until traffic conditions oblige you to slow down.
* (c) comply with the speed limit on the road you are joining.
   (d) maintain the speed of the vehicle in front of you.

Q. What should you do if you drive past your intended

ABMW0493
exit on a motorway?

Ans. (a) Stop on the hard shoulder and reverse back to the exit.

(b) Use the emergency telephone to ask for advice.

* (c) Drive on to the next exit.

(d) Carefully complete a 'U'-turn.

Q. What is the difference between driving on a

ABMW0494
motorway and driving on other types of road?

Ans. * (a) Traffic usually travels at a higher speed on a motorway.

(b) Hand-signals may not be used on a motorway.

(c) Speed limits are the same for all vehicles on a motorway.

(d) Traffic usually travels at lower speeds on a motorway
than on a dual-carriageway.

Q. What should you do when you are driving on a

ABMW0495
motorway and wish to overtake another vehicle?

Ans. (a) Use the mirror, signal and overtake in the left-hand lane
if necessary.

(b) Check for following traffic and overtake in either lane.

* (c) Use the mirror, signal and overtake in the right-hand
lane.

(d) Check for following and oncoming traffic and overtake in
either lane.

Q. The hard shoulder of a motorway may be used

ABMW0496
for .....

Ans. (a) joining the motorway.

(b) stopping to receive a call on a mobile phone.

(c) stopping the vehicle so the driver can have a rest.

* (d) stopping in an emergency.

(e) exiting the motorway.

Q. On exiting a motorway you should .....

ABMW0497

Ans.   (a) maintain motorway speeds for a few kilometres.
       * (b) be alert for oncoming and crossing traffic.
         (c) not overtake for a few kilometres.
         (d) watch for oncoming traffic on the slip road.

Q. On leaving a motorway, you should .....

ABMW0498

Ans.   (a) reduce speed gradually for a few kilometres.
         (b) drive up to 120 km/h.
       * (c) obey the reduced speed limit.
         (d) drive up to 110 km/h.

ROADS OF EQUAL IMPORTANCE

Q. You are coming to a junction where the roads are of equal importance and you wish to go straight ahead. What should you do?

ABMW0499

Ans.   (a) Carry on as normal because you have the right of way.
       * (b) Give way to traffic coming from your right.
         (c) Give way to traffic coming from your left.
         (d) Give way to traffic both left and right.

Q. What should you do when approaching a junction where the roads are of equal importance?

ABMW0500

Ans.   (a) Give way to all the traffic at the junction.
       * (b) Give way to traffic approaching from your right.
         (c) Give way to trucks and buses only.
         (d) Give way to traffic on the left.

CLEARWAY

Q.   **What is a clearway?**
ABMW0501

Ans. * (a) A road where stopping and parking is prohibited during certain periods.
    (b) A road which is reserved for pedestrians only.
    (c) A road which is reserved for buses only.
    (d) A road without road markings.

FACING DOWNHILL

Q.   **When you wish to park facing downhill, you**
ABMW0502   **should .....**

Ans.   (a) angle your wheels towards the road.
       * (b) angle your wheels towards the kerb.
        (c) angle your wheels in the straight ahead position.
        (d) wheel angle does not matter.

Q.   **When parking a vehicle on a two-way street facing**
ABMW0503   **downhill, you should .....**

Ans.   (a) put the gears in neutral.
        (b) put the gears in forward.
        (c) ensure the steering wheel is facing straight.
       * (d) turn the steering wheel to the left.
        (e) turn the steering wheel to the right.

FACING UPHILL

Q.
ABMW0504
When parking a vehicle facing uphill on a two-way street you should ensure that .....

Ans.
   (a) the steering is facing straight ahead.

   (b) the steering is turned to the left.

* (c) the steering is turned to the right.

   (d) the gears are in neutral.

   (e) the gears are in reverse.

UNMARKED ROAD

Q.
ABMW0505
You are driving on a primary road that is not marked by a central dividing line. What should you do?

Ans.
   (a) Drive on the middle of the road.

   (b) Imagine there is one there and drive on the right-hand side.

* (c) Imagine there is one there and drive on the left-hand side.

   (d) Position your vehicle midway on the left-hand side.

NARROW ROAD

Q.
ABMW0506
What should you do when you are driving on a narrow road and approaching a sharp bend?

Ans. * (a) Reduce speed, keep well to the left and watch for oncoming traffic.
     (b) Maintain your speed and flash your lights as a warning.
     (c) Wait until you are close to the bend before braking.
     (d) Move to the centre of the road to improve braking.

ROUNDABOUTS

Q.
ABMW0507
What should you do as you approach a roundabout?

Ans.   (a) Drive onto it as the traffic on it must give way to you.
  * (b) Give way to traffic already on the roundabout.
     (c) Give way only to heavy goods vehicles on the roundabout.
     (d) Give way only if taking the second or third exit.

Q.
ABMW0508
In which direction do you enter a roundabout? From the .....

Ans. * (a) Left.
     (b) Right.
     (c) Left or right.
     (d) Right, only when controlled by a traffic light.

Q.
ABMW0509

You are on a two-lane approach to a roundabout and wish to turn right. What lane should you use on your approach?

Ans. * (a) The right-hand lane.
      (b) The left-hand lane.
      (c) Either lane.
      (d) Right lane, only when controlled by a traffic light.

Q.
ABMW0510

You are coming to a roundabout and you wish to turn left. What should you do?

Ans.
      (a) Approach in any lane and give a clear signal.
      (b) Approach in the right-hand lane and give way to traffic which is already on the roundabout.
   * (c) Approach in the left-hand lane and give way to traffic which is already on the roundabout.
      (d) Approach in any lane, traffic on the roundabout must give way to you.

Q.
ABMW0511

You wish to take the second exit at a roundabout. What signals should you give?

Ans.
      (a) Give no signals.
      (b) Signal to the left as you approach the roundabout.
   * (c) Give no signal on the approach, then signal left as you pass the exit before the one you wish to take.
      (d) Signal right as you approach the first exit.

Q.
ABMW0512
You are stopped at a roundabout. Which factor is the most important in deciding whether or not to proceed?

Ans.
(a) The distance to the road from which you intend to leave the roundabout.
* (b) The distance and speed of the traffic coming from the right.
(c) The distance and speed of traffic coming from behind.
(d) The distance and speed of the traffic coming from the left.

TURNING RIGHT

Q.
ABMW0513
What is the correct road position(s) for a vehicle when turning right?

Ans.
(a) The left-hand side of the road.
(b) The right-hand side of the road.
* (c) Just left of the centre of the road.
(d) Either side of the centre of the road.

Q.
ABMW0514
You are driving on a main road and intend to turn right into a minor road. What should you do?

Ans. * (a) Yield right-of-way to oncoming traffic and to pedestrians who may be crossing at the junction.
(b) Turn in front of oncoming traffic as it must give right-of-way to you.
(c) Stop and signal traffic to exit left from the minor road.
(d) Stop and signal traffic to exit right from the minor road.

TUNNELS

Q.
ABMW0515

When entering a tunnel, you should .....

Ans. * (a) switch on your dipped headlights.
  (b) switch on your headlights.
  (c) listen to the local radio.
  (d) switch on your hazard warning lights.
  (e) switch on your hazard warning lights, if reversing.

Q.
ABMW0516

Select 2 answers. When entering a tunnel, you should .....

Ans. * (a) keep a safe distance.
  (b) wear sunglasses, if available, to prevent glare from the lights.
  (c) drive compact to the vehicle in front.
  (d) register at the first tunnel station.
 * (e) take off your sunglasses.

Q.
ABMW0517

Select 2 answers. When entering a tunnel, you should .....

Ans. (a) listen to the local radio.
 * (b) switch on your dipped headlights.
  (c) switch on your hazard warning lights.
  (d) switch on your full headlights.
 * (e) listen to the radio channel for the tunnel.

Q.

ABMW0518

Select 2 answers. When entering a tunnel, you should .....

Ans.
    (a) register at the first tunnel station.
    (b) wear sunglasses, if available, to prevent glare from the lights.
* (c) take off your sunglasses.
* (d) keep a safe distance.
    (e) drive compact to the vehicle in front.

Q.

ABMW0519

When driving through a tunnel, you should .....

Ans.
    (a) drive close to the central dividing line.
* (b) keep further back than normal from the vehicle in front.
    (c) monitor the exhaust filtering system to your vehicle.
    (d) drive with full headlights switched on.
    (e) reduce the tyre pressures to improve grip.

Q.

ABMW0520

In a tunnel if there is traffic congestion, you should .....

Ans.
    (a) keep compact to the vehicle in front.
    (b) leave your vehicle.
    (c) keep your distance.
* (d) switch on your hazard warning lights.
    (e) stop at the nearest emergency exit.

Q.

ABMW0521

In a tunnel traffic has come to a halt, you should .....

Ans.
    (a) select a low gear, and keep the engine ticking over.
    (b) switch on your fog lights.
* (c) switch off the engine.
    (d) only give hand signals.

Q.
ABMW0522
Select 3 answers. In a tunnel, in the event of a breakdown or accident, you should .....

Ans.   (a) beckon other traffic to overtake.
   *   (b) switch on your hazard warning lights.
   *   (c) move the vehicle to a lay-by or hard shoulder, if possible, to make room for overtaking traffic.
   *   (d) call for help from an emergency station.

Q.
ABMW0523
If your vehicle breaks down in a tunnel, you should .....

Ans.   (a) hitch a lift to the nearest service area and get help.
         (b) flag down a passing motorist and ask for help.
         (c) wait in the vehicle until help arrives.
         (d) walk to the end of the tunnel and call the police.
   *   (e) use the emergency telephone to call for help.

Q.
ABMW0524
Select 3 answers. In a tunnel, in the event of a breakdown or accident, you should .....

Ans. * (a) call for help from an emergency station.
         (b) reverse the vehicle, if necessary, to make room for over taking traffic.
   *   (c) move the vehicle to a lay-by or hard shoulder, if possible.
         (d) beckon other traffic to overtake.
   *   (e) switch on your hazard warning lights.

Q.
ABMW0525
While driving in a tunnel your vehicle goes on fire. You should .....

Ans.   (a) drive to the nearest emergency station.
         (b) drive to the nearest emergency exit.
         (c) wait for the tunnel traffic radio to announce procedure.
         (d) drive to nearest tunnel lay-by.
   *   (e) leave the vehicle and follow the emergency escape route lights.

VULNERABLE ROAD USERS

ALLOWING SUFFICIENT TIME FOR OTHERS

Q.
ABMW0526

You are approaching a junction where a pedestrian is walking across the road. What should you do?

Ans. * (a) Yield right-of-way to the pedestrian.
(b) Sound the horn as a warning of your approach.
(c) Carry on because the pedestrian only has right-of-way at a pedestrian crossing.
(d) Wave the pedestrian on.

Q.
ABMW0527

What should you do when you are being delayed by a cyclist just ahead?

Ans. (a) Try to squeeze past the cyclist despite oncoming traffic.
(b) Drive close behind to encourage the cyclist to pull in.
* (c) Stay well back until you have an opportunity to overtake safely.
(d) Sound the horn to encourage the cyclist to move over.

Q.
ABMW0528

You are stopped at traffic lights and the green light is about to come on as pedestrians are crossing the road. What should you do?

Ans. * (a) Wait as long as is necessary to enable them to complete the crossing.
(b) Sound the horn as a warning to them that the lights are about to change.
(c) Inch forward in your vehicle to encourage them to complete the crossing quickly.
(d) Signal the pedestrians to warn them of the light's changing and move out when it changes.

Q.
ABMW0530

You see a vehicle ahead which is being driven slowly by a learner driver. What should you do?

Ans.

    (a) Quickly overtake the vehicle to avoid being delayed.

  * (b) Be patient and allow extra time to the driver if necessary.

    (c) Drive close behind the vehicle to encourage the driver to speed up.

    (d) Sound the horn to encourage the driver to speed up.

Q.
ABMW0531

The vehicle in front of you is being driven by a learner driver and is causing an obstruction. What should you do?

Ans. *

    (a) Stay back until you can overtake safely.

    (b) Sound the horn to encourage the driver to pull in.

    (c) Drive close behind the vehicle in front and flash your headlights.

    (d) Overtake the vehicle as quickly as possible.

Q.
ABMW0532

An inexperienced learner driver is likely to react in traffic situations?

Ans.

    (a) More quickly.

  * (b) More slowly.

    (c) More correctly.

    (d) The same as an experienced driver.

Q.
ABMW0533

You see a cyclist just ahead who is about to overtake a parked vehicle. There is oncoming traffic. What should you do?

Ans.
   (a) Expect the cyclist to go on the inside of the vehicle.
   (b) Allow enough clearance to overtake both the parked vehicle and the cyclist together.
* (c) Allow the cyclist to overtake the parked vehicle, and then proceed.
   (d) Overtake the cyclist before the cyclist has a chance to overtake the parked vehicle.

Q.
ABMW0534

You are driving in slow-moving traffic in a built up area and there is a pedestrian crossing up ahead. What should you do?

Ans.
   (a) Stop your vehicle on the pedestrian crossing if necessary.
   (b) Drive close up behind the vehicle in front and move forward when it moves.
* (c) Time your stop/start movements to avoid obstructing the pedestrian crossing.
   (d) Avoid obstructing the pedestrian crossing only if there are pedestrians on the crossing.

Q.
ABMW0535

Select 3 answers. At road junctions you should take particular care for which of the following most vulnerable road users?

Ans. * (a) Pedestrians.
   (b) Tractor drivers.
   (c) Minibus or van drivers.
* (d) Cyclists.
   (e) Car drivers.
* (f) Motorcyclists.

Q.
ABMW0536

Select 3 answers. At traffic lights you should take particular care for which of the following coming up on your left?

Ans. * (a) Cyclists.
 * (b) Pedestrians.
 (c) Cars.
 * (d) Motorcyclists.
 (e) Buses or vans.

Q.
ABMW0537

At a pelican crossing or traffic lights, pedestrians are crossing after the traffic light facing you shows green. You should .....

Ans. (a) beckon them along as quickly as possible.
 (b) sound your horn as a warning and proceed with care.
 (c) move off slowly.
 * (d) wait patiently and let them cross at ease.
 (e) rev your engine to encourage them to hurry along.

Q.
ABMW0538

Select 3 answers. You wish to make a left-hand turn on a busy city street intersection. There are pedestrians and cyclists around. You should .....

Ans. * (a) watch for cyclists or pedestrians who may try to cross the road in front of you.
 * (b) watch for cyclists or pedestrians on your left.
 (c) signal left, watch the right-hand mirror and make the turn when it is clear.
 (d) stay tight on the left so as to prevent cyclists or pedestrians coming up your left side.
 * (e) allow comfort space for any pedestrians standing on the corner.

Q. In slow moving, city driving, blind spots should be
ABMW0539 checked frequently for .....

Ans.   (a) horse drawn carriages.
  * (b) cyclists, pedestrians and motorcyclists.
  (c) other large vehicles.
  (d) parking bays.
  (e) taxis.

Q. At a junction with green traffic lights in your favour
ABMW0540 elderly people are crossing. You should .....

Ans.   (a) beckon them to return to the side.
  (b) tell them to be careful and wave them across.
  (c) proceed if you can edge your way through.
  * (d) allow them to cross in their own time.

Q. Select 3 answers. At traffic lights you should take
ABMW0541 particular care for which of the following coming up
on your left?

Ans.   (a) Cars.
  * (b) Cyclists.
  (c) Minibuses or vans.
  * (d) Motorcyclists.
  * (e) Pedestrians.

Q. At a pelican crossing or traffic lights pedestrians are
ABMW0543 crossing after the traffic light facing you shows green.
You should .....

Ans. * (a) wait patiently and let them cross at ease.
  (b) beckon them along as quickly as they can.
  (c) move off slowly.
  (d) rev your engine to encourage them to hurry along.
  (e) sound your horn as a warning and proceed with care.

REDUCING SPEED HAVING REGARD TO OTHER ROAD USERS

Q.
ABMW0544

What should you do when you see an elderly person crossing the road up ahead?

Ans.

(a) Increase your speed to pass quickly.

* (b) Reduce your speed sufficiently to enable the person to complete the crossing safely.

(c) Increase your engine noise to warn the person of your approach.

(d) Sound the horn to warn them that you are approaching and maintain your speed.

Q.
ABMW0545

While driving at 80 km/h you see some children on the road ahead. What should you do?

Ans.

(a) Turn on your headlights.

(b) Maintain your speed.

* (c) Reduce speed and prepare to stop if necessary.

(d) Sound the horn to warn them of your approach and maintain your speed.

CLEARANCE

Q.
ABMW0546

What should you do when you see children just ahead on the road?

Ans. * (a) Give them a wide clearance and be prepared to slow down if necessary.
(b) Keep your course as the noise of the engine will make them keep in.
(c) Flash your lights to warn them of your presence and maintain your present speed.
(d) Flash your lights and sound your horn to warn them of your approach.

Q.
ABMW0547

You are driving on a windy day and see a cyclist ahead of you. What should you do?

Ans. * (a) Allow extra clearance in case the cyclist is blown off course.
(b) Expect the cyclist to be alert and to keep in to the left.
(c) Maintain your course but sound the horn as a warning.
(d) Maintain your course but prepare to swerve around the cyclist if necessary.

Q.
ABMW0548

What should you do when overtaking a cyclist?

Ans. (a) Sound the horn as a warning.
* (b) Allow extra clearance in case the cyclist swerves suddenly.
(c) Drive close to the cyclist and overtake promptly.
(d) Sound the horn as a warning and overtake the cyclist as quickly as possible.

Q.

ABMW0549

What should you do when you see joggers ahead on the left?

Ans. * (a) Use your mirrors, indicate, and overtake allowing sufficient clearance.
(b) Sound the horn and flash your lights to warn them of your presence.
(c) Expect them to move in so that you can pass them by.
(d) Indicate, use your mirrors and overtake allowing sufficient clearance.

Q.

ABMW0550

You are driving on a road that has a potholed surface and there is a cyclist ahead. What should you do?

Ans. * (a) Allow extra clearance in case the cyclist swerves out to avoid a pothole.
(b) Maintain your course and sound your horn to alert the cyclist of your approach.
(c) Expect the cyclist to keep to the left and maintain your speed.
(d) Change to a lower gear and overtake quickly.

ANTICIPATION OF VULNERABLE ROAD USERS

Q.
ABMW0551

Select 2 answers. What precautions should you take in relation to pedestrians when driving in slow-moving traffic?

Ans.
    (a) Allow them to cross the road only at pedestrian crossings.
* (b) Watch for pedestrians who may cross the road in front of your vehicle.
    (c) Do not leave a gap between your vehicle and the vehicle in front.
* (d) Look around and check your mirrors regularly.
    (e) Rev your engine occasionally as a warning.

Q.
ABMW0552

What should you be aware of when making a left-hand turn?

Ans. * (a) Cyclists might come up on the 'inside'.
    (b) Following traffic must have room to overtake.
    (c) You should approach with the nearside wheels brushing against the kerb.
    (d) Cyclists might come up on the 'outside'.

Q.
ABMW0553

Select 2 answers. When driving through a housing estate or play area, what hazards may arise?

Ans.
    (a) Minimum loading limits may apply.
    (b) All the traffic may be slow moving.
* (c) Children or residents may come out suddenly.
    (d) Parking fees may apply.
* (e) Vehicles may drive or reverse onto the road.

Q.
ABMW0554

When you approach a play area up ahead, you should .....

Ans. * (a) watch out for children who might suddenly dash onto the road.
(b) obey the speed limit and maintain your course.
(c) switch on your hazard warning lights.

Q.
ABMW0555

When making a left turn into a side road, you should .....

Ans. * (a) check for pedestrians or cyclists who may have come up on the 'inside'.
(b) ensure that following traffic has room to overtake if necessary.
(c) expect that traffic coming out of the other road will always stay back and allow you space.
(d) claim your right-of-way.

Q.
ABMW0556

You are driving on a country road without footpaths. What should you look out for coming towards you on your side of the road?

Ans. (a) Motorcycles.
* (b) Pedestrians.
(c) Tractors.
(d) Cyclists.

Q.
ABMW0557 Select 3 answers. What should you do when driving at night on an unlit road?

Ans.
    (a) Maintain your speed when meeting oncoming traffic.
    (b) Drive on the centre of the road.
* (c) Anticipate that there may be pedestrians up ahead who may be wearing dark clothing.
* (d) Watch for parked cars.
    (e) Drive as close as possible to the line of reflective studs.
* (f) Watch for stray animals or livestock.

Q.
ABMW0558 What could happen if you park on a footpath?

Ans.
    (a) The suspension could be weakened.
    (b) The tyres could lose air pressure.
* (c) Pedestrians could be impeded.
    (d) Traffic could be impeded.

SIGNALLING TO OTHER DRIVERS

Q.
ABMW0559 What should you do when you are driving along and see a cyclist on the road up ahead?

Ans. * (a) Use your mirrors, indicate in good time, and move out if safe to do so.
    (b) Use your mirrors, and move out to overtake without indicating.
    (c) Indicate, move out and check the mirror for following traffic.
    (d) Indicate, check the mirror and move out.

Q.
ABMW0560

If indicators are not fitted or are not working, how should signals be given?

Ans.

   (a) It is not necessary to give signals provided you look around.

   (b) Your position on the road is a signal in itself.

* (c) By hand, clearly and in good time.

   (d) Verbally, out your window.

Q.
ABMW0561

There is traffic behind you while driving on an open road. If you meet a pedestrian, you should .....

Ans.

   (a) leave a minimum safety clearance of 25 centimetres.

   (b) flash your lights so that following traffic might see the pedestrian.

* (c) signal to following traffic that you are about to overtake.

   (d) gesture to the pedestrian to move in off the road.

DRIVING IN DARKNESS

Q.
ABMW0562

Dark winter mornings and evenings .....

Ans. * (a) increase the potential of cyclists being hit by your vehicle on unlit country roads.

   (b) mean that all cyclists in the countryside will have space in the margin of the road so that you can overtake with out reducing speed and moving out.

   (c) mean that all cyclists will be wearing reflective belts and have the correct lighting on their bicycles, and will be clearly visible to you.

Q. **Dark winter mornings and evenings .....**

ABMW0563

Ans. * (a) require you to take extra care for cyclists in the countryside as they may not be clearly visible to you.

(b) mean that all cyclists you may meet in the countryside will be wearing bright clothing and be clearly visible.

(c) mean that oncoming cyclists could never be dazzled by your lights and wobble off course into your path.

Q. **Dark winter mornings and evenings .....**

ABMW0564

Ans. * (a) require you to take extra care for vulnerable pedestrians walking in the countryside.

(b) mean that all pedestrians in the countryside will be wearing reflective armbands and bright clothing, and will be clearly visible to you.

(c) have no effect on your ability to see vulnerable pedestrians.

(d) mean that there will be no pedestrians on the roads.

Q. **Dark winter mornings and evenings .....**

ABMW0565

Ans. (a) mean you should anticipate that any pedestrians up ahead will be on a footpath and will be free from danger from your vehicle.

* (b) increase the potential for school children to be hit by your vehicle on unlit country roads.

(c) do not affect your ability to see stray animals on the road.

(d) mean that you should drive with full headlights at all times in order to see pedestrians walking on unlit country roads.

NECESSARY DOCUMENTS

DRIVING LICENCE AND LEARNER PERMIT MATTERS

Q.
ABMW0566
What drivers are required to display 'L' Plates on their vehicles?

Ans.
(a) Drivers on their second Learner Permit.
(b) Learner drivers who are accompanied by the holder of a "full" licence in the relevant vehicle category.
* (c) All Learner Permit holders except those driving motorcycles, agricultural tractors and works vehicles.
(d) Drivers who have less than two years driving experience.

Q.
ABMW0567
You have passed your test on a vehicle with automatic transmission. What restriction does this put on your licence?

Ans.
(a) You may not drive at speeds of more than 80 km/h.
(b) You must continue to display 'L' plates.
* (c) You may not drive vehicles with manual transmission.
(d) You may not tow a trailer.

Q.
ABMW0568
What roads can Learner Permit drivers drive on?

Ans.
(a) All roads.
* (b) All roads except motorways.
(c) All roads except motorways and dual-carriageways.
(d) All roads except dual-carriageways.

Q.   **'L' Plates should be .....**

Ans.   (a)   a green 'L' on a white background.

           (b)   a red 'L' on a transparent background.

   *   (c)   a red 'L' on a white background.

           (d)   a white 'L' on a yellow background.

Q.   **Which of the following is correct? Learner Permit**

holders .....

Ans.   (a)   may not drive on national primary roads.

   *   (b)   may not drive on motorways.

           (c)   may not drive on dual-carriageways.

           (d)   may drive on all roads.

Q.   **What Learner Permit holders are exempt from**

having to be accompanied by qualified drivers?

Ans.   (a)   None.

           (b)   All.

   *   (c)   Learner Permit holders in categories A, A1 and M and W.

           (d)   All Learner Permit holders in category B and W.

Q.   **The 'gross vehicle weight' of your vehicle should be**

found .....

Ans. *   (a)   on a metal plate in the vehicle.

           (b)   on the Tax Disc.

           (c)   on the insurance disc.

           (d)   on the tachograph.

VEHICLE REGISTRATION AND TAX REQUIREMENTS

Q.
ABMW0586

May you use your vehicle in a public place when it does not have a current tax disc displayed?

Ans.
    (a) Yes, but for not more than one month after the expiry of your previous disc.
    (b) Yes, but for not more than 10 days after the expiry of your previous disc.
* (c) No.
    (d) Yes, but not more than 14 days after expiry of your previous disc.

Q.
ABMW0588

You wish to drive a vehicle and the tax disc is out of date. You should .....

Ans.
    (a) notify the Gardaí.
    (b) renew it within 10 days of expiry.
* (c) not drive it.
    (d) drive it only in case of an emergency.

Q.
ABMW0589

You wish to drive another vehicle which is not currently taxed. May you transfer the tax disc from your own vehicle onto it?

Ans.
    (a) Yes, on a temporary basis.
    (b) Yes, provided your own vehicle is not being used at the same time.
* (c) No.
    (d) Only when the proper form has been completed.

Q.
ABMW0590
Who should ensure that the correct tax disc is displayed on a vehicle?

Ans.
    (a) The driver, where not the owner.
  * (b) The driver and owner are equally responsible.
    (c) The owner, where not the driver.
    (d) The government.

Q.
ABMW0591
When must a current tax disc be displayed on a new vehicle on a public road?

Ans.
    (a) Not later than 3 months after registration.
    (b) Not later than 6 months after registration.
  * (c) At all times.
    (d) Only when driving on motorways.

Q.
ABMW0592
Who may demand to see your vehicle registration document or vehicle licensing certificate, whichever applies in your case?

Ans.
    (a) Any person with whom you are involved in an accident.
    (b) Any Traffic Warden.
  * (c) Any member of the Gardaí.
    (d) Anyone.

INSURANCE

Q.
You are driving a vehicle which is not your own but with the owner's consent. Who is responsible for ensuring that the vehicle in question is properly insured?

Ans.
    (a) The driver only.
* (b) Both the driver and the vehicle owner.
    (c) The vehicle owner only.

Q.
Your insurance policy has expired. Are you still covered to drive your vehicle?

Ans.
    (a) Yes, up to 10 days after expiry.
* (b) No.
    (c) Yes, up to 30 days after expiry.
    (d) Yes, up to 14 days after expiry.

Q.
You wish to drive another privately owned vehicle but you are uncertain if you are insured to drive it. You should .....

Ans.
    (a) transfer the insurance disc from your own vehicle on to it.
* (b) ensure from your own insurance company if you are covered to drive it, before driving.
    (c) drive it provided you tell your insurance company within 10 days, and agree to pay any additional premium.
    (d) drive if there is an insurance disc on the vehicle.

Q.
ABMW0596

When you wish to drive a vehicle and you are not sure if you are covered by insurance, you should .....

Ans. * (a) not drive until cover is confirmed by your insurance company.
(b) check with your local motor taxation office.
(c) check with your local Garda station.

Q.
ABMW0597

What is the minimum insurance cover which is required to drive a vehicle on a public road?

Ans. (a) Personal accident.
(b) Comprehensive.
* (c) Third-party.
(d) Third-party, fire and theft.

Q.
ABMW0598

What information are you required to give when you wish to obtain insurance cover on your vehicle?

Ans. (a) All information relating to the previous 5 years.
(b) Your age and details of your driving licence.
* (c) All information requested by the insurance company.
(d) Name, address, phone number and licence number.

Q.
ABMW0599

When you have had the engine capacity of your vehicle altered, you should .....

Ans. (a) not exceed 50 km/h for the first 1,600 kilometres after having the alteration made.
* (b) inform your local motor taxation office and your insurance company.
(c) inform your insurance company.
(d) not exceed 80 km/h for the first 1,600 kilometres after having the alteration made.

Q.
ABMW0600
What must be displayed on a vehicle's windscreen at all times?

Ans.
    (a) The insurance cover note.
* (b) The insurance disc.
    (c) The insurance certificate.
    (d) The insurance certificate and motor tax disc.

AUTOMATIC TRANSMISSION

Q.
ABMW0601
You have passed your test on a vehicle with automatic transmission. You may now drive .....

Ans.
    (a) all vehicles in the licence category.
    (b) manual vehicles only.
* (c) automatic vehicles only.
    (d) all vehicles in the licence category, but only automatic vehicles on a motorway.

ACCIDENTS

Q.
ABMW0602
Select 2 answers. At a motorcycle accident where the rider is in shock, you should .....

Ans.
    (a) move the rider to the side of the road.
* (b) ensure the helmet is not removed.
    (c) ensure the helmet is removed.
* (d) lie the rider on his side in the recovery position.
    (e) give the rider a hot drink.

WHAT ACTION TO TAKE

Q.
ABMW0611

You have been involved in an accident where nobody has been injured but the vehicles are causing danger or obstruction to other road users. What should you do?

Ans.
    (a) Halt all other traffic until blame has been established and then move the vehicles.

* (b) Mark the position of the vehicles and move them off the road.

    (c) Wait for the Gardai to arrive before moving the vehicles off the road.

    (d) Move any passengers and display a red warning triangle on the vehicle.

Q.
ABMW0612

What should you do if you are involved in an accident which you think was not your fault?

Ans.
    (a) Carry on to the nearest Garda station and report it as soon as possible.

* (b) Stop immediately and exchange particulars with the other person involved.

    (c) Carry on if you think there was no damage done to your vehicle.

    (d) Exchange licence details with the other driver.

Q.
ABMW0613

If you have been involved in a road accident, you must notify your insurance company .....

Ans.
    (a) only when renewing your policy.

* (b) as soon as possible.

    (c) only if a person has been injured.

    (d) only if you were at fault.

COLLISION - NO INJURY

Q.
ABMW0614

If you are involved in a collision where minor damage is caused to both vehicles, you .....

Ans. * (a) must stop your vehicle and exchange particulars with the driver of the other vehicle.
(b) must mark the position of the vehicles on the road and report to the Gardai.
(c) must report it to the Gardai.
(d) must share the cost of any damage caused.

Q.
ABMW0615

You have been involved in an accident where damage to property only has occurred. What should you do?

Ans. (a) Report the incident to the Gardai within 10 days.
(b) Report the incident to the Gardai within 24 hours.
* (c) It is not necessary to report the incident to the Gardai provided it is reported to the property owner.
(d) Report the incident to the Gardai within 14 days.

COLLISION - PERSON INJURED

Q.
ABMW0616

Where a person has been injured in an accident, you should .....

Ans. (a) move the vehicles out of the way to avoid causing obstruction.
(b) move the victim.
* (c) move the victim only if there is a risk of fire or further injury.
(d) move the victim and the vehicles.

Q.
ABMW0617

You come on the scene of an accident where a person has been injured. What should you give the person to drink?

Ans. * (a) Nothing.
(b) A cold drink.
(c) A non-alcoholic drink.
(d) A hot drink.

Q.
ABMW0618

You have been involved in an accident and a person is unconscious. What should you do?

Ans. * (a) Loosen any tight clothing at the neck, and keep the person warm with a blanket or overcoat.
(b) Move the person to the nearest hospital.
(c) Try to get the person to drink something warm.
(d) Raise the person's head.

Q.
ABMW0619

You have arrived at the scene of an accident and a person is bleeding heavily. What should you do?

Ans. (a) Keep the person warm and give him/her something to drink.
* (b) Try to stop the bleeding by putting on a tight bandage.
(c) Lie the person flat on the ground and prevent him/her from moving.
(d) Raise the injured part of the body with as little movement as possible.

Q. ABMW0620
You have been involved in an accident and a person has been injured. What is the most correct procedure?

Ans. * (a) Do not move the person unless there is a danger of fire or of being hit by passing vehicles.
(b) Carry the person to the side of the road.
(c) Have the person move various limbs to determine the extent of the injuries.
(d) Keep the injured person calm and give them a cold drink.

Q. ABMW0621
A person has been injured in a road accident. Who should be called first?

Ans. (a) The person's relatives.
* (b) An ambulance and the Gardai.
(c) The injured person's solicitor.
(d) The injured person's insurance provider.

Q. ABMW0622
You have been involved in an accident and a person has been injured. You should firstly .....

Ans. * (a) report it to the Gardai and the local ambulance service.
(b) report it to the local motor taxation office.
(c) report it to your insurance company.

EXCHANGE OF INFORMATION

Q.

ABMW0623

You have been involved in an accident with a visiting uninsured motorist where no injury has occurred. You should report it to .....

Ans. * (a) the Motor Insurers Bureau of Ireland and your own insurance company.
    (b) the Department of Foreign Affairs.
    (c) your local motor taxation office.
    (d) the Irish Insurance Federation and your own insurance.

Q.

ABMW0624

If you are involved in a collision with another vehicle where nobody is injured, what must you do?

Ans. * (a) Exchange all relevant particulars with the other driver.
    (b) Give your name and address only.
    (c) Report it to the Gardai.
    (d) Submit a report in written form to the Insurance Bureau of Ireland.

HAZARDOUS MATERIALS

Q.

ABMW0625

You come on the scene of an accident involving a vehicle carrying hazardous materials. What should you do?

Ans. (a) Try to establish the nature of the hazardous materials before raising the alarm.
    (b) Try to move the vehicle to a safe place.
* (c) Keep well clear and raise the alarm.
    (d) Wave a white cloth indicating hazardous materials present.

SAFETY FACTORS RELATING TO VEHICLE LOADING AND PERSONS CARRIED

SEVERE BRAKING

Q. **What danger can arise if you have to brake suddenly?**

ABMW0626

Ans. * (a) Both yourself and your passenger(s), could be thrown forward.
     (b) The passenger(s) could be thrown forward.
     (c) Both yourself and your passenger(s), could be thrown backwards.
     (d) The passenger(s) could be thrown backwards.

Q. **In order to avoid the need for harsh braking, you should ......**

ABMW0627

Ans. (a) drive with cruise control engaged.
     (b) drive with your foot resting on the clutch pedal.
* (c) look ahead and anticipate what others may do.
     (d) drive with foot resting on the brake-pedal.

LOAD CARRYING CAPACITY

Q. **What determines a vehicle's total load carrying capacity?**

ABMW0628

Ans. (a) The size of the boot.
     (b) The number of seats.
* (c) The vehicle manufacturer's specification.
     (d) The horsepower of the engine.

Q. ABMW0629 **What defines the maximum allowed towing capacity of a drawing vehicle?**

Ans.
    (a) The strength of the hitch.
* (b) The manufacturer's specifications.
    (c) The size of the tyres on the vehicle.
    (d) The combined weight of both the vehicle and its trailer.

LOAD DISTRIBUTION

Q. ABMW0630 **What effect does overloading a vehicle have on road-holding?**

Ans.
    (a) It improves the stability of the vehicle provided the load is evenly distributed.
* (b) It can make the vehicle more difficult to control.
    (c) It can make the vehicle more difficult to control only when reversing.
    (d) It can make the vehicle more difficult to control only when going downhill.

Q. ABMW0631 **What effect could overloading with passengers or goods have on a vehicle?**

Ans.
    (a) It could improve the vehicle's road-holding ability.
* (b) It could lessen the vehicle's road-holding ability.
    (c) It would not have any effect provided you drive slowly.

Q.
ABMW0632
How could an unevenly distributed load affect your vehicle?

Ans. * (a) It could make the vehicle unstable while cornering or braking.
(b) It could cause the clutch to slip while accelerating.
(c) It could cause the gearbox to overheat.
(d) It could affect fuel consumption.

TECHNICAL MATTERS, WITH A BEARING ON ROAD SAFETY

HEADLIGHTS

Q.
ABMW0633
Why is it important to ensure that your vehicle's headlights are correctly aligned?

Ans. (a) To reduce battery consumption.
(b) To enable you to drive faster in the dark.
* (c) To enable you to see properly.
(d) To increase the life span of your headlights.

Q.
ABMW0634
If your vehicle's headlights were incorrectly aimed .....

Ans. (a) the bulbs must be replaced frequently.
* (b) the headlight beams would not shine light correctly on the road ahead.
(c) a warning light appears on the dash.
(d) may cause extra wear on your headlight lens.

Q. Incorrectly aligned headlights could .....

ABMW0635

Ans. * (a) dazzle oncoming drivers.
(b) increase battery consumption.
(c) cause a fire.
(d) wear out the headlights prematurely.

Q. In general, how frequently should your vehicle's lights be checked?

ABMW0636

Ans. (a) Monthly.
(b) Annually.
* (c) Weekly.
(d) Every three months.

Q. What effect can a broken lens have on a headlight?

ABMW0637

Ans. * (a) It can reduce and distort the beam.
(b) It can increase the brightness of the beam.
(c) It can cause the bulb to overheat.
(d) It can cause the bulb to blow if not fixed immediately.

Q. You are driving at night and the right-hand headlight bulb has blown. You should .....

ABMW0638

Ans. (a) replace it temporarily with the left-hand bulb.
(b) drive with the right-hand indicators on.
* (c) not drive until you have replaced it.
(d) replace it temporarily with the brake-light bulb.

Q. Select 2 answers. Which of the following are you required to keep in good condition?

ABMW0639

Ans. (a) Upholstery.
(b) Radio.
* (c) Headlights.
* (d) Seatbelts.

BRAKE-LIGHTS

Q. How do you know if a brake-light bulb is not working?

ABMW0640

Ans.   (a) The brake-pedal feels 'soft'.

        (b) The remaining brake-light is brighter than normal.

*   (c) You press the brake-pedal while another person checks the lights from behind.

        (d) The remaining brake-light is dimmer than normal.

Q. You are changing down through the gears in order to reduce speed. How does this affect your brake-lights?

ABMW0641

Ans. * (a) It has no effect on them.

        (b) It causes them to light up.

        (c) It causes them to flash briefly.

Q. When may you drive if your brake-lights are not working?

ABMW0642

Ans.   (a) When driving in a built-up area.

        (b) When driving slowly.

*   (c) Never.

        (d) Outside of lighting up time.

WARNING LIGHTS

Q.   **This warning light would indicate .....**

ABMW0643

Ans.   (a) engine overheat.
        (b) gearbox overheat.
        (c) load insecure on trailer.
    * (d) battery malfunction.

Q.   **What does this light mean?**

ABMW0644

Ans.   (a) Reversing light switched on.
        (b) Headlights should be dipped.
    * (c) High beam headlights are switched on.
        (d) Faulty number plate light.

Q.   **What does this light mean?**

ABMW0645

Ans.   (a) Low level of battery fluid.
        (b) Excessive level of battery fluid.
        (c) Low level of brake fluid.
    * (d) Low oil level.

Q.   **What does this light mean?**

ABMW0646

Ans.   (a) Faulty indicator bulb.
    * (b) Indicator light.
        (c) Headlight bulb blown.
        (d) Brake-light bulb blown.

Q. **Warning lights are always .....**

ABMW0647

Ans. * (a) red.
(b) orange.
(c) green.
(d) blue.

Q. **If a warning light starts flashing on the dashboard of your vehicle, what should you do?**

ABMW0650

Ans. * (a) Stop and check the problem.
(b) Carry on and check the problem later.
(c) Continue for a distance to see if the light will go out.
(d) Continue to drive and listen for any unusual sounds.

Q. **If a red warning light on the dash-board lights up as you drive along, what should you do?**

ABMW0651

Ans. (a) Drive to the nearest garage and have it checked.
(b) Continue on and see if it will go out.
* (c) Stop and investigate the cause.
(d) Continue on and listen for any unusual sounds.

REFLECTORS

Q. **What is the purpose of your vehicle's reflectors?**

ABMW0652

Ans. (a) They are a substitute in case of brake-light failure.
(b) They warn the driver behind to switch to dipped headlights.
* (c) They reflect light at night in order to make other road users aware of your vehicle.
(d) They warn pedestrians of your location.

INDICATORS

Q.
ABMW0653

A rapid clicking noise when you operate the indicator switch suggests that .....

Ans. * (a) an indicator bulb has blown.
(b) the front and rear indicators are not working in tandem.
(c) the hazard warning lights are on.
(d) the voltage regulator in your car is not functioning properly.

BRAKES

Q.
ABMW0654

What does A.B.S. do?

Ans. (a) It displays the name of the radio station playing on the car radio.
(b) It locks the brakes to prevent skidding during harsh braking.
* (c) It prevents the wheels from locking under harsh braking conditions.
(d) It deploys the airbags during a collision.

Q.
ABMW0655

The brake-pedal on your vehicle feels 'soft' or 'slack' when applied. This indicates .....

Ans. (a) worn brake-pads.
(b) worn handbrake cable.
* (c) low brake fluid level.
(d) over-heated brake-pads.

Q. If the brake fluid is low, the brakes .....

ABMW0656

Ans.
    (a) are unusually sharp.
    (b) take longer than usual to release.
* (c) feel spongy and soft.
    (d) feel hard to press.

Q. A low level of which of the following could cause an

ABMW0657 accident?

Ans.
    (a) Water.
* (b) Brake fluid.
    (c) Radiator coolant.
    (d) Antifreeze.

Q. You hear a scraping noise when the footbrake is

ABMW0658 applied. What is the likely cause?

Ans.
    (a) There is too much oil on the brakes.
* (b) The brake-linings are worn.
    (c) There is not enough oil on the brakes.
    (d) The brake-pads are wet.

Q. How do you know that there is a problem in the

ABMW0659 condition of your vehicle's brakes?

Ans.
    (a) The vehicle's suspension is affected.
    (b) The vehicle is sluggish when moving off.
* (c) The vehicle's stopping ability is affected.
    (d) The brake fluid level would be low.

AUTOMATIC TRANSMISSION

Q.
ABMW0660

If driving a vehicle with automatic transmission, you should be aware that .....

Ans. * (a) engine braking power is reduced.
(b) wheel-spin occurs more often.
(c) the gearbox may overheat while being driven in low gear.
(d) an automatic transmission accelerates faster than a manual transmission.

Q.
ABMW0661

What effect does automatic transmission have on an engine's braking power?

Ans. * (a) It reduces it.
(b) It increases it.
(c) It transfers the braking ability to the handbrake.
(d) It transfers the braking ability to all the wheels.

VEHICLE CONDITION (ENGINE)

Q.
ABMW0662

This dial provides information on .....

Ans. (a) speed.
(b) fuel level.
(c) temperature.
* (d) engine revolution.

Q. A rev counter gives information
ABMW0663 on .....

Ans. (a) air pressure.
     (b) gearbox revolutions.
     (c) battery charge.
  * (d) engine revolution.

Q. When driving along you notice that your engine
ABMW0664 power is lower than normal. What should you do?

Ans. (a) Switch to a different fuel.
     (b) Adjust the fuel mixture control mechanism.
  * (c) Have the vehicle checked by a competent mechanic as soon as possible.
     (d) Replace the oil filter.

FUEL

Q. If the oil gauge shows little or no pressure, the
ABMW0665 problem may be .....

Ans. * (a) the oil level is too low.
     (b) the oil level is too high.
     (c) the oil is too thin.
     (d) the oil is too thick.

Q. Insufficient or used oil may .....
ABMW0666

Ans. (a) cause the engine to overheat.
     (b) cause excessive exhaust pollution.
     (c) increase the amount of petrol required.
  * (d) increase wear on the engine parts.

Q.   **Driving with low oil pressure could .....**

ABMW0667

Ans.   (a)   increase fuel consumption only in dry weather.

     *   (b)   increase wear and tear on the engine.

         (c)   increase fuel consumption only in wet weather.

         (d)   increase fuel consumption.

Q.   **The oil pressure gauge on your vehicle is reading low.**

ABMW0668   **You should .....**

Ans.   (a)   drive at lower speeds until the oil level is topped up.

         (b)   drive in a low gear until the oil level is topped up.

     *   (c)   stop the vehicle and check the oil level.

         (d)   drive in a low gear and at lower speeds until the oil level is topped up.

Q.   **Select 2 answers. When checking the oil level, your**

ABMW0669   **engine should be .....**

Ans.   (a)   running.

         (b)   hot.

     *   (c)   switched off.

     *   (d)   cold.

Q.   **Select 3 answers. Engine oil .....**

ABMW0670

Ans.   *   (a)   lubricates the moving crankshaft.

     *   (b)   helps to cool the moving parts of the engine.

     *   (c)   lubricates the valves.

         (d)   lubricates the exhaust system.

Q.   **An oil filter .....**

ABMW0671

Ans.   (a)   prevents the engine from being over filled.

         (b)   prevents excessive wear on the crankshaft.

         (c)   replenishes low oil level in the engine.

     *   (d)   gathers sediment.

Q.
ABMW0672

As you drive along you notice a strong smell of fuel. You should .....

Ans.
    (a) check the exhaust system.
    (b) drive at a reduced speed.
    (c) check that the fuel cap is secured properly.
* (d) stop and investigate the problem.

Q.
ABMW0673

It is recommended that you use antifreeze?

Ans.
    (a) Summer only.
    (b) Winter only.
* (c) All year round.
    (d) Only in petrol engine vehicles.

Q.
ABMW0674

The warning light/red zone on fuel gauge indicates .....

Ans.
    (a) overfilling.
    (b) leak in the fuel system.
* (c) low in fuel.
    (d) presence of leaded fuel.

Q.
ABMW0675

Select 3 answers. What happens if you have a flat battery .....

Ans. * (a) you will not be able to start the engine.
    * (b) parking lights may not work.
    * (c) hazard warning lights will not work.
      (d) the battery will have to be replaced.

Q.
ABMW0676

Select 3 answers. The battery is necessary to .....

Ans. * (a) turn the starter motor.
      (b) provide heat to the passenger compartment.
    * (c) run the parking lights.
    * (d) run the hazard warning lights.

COOLANT TEMPERATURE GAUGE

Q.
ABMW0677 The temperature gauge on your vehicle is showing in the red zone. You should .....

Ans.   (a) drive on to the nearest service depot and fill up with water.
    (b) remove filler cap from radiator and check for leakage.
    (c) not drive until anti-waxing agent is added to the coolant.
*   (d) not drive until the coolant level is topped up.

Q.
ABMW0678 The temperature gauge on your vehicle is showing in the red zone. You should .....

Ans.   (a) remove filler cap from radiator and check for leakage.
    (b) not drive until anti-waxing agent is added to the coolant.
*   (c) not drive until the coolant level is topped up.
    (d) drive on to the nearest service depot and fill up with water.

Q.   It is recommended that you use coolant?
ABMW0679

Ans.   (a) Summer only.
    (b) Winter only.
*   (c) All year round.
    (d) Only in petrol engine vehicles.

BODY CONDITION

Q.
ABMW0680

You notice that parts of your vehicle's body are affected by rust. What should you do?

Ans.
    (a) Have paint sprayed over it of the same colour.
    (b) Have it sandpapered and keep the affected area dry.
* (c) Have it assessed and treated if necessary by a competent repair shop.
    (d) Treat the area with grease and paint over it.

BATTERY

Q.
ABMW0681

What effect would a weakly charged battery have on your vehicle's driving performance?

Ans. * (a) It would have no effect.
    (b) The fuel would burn less efficiently.
    (c) Uphill acceleration would be reduced.

SHOCK ABSORBERS/SUSPENSION

Q.
ABMW0682

What effect can a worn shock absorber have on a vehicle?

Ans.
    (a) It can increase fuel consumption.
* (b) It can cause the vehicle to 'bounce' in an unstable manner.
    (c) It can cause an electrical short circuit.
    (d) It can release the airbags.

MIRRORS

Q. When driving, your mirror(s) should reflect .....
ABMW0683

Ans. (a) the position of the left side wheels.
(b) the passenger area of the vehicle.
* (c) the area behind and to each side of the vehicle.
(d) the position of all the wheels.

Q. Your vehicle's wing mirror(s) should .....
ABMW0684

Ans. (a) show the side(s) of the vehicle only.
(b) not show the sides of the vehicle.
* (c) show the side(s) of the vehicle and also the road to the side(s) and to the rear of the vehicle.
(d) be angled 60% to the car and 40% to the road.

Q. Your wing mirrors have been covered by a film of mud and dust. You should .....
ABMW0685

Ans. (a) drive on as normal, as driving in the slipstream of other traffic will clean them eventually.
(b) angle them towards the front for a distance in order to clean them.
* (c) clean them with a cloth, or tissue, before continuing on.

Q. You are making a left-hand turn. What mirrors should you particularly concentrate on?
ABMW0686

Ans. (a) The interior and right mirror.
(b) The interior mirror.
(c) The right-hand wing mirror.
* (d) The left-hand wing mirror.

Q.
ABMW0687
What effect can wet weather have on your vehicle's exterior mirrors?

Ans.
   (a) It can keep them clean.
* (b) It can make the reflected image less clear.
   (c) It can cause a short circuit in electrically heated mirrors.
   (d) It can make reflected images appear closer than they really are.

EXHAUST

Q.
ABMW0688
Blue smoke coming from your vehicle's exhaust indicates the .....

Ans.
   (a) catalytic converter is worn out.
* (b) engine is burning oil.
   (c) engine is overheating.
   (d) air filter needs to be replaced.

Q.
ABMW0689
What is the effect of a worn exhaust?

Ans. * (a) The filtering of fumes is reduced and engine noise is louder.
   (b) The engine overheats.
   (c) Gear-changing is more difficult.
   (d) Fuel efficiency is decreased.

Q.
ABMW0690
How can a faulty exhaust affect your vehicle? It can .....

Ans.
   (a) lessen engine noise.
   (b) improve fuel consumption.
* (c) increase the noise and pollution levels of the vehicle.
   (d) increase wear on the engine.

Q. What is the purpose of a catalytic converter?

ABMW0691

Ans. (a) It allows the engine to quickly reach its normal operating temperature.

(b) It increases engine power.

* (c) It filters exhaust gases thereby minimising air pollution.

(d) It decreases engine power.

TYRES

Q. The speed rating of a tyre indicates .....

ABMW0692

Ans. (a) the speed not to be exceeded at maximum loading of the vehicle.

(b) the maximum speed the tyre can take when the vehicle is unladen.

(c) the maximum speed which the tyre can take on a dry road.

* (d) the maximum speed at which the vehicle should be driven.

Q. Why should you replace the valve when replacing a

ABMW0693 tubeless tyre?

Ans. * (a) The valve may be worn.

(b) In order to ensure that the wheel nuts can be tightened correctly.

(c) In order to ensure that the wheel can be balanced correctly.

(d) In order to ensure that the wheel can be aligned correctly.

Q. ABMW0694 You have recommenced driving after having changed a wheel on your vehicle. Which of the following should you check soon afterwards?

Ans.
    (a) The brake-pad clearance.
    (b) Pressure in the tyre.
 * (c) The wheel nuts.
    (d) Tyre tread depth.
    (e) Air valve.

Q. ABMW0695 It is illegal to drive with tyres that .....

Ans.
    (a) have painted walls.
 * (b) have a large deep cut in the side wall.
    (c) are by different manufacturers.
    (d) are not manufactured in the European Union.

Q. ABMW0696 In general, tyre pressure should be checked .....

Ans. * (a) once a week.
    (b) monthly.
    (c) six monthly.
    (d) annually.

Q. ABMW0697 Tyres should be kept to the pressure specified by the manufacturer in order to help .....

Ans.
    (a) stop the vehicle from sloping to the left.
    (b) in maintaining the correct ground clearance.
    (c) reduce engine wear.
 * (d) prevent the vehicle from skidding.

Q. Select 2 answers. Uneven or excessive tyre wear can be caused by faults in the .....

ABMW0698

Ans. * (a) braking system.
   * (b) suspension.
     (c) accelerator.
     (d) gearbox.

Q. Select 2 answers. Under-inflated tyres can affect?

ABMW0699

Ans. * (a) Fuel consumption.
   * (b) Braking.
     (c) The exhaust system.
     (d) Oil pressure.

Q. Tyre pressure should be checked when .....

ABMW0700

Ans. (a) the vehicle is loaded.
     (b) the vehicle is unladen.
     (c) tyres are hot.
   * (d) tyres are cold.

Q. What effect does low tyre pressure have on a vehicle?

ABMW0701

Ans. (a) Engine noise increases.
     (b) The brakes can overheat.
   * (c) Braking and cornering of the vehicle is affected.
     (d) The vehicle accelerates faster.

Q. You notice that one of your front tyres is worn. What should you do?

ABMW0702

Ans. (a) Reduce speed on wet roads.
     (b) Fit it on one of the rear wheels.
   * (c) Have it replaced.
     (d) Check the tyre pressure to ensure it remains constant.

Q. *ABMW0703* **What effect could hitting or mounting the kerb have on your vehicle's tyres?**

Ans.
    (a) It could allow air to escape from them.
* (b) It could damage the sidewalls.
    (c) It could put them off balance.

Q. *ABMW0704* **A worn tread along the edge of a tyre suggests that .....**

Ans.
    (a) air pressure is low.
    (b) air pressure is high.
* (c) steering alignment may be faulty.
    (d) driver is driving too fast around corners.

Q. *ABMW0705* **What effect would under-inflated tyres have on your vehicle's engine transmission?**

Ans.
    (a) They would make it more difficult to change gears.
    (b) They would cause the clutch to overheat.
* (c) They would have no effect on it.

Q. *ABMW0706* **What should you do before undertaking a long journey?**

Ans.
    (a) Reduce the air pressure in your tyres.
    (b) Increase the air pressure in your tyres.
* (c) Check that your tyres have their normal air pressure.

Q. *ABMW0707* **Is it advisable to put extra air pressure into the tyres when about to undertake a long journey?**

Ans. * (a) No.
    (b) Yes.
    (c) Yes, if high speeds are anticipated.
    (d) Yes, if the tread depth is below 1.6mm.

Q.
ABMW0708
What effects do under inflated tyres have on a vehicle?

Ans.
    (a) Improved braking and steering.
* (b) Impaired braking and steering.
    (c) Improved fuel economy and braking.
    (d) Increase the rate of wear on the vehicle's engine and transmission.

Q.
ABMW0709
What effect would coasting have on your vehicles tyres?

Ans. * (a) No effect.
    (b) It would cause them to lose air pressure.
    (c) It would increase the rate of wear on them.

Q.
ABMW0710
To secure the vehicle when changing a wheel, what should you do?

Ans.
    (a) Point the front wheels towards the kerb.
    (b) Ensure that the gear lever is in neutral.
* (c) Ensure that the vehicle cannot roll when jacked up.
    (d) Point the front wheels away from the kerb.

CLUTCH

Q.
ABMW0711
When driving along, where should you normally rest your left foot?

Ans. * (a) On the floor or footrest.
    (b) On the clutch pedal.
    (c) Under the brake-pedal.
    (d) Under the clutch pedal.

STEERING

Q.
ABMW0712

What effect could hitting or mounting the kerb have on your vehicle's tyres?

Ans.   (a) It could allow air to escape from them.
*   (b) It could damage the sidewalls.
     (c) It could put them off balance.

Q.
ABMW0713

A continuous vibration in the steering while driving could indicate that .....

Ans. * (a) the wheel balance is uneven.
     (b) the shock absorbers are worn.
     (c) weight distribution is uneven.
     (d) the steering is out of alignment.

Q.
ABMW0714

What can cause heavy steering?

Ans. * (a) Under-inflated tyres
     (b) Badly worn brakes
     (c) Over-inflated tyres
     (d) Poorly oiled steering
     (e) Use of leather cover on steering wheel.

ENVIRONMENTAL MATTERS

FUEL CONSUMPTION

Q.
ABMW0715
How does harsh acceleration affect fuel consumption?

Ans.
    (a) There is no effect provided the engine is properly tuned.
    (b) Fuel consumption decreases.
* (c) Fuel consumption increases.
    (d) There is no effect, if a high gear is engaged.

Q.
ABMW0716
What should you do to achieve maximum fuel efficiency from your vehicle's engine?

Ans.
    (a) Drive with the choke out.
    (b) Change rapidly up through the gears.
* (c) Use gentle acceleration and braking.
    (d) Drive in a low gear.

Q.
ABMW0717
Continuous high speed driving .....

Ans. * (a) increases fuel consumption.
    (b) reduces fuel consumption.
    (c) increases fuel consumption only in wet weather.
    (d) reduces fuel consumption as long as the road is dry and straight.

Q.
ABMW0718

What should you do to ensure better fuel efficiency from your vehicle?

Ans. (a) Drive at higher speeds in order to reduce the time spent on the road.
* (b) Ensure that the vehicle is regularly serviced.
  (c) Ensure that heavier items are carried at the rear of the vehicle.
  (d) Ensure any load carried is equally distributed on the vehicle.

Q.
ABMW0719

Fuel efficiency is improved by .....

Ans. (a) accelerating hard up through the gears to reach the desired speed as quickly as possible.
  (b) driving the vehicle in a lower gear for as long as possible.
* (c) using gentle acceleration and making gear changes as recommended by the manufacturer's specifications.
  (d) only using an anti-waxing agent in freezing conditions.

NOISE

Q.
ABMW0720

What effect does a worn exhaust have on a vehicle?

Ans. (a) It causes oil to leak on to the road.
  (b) It causes the water coolant to leak from the engine.
* (c) It causes noise and smoke pollution levels to increase.
  (d) It increases fuel consumption.

HORN

Q.
ABMW0721
Are you allowed to sound the horn while driving in a built-up area at night?

Ans.   (a) Yes, but only between 11.30 p.m. and 7.00 a.m.
      (b) No.
* (c) Yes, but only in an emergency between 11.30 p.m. and 7.00 a.m.
      (d) Yes, but only for momentary use.

Q.
ABMW0722
When are you allowed to use a musical horn on your vehicle?

Ans. * (a) Never.
      (b) During an emergency situation.
      (c) During daylight hours.
      (d) When the vehicle is a service vehicle.

Q.
ABMW0723
You must not sound your horn .....

Ans.   (a) between 10.00 p.m. and 6.00 a.m. in a built-up area.
      (b) any time in a built-up area.
* (c) between 11.30 p.m. and 7.00 a.m. in a built-up area.
      (d) between 11.30 p.m. and 6.00 a.m. on any road.
      (e) at any time on a motorway.

Q.
ABMW0724
Which 3 of the following are adversely affected if the tyres are under-inflated?

Ans. * (a) Braking.
* (b) Steering.
* (c) Fuel Consumption.
      (d) Changing gear.
      (e) Parking.

Q. ABMW0725 **Select 2 answers. Use of motor vehicles can harm the environment by .....**

Ans. * (a) causing air pollution.
    (b) reduced health risks.
   * (c) using up natural resources.
    (d) less parking.
    (e) less gear changes.

Q. ABMW0726 **Which 3 things can you, as a road user, do to help the environment?**

Ans. * (a) Cycle when possible.
    (b) Drive on under-inflated tyres.
    (c) Use the choke for as long as possible on a cold engine.
   * (d) Have your vehicle properly tuned and serviced.
   * (e) Watch the traffic and plan ahead.
    (f) Brake as late as possible.

Q. ABMW0727 **Which 3 of the following are most likely to waste fuel?**

Ans.   (a) Reducing your speed.
   * (b) Carrying unnecessary weight.
   * (c) Under-inflated tyres.
    (d) Using different brands of fuel.
   * (e) A fitted, empty roof rack.

Q. ABMW0728 **Which 2 of the following driver actions is likely to increase fuel consumption?**

Ans.   (a) Driving at a constant speed.
    (b) Looking ahead and anticipating traffic flow.
   * (c) Harsh acceleration.
   * (d) Harsh and late braking.

Q.
ABMW0729

Select 4 answers. To help protect the environment you should .....

Ans. * (a) remove your roof rack when unloaded.
(b) don't use your indicators when turning.
* (c) use public transport.
* (d) walk or cycle to work.
(e) accelerate rapidly and brake harshly when driving.
* (f) car share.

Q.
ABMW0730

Select 3 answers. Eco-driving is a driving style that delivers benefits in terms of .....

Ans. * (a) reduced fuel consumption.
(b) increased speed.
(c) less use of indicators.
* (d) increased road safety.
* (e) reduced emissions.

Q.
ABMW0731

Select 3 key elements of eco-driving.

Ans. * (a) Selecting a high gear as soon as possible.
* (b) Maintaining a steady speed.
* (c) Looking ahead and anticipating.
(d) Braking harshly.
(e) Driving in a low gear at high speed.

Q.
ABMW0732

How can you, as a driver, help the environment? By .....

Ans. * (a) reducing your speed.
(b) braking suddenly.
(c) using your indicators sparingly.
(d) harsh acceleration.

TAKING EMERGENCY/CORRECTIVE ACTION

Q. Select 3 answers. Skids are caused by .....

ABMW0733

Ans. * (a) harsh acceleration.
    (b) not enough pressure in the tyres.
  * (c) heavy braking.
    (d) too much pressure in the tyres.
    (e) the steering wheel being too free or pliable.
  * (f) excessive speed.

Q. Your tyre bursts while you are driving. Which 2 things should you do?

ABMW0604

Ans. (a) Pull on the handbrake.
    (b) Brake as quickly as possible.
  * (c) Pull up slowly at the side of the road.
  * (d) Hold the steering wheel firmly to keep control.
    (e) Continue on at a normal speed.

Q. Which 2 things should you do when a front tyre bursts?

ABMW0605

Ans. (a) Apply the handbrake to stop the vehicle.
    (b) Brake firmly and quickly.
  * (c) Let the vehicle roll to a stop.
    (d) Hold the steering wheel lightly.
  * (e) Grip the steering wheel firmly.

Q. Your vehicle has a puncture on a motorway. What
ABMW0606 should you do?

Ans. (a) Drive slowly to the next service area to get assistance.
* (b) Pull up on the hard shoulder. Switch on your hazard
warning lights and change the wheel as quickly as
possible
(c) Stop in your lane.

Q. What 2 safeguards could you take against fire risk to
ABMW0607 your vehicle?

Ans. (a) Keep water levels above maximum mark.
* (b) Carry a fire extinguisher.
(c) Avoid driving with a full tank of petrol.
(d) Use unleaded petrol.
* (e) Check out any strong smell of fuel.
(f) Use low octane fuel.

Q. Select 2 answers. You are driving on a motorway.
ABMW0609 You should use hazard warning lights when .....

Ans. (a) a vehicle is following too closely.
* (b) you slow down quickly because of danger ahead.
(c) you are towing another vehicle.
(d) driving on the hard shoulder.
* (e) you have broken down.

Q.

ABMW0610

Your vehicle has broken down and you are awaiting assistance. You should ......

Ans.   (a)   direct traffic to pass your vehicle.

(b)   get out of the vehicle and wait at the rear of it.

* (c)   get out of the vehicle and place the red warning triangle a distance to the rear of the vehicle.

(d)   attempt to flag down drivers approaching from the rear.

MEETING EMERGENCY OR EXTRA-LARGE VEHICLES

Q. ABMW0734 **You see flashing blue lights in your rear-view mirror. You should .....**

Ans.   (a) drive on more quickly to avoid causing obstruction.
        (b) turn into the next available side-road.
        (c) beckon the driver to overtake you.
   * (d) move towards the left and reduce speed to allow the vehicle to overtake.

Q. ABMW0735 **You see road-working machinery with flashing amber lights up ahead. You should .....**

Ans.   (a) proceed at your normal speed.
        (b) do 'U'-turn because the road is blocked.
        (c) engage 1st gear immediately.
   * (d) slow down and prepare to stop if necessary.

Q. ABMW0736 **You meet a vehicle with flashing blue lights. You should .....**

Ans.   (a) flash your headlights to acknowledge that you have seen it.
   * (b) move to the left and reduce speed, stopping if necessary.
        (c) stop immediately.
        (d) switch on your hazard warning lights.

Q. ABMW0737 **You see an ambulance with flashing blue lights stopped up ahead. You should .....**

Ans.   (a) stop to see what's happening.
        (b) drive in the centre of the road to prevent other drivers from overtaking,
   * (c) reduce speed and prepare to stop if necessary.
        (d) stop to offer assistance.

Q.

ABMW0738

Emergency vehicles are identified by .....

Ans.
    (a) flashing green lights.
    (b) alternating flashing amber and white lights.
    (c) continuously lit red lights.
  * (d) flashing red or blue lights.

Q.

ABMW0739

Select 3 answers. Vehicles being used by which of the following are exempted from speed limits, and some traffic regulations when being used in an emergency?

Ans. * (a) Fire brigades.
    * (b) Ambulance services.
      (c) Doctor.
      (d) Mountain rescue.
      (e) Bus breakdown service.
    * (f) Garda.

Q.

ABMW0740

Select 2 answers. If the oil gauge shows little or no pressure, the problem may be .....

Ans.
    (a) the engine is burning oil.
    (b) the oil level is too high.
  * (c) the oil pump is out of order.
  * (d) an internal leak is sidetracking the oil flow.

CHAPTER I

PART II

CATEGORY BW

ALERT DRIVING, AND CONSIDERATION FOR ROAD USERS

Q.
BW0001
What should you do when you want to use a mobile phone while driving?

Ans. * (a) Pull in and stop in a safe place.
 (b) Reduce speed and be alert for other road users.
 (c) Allow a wider gap to open up with the vehicle in front and continue at normal speed.
 (d) Keep the conversation short.

ALERTNESS

Q.
BW0002
You have parked in a row of parked vehicles which other traffic is overtaking. You should ensure that .....

Ans. * (a) you do not open a door without proper care being taken.
 (b) the handbrake is not applied.
 (c) the gear lever is in the neutral position before getting out.
 (d) the wheels of the vehicle are angled away from the kerb.

Q.
BW0003

Where there are a number of lanes of queuing traffic you should be aware that motorcycles or bicycles may come up on .....

Ans.
(a) either side only when there is a roundabout ahead.
(b) your right.
* (c) either side.
(d) your left.

Q.
BW0004

You are driving on a dual-carriageway. What should you be aware of in this situation?

Ans.
(a) Reduced visibility.
* (b) Cross-winds may blow the rider into your lane.
(c) Oncoming traffic.
(d) The motorcyclist may perform a 'U'-turn.

OBSERVATION/FIELD OF VIEW

VISIBILITY

Q.
BW0005

What should you do when towing a caravan?

Ans.
(a) Carry all passengers in the caravan.
(b) Switch on the hazard warning lights.
* (c) Have extended mirrors fitted to your vehicle and use them regularly.
(d) Carry only adults in the caravan.

Q. You are driving a vehicle that is towing a high-sided
BW0006 trailer. You should .....

Ans. (a) drive with a red flag to the front right-hand side of the
trailer.
(b) drive with full headlights on.
* (c) make use of extended mirrors where necessary, to check
for following traffic.
(d) drive with a red flag at rear of the trailer.

Q. Why is it important to have clean, clear, windows?
BW0007

Ans. (a) To enable other road users to see you.
(b) To improve the maintenance of windows.
* (c) To ensure good all-round visibility from your vehicle.
(d) To avoid condensation.

Q. You want to undertake a journey and your vehicle
BW0008 windows are covered with ice. What should you do?

Ans. (a) Clear enough space in the windscreen to be able to see
ahead.
(b) Drive slowly until the heater and demister have cleared
the ice from the windows.
* (c) Clear the ice from the windows before starting.
(d) Use boiling water to clear the ice.

Q. What should you do if the vehicle's windows are
BW0009 covered in ice?

Ans. (a) Drive at a reduced speed until the heating system has
cleared the ice.
* (b) Switch on the heating system and use a scraper to clear
the ice before driving.
(c) Switch on the windscreen wipers.
(d) Use boiling water with salt to clear the ice.

Q. What should you do if condensation is affecting your
BW0010   vehicle's windows?

Ans.   (a) Drive for a few kilometres with a window open.
           (b) Wipe the glass with the back of your hand.
       *   (c) Dry the windows with a cloth and then use the demister
               system.
           (d) Close off the air vents.

Q. What effect can sunlight have on grimy windows?
BW0011

Ans.   (a) It can enhance visibility.
       *   (b) It can create a mirror effect and reduce visibility.
           (c) It can cause objects to seem closer than they are.
           (d) It can cause objects to seem further away than they are.

REVERSING

Q. Select 2 answers. You wish to reverse your vehicle.
BW0012   You should take observations .....

Ans. * (a) over your shoulders.
            (b) in the right hand mirror.
            (c) in the left-hand mirror.
        *   (d) in both wing mirrors.
            (e) over your right shoulder.

Q. When reversing a vehicle with an audible warning
BW0013   device sounding, you .....

Ans.   (a) need not take observations, as bystanders will be aware
                of you.
            (b) should take observations only in the blindspots.
        *   (c) should take observations to the front, sides and rear of
                the vehicle, including blindspots.

Q.
BW0014

You wish to reverse around a corner into a side road. You should .....

Ans.
(a) turn your steering fully and reverse quickly.
(b) open the door fully to look behind.
* (c) check carefully all around before and during the reverse.
(d) turn on your hazard lights to signal your reverse direction.

Q.
BW0015

You want to reverse your vehicle on a busy street. What should you do?

Ans.
(a) Sound the horn occasionally as you reverse.
* (b) Reverse slowly, checking all around for other road users.
(c) Reverse quickly to avoid delay.
(d) Give a hand signal while reversing.

Q.
BW0016

You cannot see clearly behind when reversing. What should you do?

Ans. * (a) Ask someone to direct you.
(b) Look in the nearside mirror.
(c) Open your window and look behind.
(d) Open the door and look behind.

Q.
BW0017

What should you do when reversing with a trailer?

Ans.
(a) Sound the horn as a warning.
(b) Turn the steering in the direction in which you wish to reverse.
* (c) Look all around and use the rear-view mirrors as you reverse.
(d) Keep the front of trailer in view at all times.

GOOD JUDGEMENT AND PERCEPTION

FATIGUE

Q. **What should you do to keep alert during a long**
BW0018 **journey?**

Ans. * (a) Increase the air circulation and make regular stops if necessary.
(b) Increase your speed to shorten the journey.
(c) Keep the radio turned on.
(d) Drink tea or coffee or other hot drinks.

Q. **Driving at night with a warm vehicle interior,**
BW0019 **could .....**

Ans. * (a) make you feel drowsy.
(b) reassure you that the engine is operating at normal temperatures.
(c) increase your sense of alertness.
(d) tempt you to drive at increased speed.

Q. **Exhaust gases leaking into the driver compartment**
BW0020 **of your vehicle, can cause you to .....**

Ans. (a) become more alert.
* (b) become drowsy or ill.
(c) be enticed to drive faster than normal.
(d) be enticed to drive slower than normal.

AWARENESS

Q.
BW0021

What effect can driving a smoother high powered car have on your sense of driving?

Ans.

(a) It can make you feel the brakes appear more powerful than they actually are.

* (b) It can make you think that you are driving slower than you are actually driving.

(c) It can make you think that you are driving faster than you are actually driving.

(d) It can make you think that the car is bigger than it actually is.

OBSERVANCE OF SAFE DISTANCE AND DRIVING IN VARIOUS WEATHER/ROAD CONDITIONS

ROADHOLDING

Q.
BW0022

If the road is slippery, when should you drive your tractor with the left side wheels up on the grass verge in order to improve road holding?

Ans.

(a) When not towing a trailer.

* (b) This practice should be avoided.

(c) When towing heavy loads.

(d) When towing a trailer.

Q.
BW0023

Why should you drive a tractor more slowly on uneven roads?

Ans.
    (a) To ensure that fuel does not spill from the tank.
* (b) To avoid severe bouncing.
    (c) To reduce noise.
    (d) To avoid reduced tyre pressure.

Q.
BW0024

Should the handbrake be used to bring the vehicle to a halt?

Ans. * (a) No.
    (b) Yes, only when going downhill.
    (c) Only at speeds below 10 km/h.
    (d) Yes.

Q.
BW0025

If you apply the handbrake while the vehicle is moving at speed .....

Ans.
    (a) the A.B.S. could disconnect.
* (b) the back wheels could lock causing the vehicle to skid.
    (c) the vehicle will not skid.
    (d) the engine will stall.

DRIVING RISK FACTORS RELATED TO VARIOUS ROAD CONDITIONS, IN PARTICULAR AS THEY CHANGE WITH THE WEATHER AND THE TIME OF DAY OR NIGHT

DRIVING IN FOG

Q.
BW0026
Rear fog lamps should be used .....

Ans. (a) always when driving at night.
  (b) when the vehicle behind is too close.
* (c) only in fog.
  (d) only in light fog.

Q.
BW0027
When may you drive your vehicle showing a high intensity fog light to the rear?

Ans. (a) When the tail-light is broken.
* (b) In fog.
  (c) Never.
  (d) At dusk and dawn.

DRIVING AT NIGHT

Q.
BW0028
You are driving at night and the right hand headlight bulb has blown. You should .....

Ans. * (a) not drive until you have it replaced.
  (b) drive with the right hand indicators on.
  (c) replace it temporarily with the brake-light bulb.
  (d) replace it temporarily with the left-hand bulb.

Q.
BW0029

What should you do if you are dazzled by headlights reflecting in the rear-view mirror of your car?

Ans.

   (a) Turn on your rear fog lights to signal to the following driver to turn off his headlights.

* (b) Adjust the night driving mode on your mirror.

   (c) Adjust your mirror to reflect the light back towards the following driver.

   (d) Switch your lights off and on to remind the following driver to dip his lights.

Q.
BW0030

What should you do if dazzled by lights reflecting in your mirror?

Ans.

   (a) Adjust your mirror to reflect the light back to the following driver.

   (b) Switch on your rear lights.

* (c) Temporarily adjust the angle of your mirror.

   (d) Switch on a reversing light.

Q.
BW0031

When driving a car at night, what effect could driving with a single headlight have on oncoming drivers?

Ans.

   (a) It could enable them to see your vehicle more clearly.

   (b) It could dazzle them.

* (c) They could mistake your vehicle for a motorcycle.

   (d) This will have no effect on oncoming drivers.

Q.
BW0032

Generally, what lighting must a car, tractor or works vehicle have when driving at night?

Ans. * (a) Headlights, side lights front and rear, rear number plate light, red rear reflectors, brake-lights and indicators.

   (b) Headlights only.

   (c) Headlights and a reversing light.

   (d) Headlights, brake-lights and indicators.

Q. What lights must show when parking your car,

BW0033
tractor or work vehicle at night on an unlit public road?

Ans. * (a) At least one side-lamp front and rear on the side nearest the centre of the road.
(b) Tail lights only.
(c) Dipped head lights.
(d) At least one side-lamp front and rear on the side nearest the kerb.

CHARACTERISTICS OF VARIOUS TYPES OF ROAD

HUMPBACK BRIDGE

Q. What should you be aware of when driving a tractor over a humpbacked bridge while towing a trailer?

BW0034

Ans. (a) Tail-swing.
* (b) The trailer could become detached if a severe bump is encountered at speed.
(c) The tractor's suspension will smooth out the bump.
(d) The trailer brakes might engage.

TUNNELS

Q. You intend to drive through a tunnel. You should .....

BW0035

Ans. * (a) check that the height of your vehicle is suitable for the tunnel.
(b) stop regularly to inspect the load.
(c) carry the minimum amount of fuel in case of fire.
(d) drive in a lower gear than normal to reduce exhaust pollution.
(e) drive close to the vehicle in front to reduce congestion.

Q. You intend to drive through a tunnel. You should .....

BW0036

Ans. (a) carry extra fuel containers in the cab.
* (b) check the tunnel height before starting your journey.
(c) check the tachograph to find out height of the vehicle.
(d) disengage the global positioning system.

NECESSARY DOCUMENTS

DRIVING LICENCE AND LEARNER PERMIT MATTERS

Q. <small>BW0037</small> **'L' plates should be displayed on cars .....**

Ans.
    (a) on the front only.
    (b) on the rear only.
 * (c) both front and rear.
    (d) on the driver's side only.

Q. <small>BW0038</small> **A Learner Permit car driver must display 'L' plates on the vehicle .....**

Ans. * (a) at all times.
    (b) while driving unaccompanied by a qualified driver.
    (c) during the term of the driver's first Learner Permit only.

Q. <small>BW0039</small> **The maximum permitted weight of the vehicle .....**

Ans.
    (a) refers to the unladen weight of the vehicle.
 * (b) refers to the weight of the vehicle plus the weight of the load which may be carried.
    (c) refers to the unladen weight of the vehicle plus the weight of the fuel.
    (d) refers to the weight of the load which may be carried.

Q. <small>BW0040</small> **What is the maximum design gross vehicle weight that the holder of a category B licence may drive?**

Ans. * (a) 3,500 kilogrammes.
    (b) 2,500 kilogrammes.
    (c) 4,500 kilogrammes.
    (d) 4,750 kilogrammes.

Q.
BW0044

What is the maximum number of passengers that the holder of category B licence may carry in a vehicle?

Ans.
     (a) 5.
     (b) 9.
  * (c) 8.
     (d) 7.

Q.
BW0045

A category W Learner Permit holder may not carry a passenger unless .....

Ans.
     (a) such person holds a category W driving licence.
  * (b) such person holds a category W driving licence and the vehicle is constructed or adapted to carry a passenger.
     (c) such person holds a category M driving licence and the vehicle is constructed or adapted to carry a passenger.

Q.
BW0582

What is the maximum design gross vehicle weight that the holder of a category B licence may drive?

Ans. * (a) 3,500 kilogrammes.
     (b) 2,500 kilogrammes.
     (c) 4,500 kilogrammes.
     (d) 4,750 kilogrammes.

Q.
BW0584

What is the maximum number of passengers that the holder of category B licence may carry in a vehicle?

Ans.
     (a) 5.
     (b) 9.
  * (c) 8.
     (d) 7.

ACCIDENTS

Q.

BW0046

You have stalled in the middle of an unguarded level crossing and cannot restart the engine. The warning bell is ringing. You should .....

Ans. * (a) walk clear of the crossing and phone the signal operator so that trains can be stopped.
     (b) stay at vehicle and warn the approaching train.
     (c) try to restart the engine in first gear.
     (d) push the vehicle clear of the crossing.

SAFETY FACTORS RELATING TO VEHICLE AND PERSONS CARRIED

CHILD PASSENGERS

Q.

BW0047

What is the greatest danger in allowing children to stand in the space between the front seats of a vehicle?

Ans.   (a) They could become ill.
  * (b) They could be thrown forward if the brakes are applied suddenly.
    (c) They could be thrown backwards if the brakes are applied suddenly.
    (d) They could distract the driver thus drawing attention away from the road.

Q. BW0048

When should you allow children to stand with their heads up through an open sun-roof?

Ans.
    (a) When travelling at speeds below 50 km/h.
    (b) When they are wearing eye protection.
* (c) Never.
    (d) When they are aged more than 12 years.

CARRYING OF PASSENGER

Q. BW0049

When may a category W Learner Permit holder carry a passenger on a tractor or works vehicle?

Ans.
    (a) When the passenger has personal insurance cover.
    (b) When the passenger holds a full category M licence and personal insurance cover.
* (c) When there is proper passenger seating and the passenger holds a full category W licence.
    (d) When there is a need for their assistance.

Q. BW0050

Children should be left unattended in a vehicle .....

Ans.
    (a) only when there is adequate ventilation.
    (b) only when the vehicle is not parked on a hill.
* (c) never.
    (d) only when the vehicle is parked in a supervised car park.

Q. Your vehicle has broken down on an automatic railway level crossing. What should you do first?

BW0051

Ans. * (a) Get passengers clear of the crossing and phone the signal operator so that trains can be stopped.
(b) Walk along the track to give warning to any approaching trains.
(c) Try to push the vehicle clear of the crossing as soon as possible.
(d) Turn on the warning bells at the crossing.

CHILDREN DRIVING

Q. When should children be allowed to drive a tractor?

BW0052

Ans. * (a) Never.
(b) When it is off the public road.
(c) When it is being driven at very slow speeds and not towing a trailer.
(d) When it is being driven at very slow speeds and without a front loader.

EFFECT OF IMPACT ON PASSENGERS

Q. What is the immediate effect of a head-on impact of two cars at speed?

BW0053

Ans. * (a) All persons in the vehicles are thrown violently forward.
(b) All persons in the vehicles are thrown violently backward.
(c) Only back seat belts will activate.
(d) Only front seat belts will activate.

SAFETY

Q.
BW0054

What danger can arise with the power takeoff of a tractor?

Ans. * (a) Clothing can get caught in it if it is not covered.
(b) If not disengaged, it can cause the battery to short-circuit.
(c) If not disengaged, it can cause the steering wheel to lock.
(d) If not disengaged, it can cause the tractor to increase speed rapidly.

Q.
BW0055

Select 4 answers. When changing a wheel on your car, on a public road, you should .....

Ans. * (a) turn on your hazard warning lights.
* (b) wear reflective clothing, if available.
* (c) place a red warning triangle to the right side rear of the vehicle.
* (d) secure the handbrake and place a chock or small wooden block at the front of the wheels.
(e) place a red warning triangle to the left of the vehicle.

LOADING

Q.
BW0129

When is a red flag a sufficient marker for a rear-load overhang that exceeds one metre?

Ans. (a) At all times.
* (b) Only during the day.
(c) When glass or fragile material is overhanging.
(d) Only at night.

Q.
BW0131
You are driving a fully loaded vehicle. In order to avoid excessive stress on the steering and suspension, you should negotiate bends .....

Ans.
    (a) at a faster speed than when empty.
* (b) at a slower speed than when empty.
    (c) by cutting the corner.
    (d) by following a wide arc along the centre of the road.
    (e) at the same speed as when empty.

LOAD CARRYING CAPACITY

Q.
BW0056
When is it permissible to carry more passengers in your car than there are seats available?

Ans.
    (a) When the passengers do not interfere with your visibility.
* (b) Never.
    (c) When you have appropriate insurance cover.
    (d) When you are carrying children.

Q.
BW0057
You have been asked to drive a vehicle which you feel is overloaded. You should .....

Ans.
    (a) drive at a slower speed than you normally would.
* (b) refuse to drive the vehicle.
    (c) advise the person who asked you that you will not be held responsible if an accident occurs.
    (d) ensure that the load is properly covered.

LOAD DISTRIBUTION

Q.
BW0058

How could towing an overloaded trailer affect your vehicle?

Ans.
    (a) It could improve the vehicle's fuel consumption.
    (b) It could improve road holding on bends.
* (c) It could impair the vehicle's steering and braking.
    (d) It can improve braking ability when going downhill.

Q.
BW0059

You are carrying some small packages in your vehicle. Which of these is the safest place to put them?

Ans. * (a) On the rear seat or on the floor.
    (b) On the rear window ledge.
    (c) On the front windscreen ledge.

Q.
BW0130

Vehicle load is more likely to shift when .....

Ans.
    (a) reversing.
    (b) driving on the straight.
    (c) braking gently.
    (d) overtaking.
* (e) cornering.

TRAILERS

Q.
BW0060

What should you ensure when attaching a trailer to a car?

Ans.
   (a) That the trailer springs are well greased.
   (b) That the trailer has a spare wheel.
* (c) That any load in the trailer is evenly spread so that the hitch will not become detached.
   (d) That the load is positioned to the front of the trailer and that the trailer pin is tightly secured.

Q.
BW0061

What should you ensure when attaching a trailer to a car?

Ans.
   (a) That the trailer springs are well greased.
   (b) That the trailer has a spare wheel.
* (c) That the trailer pin is tightly inserted.
   (d) That the load is positioned to the front of the trailer and that the trailer pin is tightly secured.

Q.
BW0062

What should you do first before un-hitching a trailer from a towing vehicle?

Ans.
   (a) Disconnect the electrical supply to the trailer lights and lower the jockey wheel.
* (b) Apply the handbrake with a low gear engaged and switch off the ignition.
   (c) Lower the jockey wheel and then switch off the ignition.
   (d) Apply the handbrake, switch off the engine and lower the jockey wheel.

Q.
BW0063

When is it permissible for you to carry a passenger on a trailer drawbar?

Ans. * (a) Never.
   (b) When the person has a category B driving licence.
   (c) When towing a trailer off-road and the person has a category B driving licence.
   (d) When towing a trailer off-road.

VEHICLE HANDLING

Q.
BW0064

Select 2 answers. When is a tractor most likely to overturn?

Ans.   (a) When speeding on the flat.
   * (b) When speeding downhill.
   * (c) When turning sharply.
      (d) When speeding uphill.

Q.
BW0065

What should you do to avoid possible roll-over on entering a roundabout when driving a tractor with a trailer?

Ans. * (a) Reduce speed.
   (b) Increase speed.
   (c) Engage the parking brake.
   (d) Drive in a high gear.

Q. **Jack-knifing is .....**

BW0066

Ans. (a) when the trailer is too heavy to be drawn by the tractor.

* (b) when the trailer is travelling faster than the drawing tractor.

(c) when the jack is not strong enough to lift an axle.

(d) when the vehicle slides due to ice or water on the road.

Q. **When is jack-knifing most likely to occur?**

BW0067

Ans. (a) When travelling sideways across a slope.

(b) When travelling uphill.

* (c) When trying to reduce speed sharply while travelling downhill.

(d) When the trailer springs are over greased.

Q. **You wish to turn right when driving a tractor with a wide load which is blocking your view to the rear. What should you do?**

BW0068

Ans. (a) Dismount and check for following traffic before turning.

(b) Complete the turn if there is no traffic coming towards you.

* (c) Have a person advise you of traffic from behind while you check for oncoming traffic.

(d) Have a person stop following traffic while you complete the turn.

TECHNICAL MATTERS, WITH A BEARING ON ROAD SAFETY

SIDELIGHTS

Q. You should drive with side-lights on when .....

BW0069

Ans. * (a) daylight is fading.
(b) driving in an unlit area at night.
(c) driving at more than 50 km/h.
(d) driving in fog.

Q. How do you know if a side-lamp bulb has failed?

BW0070

Ans. (a) None of the lights operate when switched on.
(b) A warning buzzer sounds when the sidelights are switched on.
* (c) By checking the sidelights when switched on.
(d) By checking the sidelights when reversing the vehicle.

HAZARD WARNING LIGHTS

Q. Select 2 answers. You are driving on a motorway. You should use hazard warning lights when .....

BW0071

Ans. (a) a vehicle is following too closely.
* (b) you slow down quickly because of danger ahead.
(c) you are towing another vehicle.
(d) driving on the hard shoulder.
* (e) you have broken down.

Q.
BW0072
What effect do the hazard warning lights on your vehicle have on the brake-lights?

Ans. * (a) No effect.
     (b) It causes them to flash repeatedly.
     (c) It causes the left and right brake-lights to flash alternately.

Q.
BW0073
Select 2 answers. When should you use your hazard warning lights?

Ans. (a) When your brake-lights are not working.
     (b) When about to pull in and stop.
* (c) When you have broken down.
     (d) When parking for a short period on a single yellow line.
* (e) When causing an unavoidable obstruction.

Q.
BW0074
Your hazard warning lights enable you to .....

Ans. (a) double park when making a delivery.
     (b) park inside a continuous white line.
     (c) park on a double yellow line.
* (d) warn road users of your vehicle breakdown.
     (e) park on the brow of a hill.

Q.
BW0075
You should use your vehicle's hazard warning lights when .....

Ans. (a) you are double-parking.
* (b) you have broken down.
     (c) your brake-lights are not working.

Q.
BW0076

Select 2 answers. You should use the hazard warning lights when the vehicle is .....

Ans.
   (a) reversing into a narrow road.
* (b) being towed by another vehicle.
   (c) parked at a bend or corner.
* (d) broken down and causing an obstruction.
   (e) moving slowly.

LIGHTS

Q.
BW0077

What lighting should be on a car-trailer?

Ans.
   (a) Reversing light
   (b) Indicators and rear number plate light only.
* (c) Indicators, brake-lights, rear number plate light, red reflectors, and rear tail lights.
   (d) Brake-lights and indicators only.

Q.
BW0078

What lighting should be on a tractor trailer during lighting up hours?

Ans.
   (a) An unloading light.
   (b) Indicators and rear number plate light only.
* (c) Indicators, brake-lights, rear number plate light, red reflectors, and rear tail light.
   (d) Brake-lights and indicators only.

WARNING LIGHTS

Q. This warning light indicates .....
BW0154

Ans.   (a) low oil pressure.
          (b) low level of water coolant.
          (c) defective indicator bulb.
   * (d) fault in the braking system.

Q. What does this light mean?
BW0155

Ans. * (a) Check lights.
          (b) Check wheels.
          (c) Faulty power steering.
          (d) Faulty cooling system.

BRAKES

Q. Generally, the handbrake operates on .....
BW0079

Ans.   (a) the front wheels.
   * (b) the rear wheels.
          (c) all the wheels.
          (d) the rear right-hand wheel.

Q. In general, trailers above what gross vehicle weight
BW0080 must have brakes fitted?

Ans.   (a) 500 kg.
   * (b) 750 kg.
          (c) 900 kg.
          (d) 850 kg.

AUTOMATIC TRANSMISSION

Q.
BW0081

What is the recommended method of driving a vehicle with automatic transmission?

Ans. * (a) Operate the accelerator and brake with the right foot.
(b) Operate the accelerator and brake with the left foot.
(c) Operate the accelerator with the right foot and the brake with the left foot.
(d) Use the handbrake to bring the vehicle to a halt.

FUEL

Q.
BW0082

When driving a diesel engine vehicle in freezing weather, you should ensure that .....

Ans. * (a) the fuel is treated with an anti-waxing agent.
(b) the fuel filter is drained.
(c) the fuel level in the tank does not drop below quarter full.
(d) you use a diesel with a high sulphur content.

Q.
BW0083

Overfilling the engine with oil could .....

Ans. * (a) damage the catalytic converter.
(b) damage the oil pump.
(c) reduce oil pressure.
(d) burst the oil filter.

Q.
BW0084

**Your fuel system has become air-locked.
You should .....**

Ans.
   (a) drain the fuel filter.
   (b) loosen the fuel pump.
* (c) bleed the air out of the fuel system.
   (d) increase the air pressure.
   (e) tighten the injector pipes.

Q.
BW0085

Rebated (green) diesel fuel .....

Ans. * (a) may never be used in a car.
   (b) would reduce engine performance.
   (c) would enhance engine performance.
   (d) should only be used in cold weather.

HEAD RESTRAINT

Q.
BW0086

**To reduce the risk of neck injury in a rear end
collision, you should .....**

Ans. * (a) use a properly adjusted head restraint.
   (b) ensure the vehicle has anti-lock brakes.
   (c) ensure the vehicle has a rear spoiler.
   (d) if airbags are not fitted, use a properly adjusted head
       restraint.

MIRRORS

Q.
BW0087
When must a tractor or works vehicle be fitted with a rear-view mirror?

Ans.
    (a) It is not required.
   * (b) Always.
    (c) Only when towing a trailer.
    (d) Only when towing a trailer over eight metres long.

TYRES

Q.
BW0088
What is the minimum legal tread depth for tyres on cars?

Ans.
    (a) 0.8 millimetres.
    (b) 1 millimetre.
   * (c) 1.6 millimetres.
    (d) 1.8 millimetres.

Q.
BW0089
What is the minimum tread depth required for tractor tyres?

Ans.
    (a) 1 millimetre.
    (b) 0.8 millimetres.
   * (c) 1.6 millimetres.
    (d) 2 millimetres.

Q.
BW0091
The load index of a tyre indicates the maximum .....

Ans.
    (a) load of the vehicle.
    (b) load per axle.
   * (c) load which a tyre may take.
    (d) air pressure of the tyre.

Q. When should both cross-ply and radial tyres be fitted
BW0092 to a vehicle?

Ans. (a) When heavy loads are being carried.
    (b) In icy or slippery road conditions.
  * (c) Never.
    (d) When towing a trailer in snow.

CLUTCH

Q. Resting your foot on the clutch pedal .....
BW0093

Ans. (a) facilitates quicker gear changes.
  * (b) wears out the clutch quicker.
    (c) allows downhill speeds to be controlled more effectively.
    (d) allows corners to be taken without reducing speed.

STEERING

Q. How would you check that the power-assisted
BW0094 steering is working effectively? Ensure the fluid
reservoir is full to the mark and .....

Ans. (a) turn the steering from lock to lock with the engine
switched off.
  * (b) turn the steering from lock to lock with the engine
running.
    (c) turn the steering with the brake-pedal lightly pressed.
    (d) turn the steering with the brake-pedal fully pressed.

Q.
BW0095

The power assisted steering (P.A.S.) becomes more difficult to turn as you drive along. You should .....

Ans.
(a) drive in a lower gear with increased engine revs.
(b) increase the front tyre pressure.
* (c) check the level of the fluid, and if necessary stop and call for mechanical assistance.
(d) drive in a higher gear with reduced engine revs.
(e) reduce the front wheel pressure.

SEAT

Q.
BW0096

Select 2 answers. An incorrectly adjusted driver's seat can .....

Ans. * (a) cause a delay in the driver operating a control.
(b) enable the driver to relax more on a long journey.
(c) afford the driver a better view in the rear-view mirror.
* (d) affect the driver's ability to check for traffic behind.

WIPERS

Q.
BW0097

You are driving in the rain and your wiper blades are worn. You should .....

Ans.
(a) stop and wipe the windscreen with newspaper.
(b) use the windscreen washer system all the time while it rains.
* (c) drive slowly to the nearest garage and have the blades replaced.
(d) roll down the window and drive slowly.

Q.
BW0098
If the wipers are frozen to the windscreen, what should you do?

Ans.
    (a) Switch the wipers to high speed to free them.
* (b) Defrost the windscreen before switching on the wipers.
    (c) Pull the wipers free before switching them on.
    (d) Roll down the window and drive slowly with your head out the window.

Q.
BW0099
When a wiper blade fails to clear the windscreen satisfactorily, what should you do?

Ans.
    (a) Apply a light film of oil to the blade.
    (b) Bend the wiper arm.
* (c) Have the blade replaced as soon as possible.
    (d) Switch the wipers to the highest speed.

Q.
BW0100
What problem is indicated when wipers suddenly cease to function?

Ans.
    (a) The windscreen washer reservoir is dry.
    (b) The alternator is faulty.
* (c) A fuse has blown.
    (d) The wiper blades need to be replaced.

Q.
BW0101
In freezing weather, the windscreen washer fluid should .....

Ans.
    (a) have hot water added.
    (b) be diluted with methylated spirits.
* (c) contain a mild anti-freeze agent.
    (d) contain extra detergent.

Q. The purpose of the washer fluid is to .....

BW0102

Ans. * (a) clean head lamps and windscreens.
     (b) cool the engine.
     (c) lubricate the engine.
     (d) wash the bodywork.

Q. The wiper blade on the driver's side is partly torn.
BW0103   You should .....

Ans.   (a) repair it with sticky tape.
     (b) switch the driver and passenger wiper blades.
* (c) have it replaced with a new one.

WINDSCREEN

Q. A laminated windscreen .....
BW0104

Ans. * (a) is designed not to shatter into large fragments when struck by an object.
     (b) is glass which has the registration number of the vehicle etched on to it.
     (c) shatters into large fragments when struck by an object.
     (d) blocks the harmful rays coming from the sun.

Q. Select 4 answers. Which of the following must be in
BW0105   good working order for your vehicle to be roadworthy?

Ans. * (a) Speedometer.
     (b) Upholstery.
* (c) Windscreen washer.
* (d) Horn.
* (e) Windscreen wipers.
     (f) Internal light.

WHEELS

Q.
BW0111

Wheel nuts should be tightened .....

Ans. * (a) diagonally.
(b) in sequence.
(c) beginning nearest the valve.
(d) beginning nearest the ground.

Q.
BW0112

Select 4 answers. When changing a wheel on your vehicle, on a public road, you should .....

Ans. * (a) turn on your hazard warning lights.
* (b) wear reflective clothing, if available.
(c) secure the handbrake and place a chock or small wooden block at the rear of the wheels.
* (d) place a red warning triangle to the right side at the rear of the vehicle.
* (e) secure the handbrake and place a chock or small wooden block at the front of the wheels.
(f) place a red warning triangle to the left of the vehicle.

ENVIRONMENTAL MATTERS

Q.
BW0107

What should you do to avoid excessive exhaust pollution from your vehicle?

Ans. (a) Drive at a higher speed in order to reduce the time spent on the road.
(b) Use a fuel additive to increase the fuel octane rating.
* (c) Change your vehicle's air filters regularly.
(d) Use a lower octane rated fuel.

Q. How regularly should your vehicle's engine be serviced?

BW0108

Ans.   (a) Every 30,000 kilometres.
   (b) Every year.
* (c) As often as indicated in the manufacturer's specification.
   (d) Every 60 months.

Q. The purpose of a catalytic converter is to .....

BW0109

Ans.   (a) curb exhaust noise levels only on diesel vehicles.
   (b) allow the exhaust system to be reconditioned.
* (c) reduce harmful exhaust emissions.
   (d) curb exhaust noise levels.

NOISE

Q. What type of noise might fast cornering induce?

BW0110

Ans. * (a) Tyre squeal.
   (b) Brake squeal.
   (c) Exhaust backfire.
   (d) Engine whine.

GETTING OUT FROM, OR OFF, THE VEHICLE

Q.
BW0113

You have just stopped and wish to get out of your vehicle. What should you do?

Ans. * (a) Check your side mirror and look behind before opening the door.
    (b) Check your inside mirror before opening the door.
    (c) Open the door part way and then look behind.
    (d) Open your door and exit the vehicle without delay.

Q.
BW0114

What should you do to secure the vehicle before getting out of it?

Ans.   (a) Engage low gear and switch off the ignition.
  * (b) Apply the parking brake, and switch off the ignition, engage a low gear.
    (c) Make sure all valuables are out of sight and that the steering lock is engaged.
    (d) Angle the wheels away from the kerb and switch off the ignition.

Q.
BW0115

What precautions should you take when getting out from your vehicle?

Ans.   (a) Open the door and try to get out as speedily as possible.
    (b) Ensure the gear lever is in neutral.
  * (c) Check all around for oncoming traffic/pedestrians before opening the door.
    (d) Ensure all valuables are secured and out of sight.

Q.
BW0116

You are driving on a busy road and you wish to stop to allow passengers out of your vehicle. What should you do?

Ans.   (a) Stop and allow them to get out from whichever side of the vehicle they are sitting on.

*   (b) Stop and allow them to get out on the side nearest the kerb.

(c) Stop and ask them to get out as quickly as possible.

(d) Signal to following traffic to overtake, before letting your passengers out.

VEHICLE SAFETY EQUIPMENT

SEAT-BELTS

Q.
BW0117

What cars are required to have rear seat-belts fitted?

Ans. * (a) Cars first registered after 1st January 1992.

(b) Cars first registered prior to 1st January 1992.

(c) All cars.

(d) Cars first registered prior to 1st January 1995.

Q.
BW0118

All adult car occupants must normally wear seat-belts where they are fitted .....

Ans.   (a) on long journeys only.

(b) except in built-up areas.

*   (c) at all times.

(d) for all journeys exceeding 10 kilometres.

Q.
BW0119

What is the purpose of a seat-belt?

Ans. * (a) To prevent the wearer from being thrown forward in the event of an accident or abrupt deceleration.
(b) To keep the seat upright in the event of an accident.
(c) To prevent the seat from moving forward when the brakes are applied.
(d) To prevent the wearer from being thrown backwards in the event of an accident.

Q.
BW0120

When starting off in your car, you should put on your seat-belt .....

Ans. * (a) before you move off.
(b) not later than the time you engage top gear.
(c) once your speed has exceeded 50 km/h.
(d) when driving outside an urban area.

Q.
BW0121

When carrying passengers who are aged 17 years or more, the responsibility for wearing a seat-belt is .....

Ans. (a) on the driver only.
* (b) on the passengers only.
(c) on both the driver and the passengers.
(d) on the driver when the passenger is in the front seat.

Q.
BW0122

When carrying passengers who are under 17 years of age, who is responsible for ensuring that they are wearing seat-belts?

Ans. * (a) The driver.
(b) The passengers themselves.
(c) The passengers' parents.
(d) The driver, when the passenger is in the front seat.

CHILDREN'S SAFETY SEATS

Q.
BW0123
Who is responsible for ensuring that a child wears a child restraint system in a vehicle?

Ans.
    (a) The child, if aged over 12 years.
* (b) The driver.
    (c) The child's parent(s).
    (d) The child, if aged over 15 years.

Q.
BW0124
In general, how should infants be secured in a vehicle?

Ans.
    (a) They should always be carried on an adults lap.
    (b) They should always be placed in the front passenger seat.
* (c) They should always be secured in a child restraint system.
    (d) They should always be placed in the front passenger seat wearing a seat-belt.

Q.
BW0125
Should infants who are not secured in a child restraint system be carried in the front passenger seat?

Ans.
    (a) Yes.
    (b) Yes if held by an adult.
* (c) No.
    (d) Yes, only if the vehicle is fitted with airbags.

Q.
BW0126
How should a child's restraint system be secured in a vehicle?

Ans.
    (a) It should be placed on a normal passenger seat.
* (b) It should be secured with the existing seat belts, or with additional straps.
    (c) It should be left unsecured.
    (d) It should be placed on the floor.

Q.

BW0127

What should you do when driving a vehicle that is carrying young children?

Ans.

(a) Make certain that an older passenger is sitting next to them.

(b) Check in your rear-view mirror to ensure the children seated in the back seat are safe.

* (c) Make sure each child is wearing a seat-belt or using an appropriate restraint system.

(d) Make sure the eldest children are seated in the back seat.

SIDE IMPACT PROTECTION BARS

Q.

BW0128

What is the purpose of side impact protection bars?

Ans.

(a) To make sure that the vehicle cannot be overturned when hit from the side.

(b) To increase the weight of the vehicle thereby improving its grip on the road.

* (c) To protect the occupants when the vehicle is hit from the side.

(d) To protect the doors from becoming damaged in the event of a crash.

TAKING EMERGENCY/CORRECTIVE ACTION

Q.
BW0132
Your tyre bursts while you are driving. Which 2 things should you do?

Ans.
    (a) Pull on the handbrake.
    (b) Brake as quickly as possible.
* (c) Pull up slowly at the side of the road.
* (d) Hold the steering wheel firmly to keep control.
    (e) Continue on at a normal speed.

Q.
BW0135
When braking with a vehicle fitted with A.B.S you should .....

Ans.
    (a) press and release the brake at rapid intervals.
    (b) press and release the brake at slow intervals.
* (c) press the brake-pedal firmly and hold.
    (d) press the brake-pedal only lightly.

Q.
BW0136
You are driving along and you get a four wheel sideways skid, you should .....

Ans.
    (a) turn the steering wheel in the opposite direction and apply the handbrake to bring the car to a halt.
    (b) pump the brakes gently so that the wheels turn and grip the road again.
    (c) apply the footbrake firmly keeping the steering wheel straight ahead.
* (d) turn the steering wheel in the same direction as the skid.
    (e) turn the steering wheel in the opposite direction to improve tyre grip.

Q.
BW0137

Select 2 answers. You are driving along and you get a front wheel sideways skid. You should .....

Ans. * (a) turn the steering wheel in the same direction in which the vehicle is heading.
* (b) push in the clutch and take your foot off the accelerator.
(c) turn the steering wheel in the same direction and apply the handbrake to bring the car to a halt.
(d) apply the footbrake strongly.
(e) push in the clutch and apply the handbrake to bring the car to a halt.

Q.
BW0138

Select 2 answers. You are driving along and you get a rear wheel sideways skid. You should .....

Ans. (a) apply the footbrake strongly to bring the car to a halt.
* (b) push in the clutch and take your foot off the accelerator.
* (c) turn the steering wheel in the same direction in which the rear wheels are heading.
(d) turn the steering wheel in the same direction in which the front wheels are heading.
(e) turn the steering wheel in the opposite direction in which the front wheels are heading.

Q.
BW0139

You are driving along in a car without A.B.S. and get a front wheel skid. You should .....

Ans. * (a) release the footbrake.
(b) turn the steering gently left or right.
(c) push in the clutch and take your foot off the accelerator.
(d) apply the footbrake strongly.

Q. Select 2 answers. You are driving along and you get a
BW0140 tyre blow out. You should .....

Ans. * (a) apply the footbrake gently and bring the vehicle to a
halt.
(b) apply the footbrake firmly.
* (c) steer the vehicle to the side of the road when you have
reduced speed.
(d) apply the handbrake immediately to help bring the
vehicle to a halt.
(e) switch off the engine ignition to help bring the vehicle to
a halt.
(f) bring the vehicle to a halt.

Q. Select 3 answers. A front tyre blow-out could
BW0141 cause .....

Ans. * (a) the vehicle to sway from side to side.
(b) the vehicle to pull to the rear away from the front
blow-out.
* (c) your vehicle to go out of control.
(d) the wheels to lock.
* (e) the vehicle to pull towards the side with the blow-out.

Q. Select 2 answers. A rear tyre blow-out could
BW0142 cause .....

Ans. (a) the car to pull away from the side with the blow-out.
(b) the car to pull towards the side with the blow-out.
* (c) the car to sway from side to side.
(d) the wheels to lock.
* (e) your car to go out of control.

Q.
BW0143

Select 2 answers. Your vehicle engine cuts out suddenly while you are driving along. You should .....

Ans. * (a) put the gears in neutral.
  (b) check that the handbrake is fully off.
  (c) engage a lower gear.
  (d) depress the accelerator and then release it.
  * (e) signal and steer the car to the side of the road.

Q.
BW0144

Select 2 answers. The engine of your vehicle, which has power steering, cuts out suddenly while you are driving along. You should .....

Ans. * (a) steer as best you can to the side of the road.
  (b) engage a lower gear.
  (c) turn the steering fully and then turn the ignition key.
  * (d) grip the steering wheel tightly.

Q.
BW0145

Select 2 answers. If your brakes fail while you are driving along, you should .....

Ans. (a) check that the handbrake is fully off.
  * (b) engage a lower gear.
  (c) engage a higher gear.
  (d) engage neutral gear.
  * (e) pump the brakes firmly and quickly.

Q.
BW0146

Select 2 answers. If your brakes fail while you are driving along, you should .....

Ans.

    (a) use a hand signal to following traffic that you intend to slow down or stop.

* (b) switch on your hazard warning lights.

    (c) signal to following traffic to overtake you.

    (d) press the footbrake firmly then release it.

    (e) depress the accelerator and then release it.

* (f) steer for vacant openings on the left.

Q.
BW0147

Select 3 answers. If your accelerator jams while you are driving along, you should .....

Ans.

    (a) leave the vehicle in gear and apply the brakes.

* (b) engage a neutral gear and apply the brakes.

    (c) engage a low gear and depress the clutch.

* (d) try and flick the accelerator with your foot.

    (e) try and flick the accelerator and the brakes with your foot.

* (f) switch off the engine.

Q.
BW0148

Select 2 answers. You are driving along and find yourself heading towards a head-on crash. You should .....

Ans.

    (a) switch off the engine ignition to help bring the vehicle to a halt.

    (b) apply the footbrake gently to bring the vehicle to a halt.

* (c) apply the footbrake firmly.

* (d) flash your headlights and sound the horn to attract the attention of the other driver.

    (e) apply the handbrake immediately to help bring the car to a halt.

    (f) apply the footbrake and handbrake together.

Q.
BW0149

You are suddenly confronted with an obstacle on the road as you drive along. You should .....

Ans.
    (a) apply the handbrake and the footbrake together.
    (b) apply the footbrake and switch off the ignition.
    (c) switch off the ignition.
* (d) apply the footbrake firmly.

Q.
BW0150

You are required to stop suddenly as you drive along. You should .....

Ans.
    (a) apply the handbrake and footbrake.
    (b) steer sharply to one side and apply the handbrake.
* (c) apply the footbrake firmly.
    (d) depress the clutch and apply the footbrake.

Q.
BW0151

To stop in an emergency, you should .....

Ans. * (a) maintain firm pressure on the footbrake.
    (b) press and release the footbrake.
    (c) maintain a firm grip on the steering and depress both the clutch and footbrake.
    (d) flash the headlights and the brake-lights.

Q.
BW0152

When required to stop in an emergency, you should .....

Ans.
    (a) switch off the A.B.S. system.
* (b) press the footbrake firmly.
    (c) depress the clutch pedal and engage a lower gear.
    (d) press the footbrake and engage a higher gear.

Q.
BW0153

Select 2 answers. To help to avoid having to make an emergency stop, you should .....

Ans.   *   (a)   keep a safe distance from the vehicle in front.

          (b)   drive with your left foot covering the brake-pedal.

          (c)   drive with your left foot covering the clutch pedal.

          (d)   keep your left-hand available to apply the handbrake.

    *   (e)   scan the road well ahead.

CHAPTER I

PART III

CATEGORY AM

TECHNICAL MATTERS, WITH A BEARING ON ROAD SAFETY

PROTECTION/CLOTHING

Q.
AM0001
Which of the following should you always wear while riding a motorcycle?

Ans.   (a) Boots and protective clothing.
  * (b) Gloves, boots, helmet and protective clothing.
      (c) Protective clothing and gloves.
      (d) Protective clothing with yellow and orange fluorescent stripes.

Q.
AM0002
It is recommended that the protective clothing which you wear while riding a motorcycle should have .....

Ans.   (a) yellow and green stripes.
      (b) yellow and orange stripes.
      (c) a chest protector.
  * (d) a CE mark i.e. European Union standard mark.

Q. You should wear protective clothing while riding your
AM0003   motorcycle .....

Ans.   (a) in wet weather only.
   (b) in wet or icy weather only.
 * (c) at all times.
   (d) in cold weather only.

Q. Which of the following footwear should you wear
AM0004   when riding a motorcycle .....

Ans.   (a) sandals.
   (b) shoes.
 * (c) protective boots.
   (d) runners.

Q. Select 2 answers. Gloves should be worn .....
AM0005

Ans. * (a) to protect your hands from the cold and wet.
 * (b) to protect your hands if you fall off.
   (c) when the steering is tight.
   (d) if there is no wind shield on the motorcycle.

Q. Gloves should be worn .....
AM0006

Ans.   (a) only in poor weather conditions.
 * (b) at all times.
   (c) in hot weather to avoid sunburn.
   (d) when changing a wheel.

Q. How do you ensure protection for your eyes when
AM0007   riding a motorcycle?

Ans. * (a) Wear a helmet with an adjustable visor.
   (b) Keep your head angled downwards.
   (c) Keep your eyes partially closed.
   (d) Always wear sun glasses or bi-focals.

Q. When is it permissible for you to drive a moped or
AM0008 motorcycle in a public place without wearing a
helmet?

Ans. (a) When driving a moped in a 50 km/h or less, speed limit
area.
(b) When travelling on minor roads at speeds below
50 km/h.
* (c) Never.
(d) When the temperature exceeds 25 degrees centigrade.

MOTORCYCLE FEATURES, TAKING CARE OF THE MACHINE AND SAFETY

Q. This green light shows when the machine is .....
AM0009

Ans. * (a) in neutral gear.
(b) in first gear.
(c) in stop gear.
(d) in reverse gear.

Q. This switch operates ......
AM0010

Ans. (a) rear fog light.
* (b) headlights.
(c) hazard warning light.
(d) front fog light.

Q. This lever operates .....
AM0011

Ans. (a) the throttle.
(b) the rear brake.
(c) the front brakes.
* (d) the clutch.

Q. This switch operates the .....

AM0012

Ans.   (a) hazard warning lights.

      (b) choke.

   * (c) emergency engine stop.

      (d) headlights.

Q. This lever operates the .....

AM0013

Ans.   (a) rear brake.

   * (b) front brake.

      (c) clutch.

      (d) throttle.

Q. Which fluid is contained here .....

AM0014

Ans.   (a) water coolant.

      (b) clutch fluid.

      (c) gear oil.

   * (d) brake fluid.

Q. The foot lever on the nearside of your motorcycle operates the .....

AM0015

Ans.   (a) clutch.

      (b) brakes.

      (c) accelerator.

   * (d) gears.

Q. The foot lever on the offside of your motorcycle operates the .....

AM0016

Ans.   (a) clutch.

   * (b) brakes.

      (c) accelerator.

      (d) gears.

Q. What does this light mean?

AM0017

Ans.   (a) Faulty clutch.
          (b) Engine temperature too low.
          (c) Engine temperature too high.
    * (d) A gear is not engaged.

Q. Select 2 answers. You are driving along and you get a

AM0018

front wheel sideways skid. You should .....

Ans. * (a) turn steering in the same direction in which the vehicle
              is heading and release the throttle.
    * (b) pull in the clutch and ease off on the throttle.
        (c) apply the footbrake strongly.
        (d) pull in the clutch and apply the handbrake.

Q. Your weekly inspection of the motorcycle should

AM0019

cover .....

Ans. * (a) petrol, oil, water, damage, electrics and tyres.
        (b) petrol, footstand and chain.
        (c) petrol, oil and brake fluid.
        (d) petrol, tyres and chain.

Q. Good practice for the care of your motorcycle would

AM0020

be .....

Ans. * (a) to visually inspect the motorcycle daily and to carry out
              an inspection once a week.
        (b) to carry out an inspection of the motorcycle every 2,000
              kilometres.
        (c) to carry out an inspection of the motorcycle once a
              month.
        (d) to visually inspect the motorcycle once a month.

Q. AM0021

Select 2 answers. When starting the engine, you should .....

Ans.

     (a) hold the starter button on for a few moments after the engine has started.

     (b) select first gear.

     (c) be standing beside the machine.

* (d) select neutral gear.

* (e) be sitting astride the machine.

Q. AM0022

If you do not lubricate the chain of your motorcycle .....

Ans.

     (a) the chain will become flexible in dry weather.

* (b) it will increase the rate of wear.

     (c) the chain will become flexible in wet weather.

     (d) the chain will tighten and contract.

Q. AM0023

If the drive chain on your motorcycle is loose. This could cause .....

Ans. * (a) the rear wheel to lock.

     (b) the brakes to fail.

     (c) the front wheel to lock.

     (d) both wheels to lock.

     (e) the gears to tighten.

Q. AM0024

Riding a motorcycle which has a slack chain could .....

Ans.

     (a) cause the front wheel to lock.

* (b) cause the rear wheel to lock.

     (c) cause both wheels to lock.

     (d) cause the brakes to lock.

Q.
AM0025

Select 3 correct answers. If the drive chain is incorrectly adjusted this may .....

Ans.
* (a) give rise to an accident.
* (b) cause a rattling noise.
  (c) cause excessive use of the choke.
  (d) cause the wheels to wobble.
  (e) make gear changing difficult.
* (f) cause the rear wheel to lock.

Q.
AM0026

Select 2 correct answers. A motorcycle drive chain with wear may .....

Ans.
(a) affect gear change.
(b) tighten.
* (c) stretch.
* (d) become noisy.
(e) lock the front wheel.

Q.
AM0027

Having adjusted the drive chain, you should check .....

Ans.
* (a) wheel alignment.
(b) position of rear brake-pedal.
(c) position of gear selector.
(d) the kick-start lever

Q.
AM0028

Select 3 correct answers. Applying the choke for a long period can cause .....

Ans.
(a) increased wear on the engine cut-off switch.
* (b) more fuel to be used and increased pollution.
* (c) increased wear on the engine.
(d) increased wear on the transmission system.
* (e) the engine to run too high when you are slowing down.
(f) the engine to run too slow when you are slowing down.

Q.   **Leaving the choke on will .....**

AM0029

Ans.   (a) improve fuel consumption.

         (b) save on oil on the drive chain.

         (c) improve valve performance.

         (d) prevent the engine cutting out in wet weather.

    * (e) cause engine wear and waste fuel.

Q.   **Select 2 correct answers. Cable operated brakes .....**

AM0030

Ans.   (a) tighten in use.

    * (b) stretch in use.

         (c) should never be oiled.

    * (d) require regular oiling.

         (e) require weekly adjustment.

Q.   **Which 2 of the following should be kept clean?**

AM0031

Ans.   (a) Engine.

         (b) Fairing.

    * (c) Headlights.

         (d) Mud Guards.

    * (e) Number Plate.

Q.   **Which 2 of the following should be kept clean?**

AM0032

Ans.   (a) Engine.

         (b) Fairing.

    * (c) Brake-light.

         (d) Mud Guards.

    * (e) Indicators.

Q. Select 2 correct answers. Incorrect wheel
AM0033 alignment will .....

Ans. (a) cause passenger discomfort.
    (b) increase mud spray.
    (c) reduce fuel consumption.
  * (d) reduce road holding.
  * (e) give excessive tyre wear.

Q. Refitting which of the following could put wheel
AM0034 alignment off?

Ans. * (a) Rear wheel.
    (b) Front wheel.
    (c) Rear brakes.
    (d) Front brakes.
    (e) Sports fairings.

Q. Worn bearings in the steering head can .....
AM0035

Ans. (a) cause the front brake lever to loosen.
  * (b) make the motorcycle more difficult to control.
    (c) cause the clutch lever to tighten.
    (d) cause the front brake-lever to tighten.
    (e) cause the clutch lever to loosen.

Q. Which of these would cause the steering to feel
AM0036 wobbly?

Ans. (a) Putting the foot down sharply on the kick-start
       lever.
  * (b) Worn steering head bearings.
    (c) Over inflated tyres.
    (d) Over oiled head bearings.

Q. You should use the engine cut-out switch to stop the
AM0037 engine .....

Ans. (a) when stopping on a hill.
        (b) after long journeys only.
        (c) after short journeys only.
    *   (d) in an emergency only.
        (e) in cold weather.

Q. Your side stand should be fully raised .....
AM0038

Ans. (a) to avoid causing noise
        (b) when not carrying a pillion passenger.
    *   (c) to avoid jarring the ground and destabilising the
            motorcycle when cornering.
        (d) to avoid the chain getting caught in the stand.

Q. Tyre pressure should be increased when .....
AM0040

Ans. (a) in very hot weather if the road surface has softened.
    *   (b) you are carrying a pillion passenger.
        (c) you propose to go over rough terrain.
        (d) the drive chain is worn.
        (e) in snow.

Q. What is the minimum legal tyre tread depth for
AM0041 motorcycles?

Ans. (a) 1.6 millimetres.
        (b) 0.8 millimetres.
    *   (c) 1 millimetre.
        (d) 1.4 millimetres.

Q.   **A side-car may be fitted to a motorcycle .....**
AM0042

Ans.   (a)   only if fitted with a canopy.
            (b)   on either side.
            (c)   only if fitted with a visor.
            (d)   only on the right-hand side.
    *   (e)   only on the left-hand side.

Q.   **Traction control systems help to prevent .....**
AM0043

Ans.   *   (a)   the rear wheel from spinning when moving off.
            (b)   electric short circuits.
            (c)   oil leakage.
            (d)   petrol leakage.
            (e)   tyre wear.

RIDING YOUR MOTORCYCLE

MOVING OFF

Q.   **Select 2 answers. Before turning on the engine you**
AM0044   **should check if the ......**

Ans.   (a)   passenger seat is clean.
    *   (b)   back wheel turns freely.
            (c)   parking lights are on.
    *   (d)   gear selector is in neutral.
            (e)   fuel tap is off.

Q. When in busy moving traffic you wish to change
AM0045 lanes. Looking over your shoulders would help
because your ......

Ans. (a) body would be more relaxed.
* (b) mirrors may not cover blind spots.
(c) balance would be improved for moving across lanes.

Q. Before moving off from a parked position you
AM0046 should .....

Ans. * (a) look over your shoulder for a final glance.
(b) check that the right foot is on the ground.
(c) ensure that the visor is up.
(d) ensure that the front brake-lever is engaged.

Q. A lifesaver is .....
AM0047

Ans. (a) a retarder for controlling speed.
(b) a fluorescent reflective belt.
(c) a brake engaged on long descents.
* (d) a look over your shoulder before moving off, turning or
changing direction.

Q. You should give a lifesaver .....
AM0048

Ans. * (a) when changing direction on your motorcycle.
(b) only to a person with breathing difficulties following an
accident
(c) only to your passenger if injured in an accident.
(d) only to a person with non-head injuries.

ROAD POSITION

Q.   **In this situation, the rider is .....**
AM0049

Ans.   *   (a)   midway between the nearside
           edge and the centre of the road.
       (b)   in the nearside position.
       (c)   in the offside position.

Q.   **In this situation, the rider is .....**
AM0050

Ans.   (a)   midway between the nearside
           edge and the centre of the road.
    *   (b)   in the offside position.
       (c)   in the nearside position.

Q.   **In this situation, the rider is .....**
AM0051

Ans.   (a)   midway between the nearside
           edge and the centre of the road.
       (b)   in the offside position.
    *   (c)   in the nearside position.

Q.   **In this situation the motorcyclist**
AM0052   **is ......**

Ans.   *   (a)   in the normal position.
       (b)   too far to the left.
       (c)   too far to the right.
       (d)   sitting too straight.

Q.   **What should you do in this**
AM0053   **situation .....**

Ans.   (a)   stay close to the wall.
         (b)   drive on the right-hand side of
             the road.
         (c)   raise both feet off the footrests.
   *   (d)   pick the best road surface available.

Q.   **When stopped at traffic lights, stop**
AM0054   **signs, or in traffic, you should .....**

Ans.   (a)   have both feet down.
         (b)   have both feet up.
         (c)   have the right foot down.
   *   (d)   have the left foot down.

Q.   **When driving along you**
AM0055   **should .....**

Ans.   (a)   have both feet down.
   *   (b)   have both feet up.
         (c)   have the right foot down.
         (d)   have the left foot down.

Q.   **Select 2 answers. In this situation .....**
AM0056

Ans.   *   (a)   stability is reduced.
         (b)   stability is increased.
         (c)   braking takes longer.
   *   (d)   your feet may be injured by
             hitting the road.

Q.
AM0057

In this situation the motorcyclist is .....

Ans. * (a) in the correct position.
       (b) too far to the left.
       (c) too far to the right.

Q.
AM0058

In this situation the motorcyclist is .....

Ans.   (a) in the correct position.
   * (b) too far to the left.
       (c) too far to the right.

Q.
AM0059

In this situation with oncoming traffic, the motorcyclist is .....

Ans. * (a) in the normal position.
       (b) too far to the left.
       (c) too far to the right.
       (d) may be dazed by oncoming lights.

Q.
AM0060

On this type of road you should .....

Ans. * (a) avoid the grass in the centre of the road.
       (b) drive on the grass in the centre of the road.
       (c) drive on the grass on the left hand verge.
       (d) drive in a high gear to improve stability.

Q. AM0061 **In this situation, your position is .....**

Ans.
    (a) too far to the right.
  * (b) too close to the vehicle in front.
    (c) correct.
    (d) too close to the oncoming vehicle.

Q. AM0062 **In this situation, your position .....**

Ans. * (a) allows proper observation to hazards left and right.
    (b) does not allow good observation to hazards on the left.
    (c) should be at the yellow broken line.
    (d) should be closer to the vehicle in front.

Q. AM0063 **In this situation the motorcyclist's position .....**

Ans. * (a) allows for good margins of safety to the rider.
    (b) is too far to the left.
    (c) is too far to the right.

Q. AM0064 **In this situation your position .....**

Ans. * (a) allows better visibility along the inside of the truck.
    (b) allows better visibility along the outside of the truck.
    (c) allows better visibility along both sides of the truck.
    (d) reduces clearance from oncoming traffic.

Q.
AM0065

In this situation your position .....

Ans.

  (a) reduces clearance from oncoming traffic.

  (b) allows better visibility to following traffic.

  (c) allows better visibility to oncoming traffic.

* (d) allows more clearance from oncoming traffic.

Q.
AM0066

You are turning left. In this position you are .....

Ans.

  (a) in the correct position.

  (b) too far to the left.

* (c) too far to the right.

Q.
AM0067

You intend to turn left at the junction ahead. Your position is .....

Ans. * (a) correct.

  (b) too far to the left.

  (c) too far to the right.

Q.
AM0068

You are going straight ahead at the junction. Your position is .....

Ans.

  (a) correct.

* (b) too far to the left.

  (c) too far to the right.

Q. You intend to overtake the tractor ahead.
AM0069 You should .....

Ans. (a) drive closer to the vehicle
before moving out.
(b) move out from this position.
* (c) have moved out earlier.
(d) give a 'lifesaver' over your left
shoulder, and move out.

Q. The normal safety position on the road is .....
AM0070

Ans. * (a) midway between near side edge and centre of the road.
(b) near side edge.
(c) centre of the road.
(d) any position to the left of the centre line.

Q. You should generally position your machine to the
AM0071 rear off side of the vehicle you are following .....

Ans. (a) unless your machine has a side car.
(b) so that you are visible through the inside and outside
door mirrors of the vehicle in front.
* (c) so that you are able to move into an overtaking position
without changing position on the road.
(d) so that you are able to escape to either side in an
emergency.

Q. When you intend to overtake, you should generally
AM0072 position your machine to the .....

Ans. (a) near side of the vehicle in front.
(b) centre of the vehicle in front.
(c) near side or centre.
* (d) off side of the vehicle in front.

Q.
AM0073

Select 3 answers. The advantages of near side position are .....

Ans. * (a) near side views past trucks and buses.
* (b) early views through right-hand bends.
* (c) extra space for oncoming vehicles.
(d) early views through left-hand bends.

Q.
AM0074

Select 3 answers. Near side position should be taken .....

Ans. (a) for the best position for left-hand bends.
* (b) to give extra clearance for overtaking traffic.
* (c) to give extra clearance for oncoming traffic straddling the central line on right-hand bends.
* (d) for the best position for turning left.

Q.
AM0075

Select 2 answers. In wet weather, when should you not ride in the central position i.e. midway between the near side edge and the centre line of the road .....

Ans. * (a) on the straight because oil and diesel may gather.
* (b) near junctions and bends because oil and diesel may gather.
(c) on the straight so as to avoid spray.
(d) as visibility is reduced.

Q.
AM0076

Riding in the central position i.e. midway between the near side edge and the centre line of the road .....

Ans. (a) always maximises rider safety.
(b) always allows sufficient clearance for oncoming traffic straddling the central line of the road.
(c) allows near side views past trucks and buses.
* (d) gives the rider good margins of safety on both sides.

Q. The offside position .....

Ans. (a) should only be used when there is debris, dust or grit in the near side, and central position.
* (b) gives early views on the approach to left-hand bends.
(c) gives early views on the approach to right-hand bends.
(d) should only be used when positioning to overtake.

Q. Select 2 correct answers. The offside position .....

AM0078

Ans. * (a) provides increased safety margins away from near side hazards.
* (b) is generally the best position for turning right.
(c) always allows clear views past trucks and buses.
(d) is generally the best position for turning left.

Q. When cornering, a motorcyclist should .....

AM0079

Ans. * (a) lean in the direction of the turn.
(b) lean in the opposite direction to the turn.
(c) remain in an upright position.
(d) accelerate.

Q. Select 2 answers. When cornering at speed i.e. riding a motorcycle round a corner, curve or bend, your machine .....

AM0080

Ans. * (a) has less stability.
(b) increases fuel consumption.
(c) maintains stability.
* (d) puts extra demands on tyre grip.

Q.
AM0081

When cornering on right-hand bends you should position yourself towards the .....

Ans. * (a) near side position.
     (b) near side, unless riding with sidecar.
     (c) central position.
     (d) off side, unless riding with sidecar
     (e) off side position.

Q.
AM0082

Select 3 answers. Before cornering on a bend, you should be in the correct .....

Ans. * (a) speed.
   * (b) gear.
   * (c) position on the approach.
     (d) rev counter reading.

Q.
AM0083

During cornering on a bend .....

Ans. * (a) speed should be constant.
     (b) speed should be reduced.
     (c) gears should be raised.
     (d) gears should be lowered.

Q.
AM0084

Select 3 answers. When cornering on a bend, you should allow for .....

Ans. * (a) a change to poor road conditions.
     (b) use of front brakes only.
   * (c) pedestrians or parked vehicles.
     (d) another rider to pass on the inside.
   * (e) blind junctions or exits.

Q.
AM0085

Select 2 correct answers. Positioning correctly while cornering .....

Ans.
    (a) reduces fuel consumption.
* (b) gives an earlier and more extended view.
* (c) improves stability.
    (d) reduces stopping distance.
    (e) reduces banking.

Q.
AM0086

When cornering on left-hand bends, you should position yourself towards the .....

Ans.
    (a) central position.
    (b) off side, unless riding with sidecar.
    (c) near side position.
* (d) off side position.
    (e) near side, unless riding with sidecar.

Q.
AM0087

Select 2 answers. Before taking position on a left hand bend you should consider .....

Ans. * (a) whether any advantage would be gained at low speed even where there is unrestricted views across the bend.
    (b) whether indicator signals should not be given, so that machine stability is maintained.
* (c) approaching traffic which requires a margin of safety.
    (d) whether indicator signals should be given, so that machine stability is maintained.

Q. Select 2 answers. Before taking position on a left
AM0088 hand bend you should consider .....

Ans. (a) whether indicator signals should not be given, so that
machine stability is maintained.

* (b) off side hazards which require a margin of safety.

* (c) whether your position might mislead other traffic of
your intentions.

(d) whether indicator signals should be given, so that
machine stability is maintained.

Q. How would you gauge the severity of a bend?
AM0089

Ans. (a) By maintaining a course along the centre of the road.

(b) By noting the banking of the motorcycle.

* (c) By noting where the near side and off side verges appear
to meet and how this changes as you approach.

(d) By noting the speed of oncoming traffic.

Q. Special care is required when taking bends on a
AM0090 motorcycle with a side-car attached because .....

Ans. (a) the position of the side-car could interfere with the
movement of the handlebars.

(b) when the motorcycle leans over the side-car may
become detached.

* (c) the side-car compartment cannot be leaned over.

(d) the weight of the side-car increases instability.

Q. Extra special care is required when taking left-hand bends on a motorcycle with a side-car attached because .....

AM0091

Ans. * (a) the weight being thrown outwards will tend to lift the side-car off the road.
  (b) the side-car could become detached when the motorcycle leans over.
  (c) the position of the side-car could interfere with the movement of the handlebars.
  (d) the side-car outfit cannot be leaned over.

OVERTAKING

Q. Select 2 answers. When overtaking, you should avoid causing .....

AM0092

Ans. * (a) approaching traffic to alter course or speed.
  * (b) traffic being overtaken to alter course or speed.
  (c) your machine to alter course or speed.

Q. Select 2 answers. When overtaking, you should .....

AM0093

Ans. (a) avoid abandoning the overtaking manoeuvre once commenced.
  * (b) avoid making a third line of vehicles abreast, if possible.
  * (c) always be able to move back to the near side in plenty of time.
  (d) proceed so long as there is no oncoming traffic straddling the centre line.

Q. Where would you position yourself for a view along
AM0094 the offside of a truck which is following a right-hand
bend?

Ans. (a) In the offside position.
    * (b) In the nearside position.
    (c) In the central position.

Q. You propose to overtake a truck which has
AM0095 commenced following a right-hand bend on the road
where there is a restricted view. You should .....

Ans. * (a) position yourself for the earliest possible view along the
truck's off side.
(b) position yourself in the central position.
(c) alternate your position between near side and off side
for views each side of the truck.
(d) position yourself for the earliest possible view along the
truck's near side.

Q. You propose to overtake a truck which has
AM0096 commenced following a left-hand bend on the road
where there is a restricted view. You should .....

Ans. * (a) position yourself for the earliest possible view along the
truck's near side.
(b) position yourself in the central position between near
side and off side.
(c) alternate your position between near side and off side
for views each side of the truck.
(d) position yourself for the earliest possible view along the
truck's off side.

Q.
AM0097

You are in the near side position behind a truck and decide to take up the off side position. You should be aware that .....

Ans.

   (a) you should take up the central position for a time before moving to off side.

   (b) you must indicate that you are moving from near side to off side.

* (c) areas of the road will be lost from view while you change position.

   (d) you should watch the tail lights of the truck for an indication that it may be suddenly braking.

Q.
AM0098

Select 4 answers. When considering overtaking a slow moving truck, a hazard may arise because .....

Ans.

   (a) the truck is a left-hand drive and the driver would not see you in an off side position.

* (b) the truck in front of you may turn right with very late or no indication.

* (c) the driver of a vehicle turning left up ahead to face you may only have taken observations to his right.

* (d) a slow moving vehicle may be turning left onto your road up ahead.

* (e) the driver of a vehicle on a road to your left up ahead is turning right and you are not in his sight.

Q.
AM0099

You have just overtaken another large vehicle and you wish to move back to the left-hand lane. You should .....

Ans. * (a) check the left-hand mirror, signal and move back when it is safe to do so.

   (b) wait until the driver of the large vehicle signals to you to move back into the left-hand lane.

   (c) accelerate, signal and move back quickly.

   (d) signal left, and gradually move back.

Q.
AM0100

Select 4 answers. You have moved close to the vehicle in front in order to overtake. You should be aware that .....

Ans. * (a) the driver may brake suddenly.
(b) you should only indicate when the way is clear to overtake.
* (c) the driver may increase speed.
* (d) the driver may reduce speed.
* (e) an unanticipated hazard may come into view.

TAKING EMERGENCY/CORRECTIVE ACTION

Q.
AM0101

If you get a sudden and severe puncture while riding along, you should .....

Ans. (a) use the engine cut-out switch.
* (b) close the throttle and ease to a stop.
(c) change to a lower gear and ease to a stop.
(d) brake immediately.
(e) turn off the fuel tap and ease to a stop.

Q.
AM0102

Select 2 answers. When stopping the engine, you should .....

Ans. * (a) turn off ignition.
(b) de-clutch after you have stopped the engine.
(c) use the engine cut-off switch, except in an emergency.
* (d) not use the engine cut-off switch, except in an emergency.

Q.
AM0103

To stop your motorcycle quickly in an emergency, you should .....

Ans.
     (a) use both brakes together in short bursts.
     (b) use the rear brake only.
     (c) use the front brake only.
  * (d) use the front brake followed by the rear brake.
     (e) use the rear brake followed by the front brake.

Q.
AM0104

Select 2 answers. Your vehicle engine cuts out suddenly while you are riding along. You should .....

Ans. * (a) put the gears in neutral.
     (b) check that the handbrake is fully off.
     (c) engage a lower gear.
     (d) depress the accelerator and then release it.
  * (e) signal and steer the motorcycle to the side of the road.

Q.
AM0105

Select 2 answers. You are riding along and you get a front wheel sideways skid. You should .....

Ans. * (a) turn the steering in the same direction in which the bike is heading.
  * (b) roll off the throttle.
     (c) turn the steering in the opposite direction to which the bike is heading.
     (d) apply the footbrake strongly.
     (e) push in the clutch and apply the footbrake to bring the bike to a halt.

Q.
AM0106
Select 2 answers. You are riding along and you get a rear wheel sideways skid. You should .....

Ans.
   (a) apply the footbrake strongly to bring the bike to a halt.
* (b) roll off the throttle.
* (c) turn the steering in the same direction as the rear wheel is heading.
   (d) turn the steering in the same direction in which the front wheel is heading.
   (e) turn the steering in the opposite direction to which the front wheel is heading.

DEALING WITH HAZARDS

Q.
AM0107
You are approaching the truck on a narrow road. You should .....

Ans. * (a) slow down.
   (b) stop and alight from the machine.
   (c) expect the truck to stop.
   (d) expect the truck driver to keep close to his left.

Q.
AM0108
In this situation ......

Ans. * (a) your visibility ahead is reduced.
   (b) you can clearly see all hazards ahead.
   (c) another vehicle would not attempt to overtake the truck.
   (d) you would not be affected by the truck slipstream.

Q. In this situation you should be aware of .....

AM0206

Ans.
    (a) road flooded.
    (b) glare from sun.
    (c) dry grass.
 * (d) poor quality of the road
        surface on your left.

Q. Select 2 answers. What hazards should you be aware of in this situation .....

AM0109

Ans.
 * (a) wet road surface.
 * (b) exits left and right.
    (c) melting tar on the road.
    (d) glare from the sun.

Q. Select 2 answers. What hazards should you be aware of in this situation .....

AM0110

Ans.
 * (a) wet road surface.
    (b) melting tar on the road.
    (c) glare from the sun.
 * (d) absence of road markings.

Q. Select 2 answers. Why should you slow down in this situation .....

AM0111

Ans.
 * (a) you are approaching a yield sign.
 * (b) the road is severely flooded.
    (c) visibility ahead is reduced.
    (d) speed limit sign ahead.

Q.
AM0112

Select 2 answers. What hazards should you be aware of in this situation .....

Ans.
    (a) oncoming traffic.
    (b) none.
* (c) junction ahead on the right.
* (d) fallen leaves on the road.

Q.
AM0113

Select 3 answers. What hazards are presented to this rider .....

Ans. * (a) potholes.
    * (b) loose gravel.
    * (c) wet grass.
    (d) dry grass.

Q.
AM0114

In this situation .....

Ans.
    (a) you are safe to overtake.
* (b) you may be blown off course by wind turbulence from the truck.
    (c) you are safe to overtake as long as you do not cross the continuous white line.

Q.   **Select 2 answers. You are approaching a railway**

AM0115   **crossing. What should you be aware of .....**

Ans.   *   (a)   the tracks may not be flush
with the road.

      *   (b)   the barriers may come down.

        (c)   you should use a high gear.

        (d)   to avoid stalling on the tracks,
you should accelerate.

OBSERVANCE OF SAFE DISTANCE AND DRIVING IN VARIOUS WEATHER/ROAD CONDITIONS

WEATHER CONDITIONS

Q.
AM0117
Select 3 answers. Riding your motorcycle in a flood, you should .....

Ans.
    (a) keep the engine running slowly.
* (b) keep the engine running fast.
* (c) ride slowly.
    (d) ride fast.
* (e) test your brakes when you are out of the water.
    (f) gently apply the brakes at all times.

Q.
AM0118
Having gone through floods, how would you dry the brakes?

Ans.
    (a) Let the brakes dry naturally as you ride along.
* (b) Drive slowly while applying the brakes briefly.
    (c) Stop at a lay-by and use a towel.
    (d) Increase your speed so as to cause wind draught.
    (e) Use an air hose.

Q.
AM0119
Select 2 answers. In hot weather melting tar on the road?

Ans.
    (a) Improves tyre grip.
    (b) Improves braking efficiency.
    (c) Reduces stopping distance.
* (d) Reduces tyre grip.
* (e) Increases stopping distance.

Q. In hot weather soft tar on the road can affect .....
AM0120

Ans. * (a) braking.
    (b) the catalytic converter.
    (c) visibility.
    (d) the traction control system.

Q. **Select 3 answers. When riding in windy conditions**
AM0121 **you should .....**

Ans. * (a) watch for areas where there may be a sudden gust of wind.
    (b) put extra pressure in the tyres.
    (c) ride abreast of another motorcycle, if possible.
  * (d) drive at a lower speed.
    (e) drive at a higher speed.
  * (f) look ahead and anticipate crosswinds.

Q. **Select 2 answers. How might you know if there is**
AM0122 **black ice on the road?**

Ans. * (a) You will not be able to hear the noise of the tyre on the road.
    (b) Tyre pressure will seem heavier.
    (c) There will be louder tyre noise on the road.
  * (d) Steering will seem lighter.
    (e) Steering will be heavy.

KEEPING YOUR DISTANCE, BRAKING, AND STOPPING

Q.
AM0124

Select 2 answers. Should you keep a distance from the vehicle in front?

Ans. * (a) Yes, so as to suffer less from the spray from the vehicle in front in wet weather.
    (b) No, you should remain close to the proceeding vehicle so as not to be unsteadied by turbulence.
    (c) No, so that following traffic may overtake you and the vehicle in front.
* (d) Yes, so that you can stop your machine safely if the driver in front brakes without warning.

Q.
AM0125

Select 2 answers. By staying well back from the vehicle in front, you can .....

Ans.   (a) be in the blind spot of the driver in front.
* (b) extend your braking distance so that the driver behind has more time to react.
* (c) see when it is safe to move up into the overtaking position.
    (d) cause a build up of following traffic.

Q.
AM0126

Select 2 answers. By staying well back from the vehicle in front, you can .....

Ans. * (a) give the driver behind you more stopping distance.
* (b) have a good view and can increase it along both sides by slight changing of position.
    (c) give the driver in front more stopping distance.
    (d) drive safely watching the tail lights of the vehicle ahead.

Q.
AM0127

Select 2 answers. By staying tight to the vehicle in front, you would be .....

Ans.
   (a) fully aware of what is happening on the road ahead.
* (b) in the blind spot of the driver of the vehicle in front.
   (c) able to escape to either side of that vehicle in an emergency.
   (d) in the best position for overtaking.
* (e) reducing your visibility to oncoming traffic.

Q.
AM0128

You are following a vehicle on a wet road. An overtaking vehicle pulls into the gap you had left. You should .....

Ans.
   (a) continue on regardless.
   (b) move closer to prevent a repeat.
   (c) show your discomfort.
* (d) ease back to regain a safe distance.

BRAKING AND STOPPING

Q.
AM0129

The rear brake should be used on its own .....

Ans.
   (a) when banking over.
   (b) in strong winds.
   (c) when tank bags are fitted.
* (d) during slow manoeuvres.
   (e) when going downhill.

Q.
AM0130

The front brake should not be used .....

Ans. (a) when carrying a passenger.
(b) in wet weather.
* (c) when the motorcycle is banked over, turning, or on loose surfaces.
(d) when going downhill.

Q.
AM0131

When the motorcycle is banked over, which of the following should be avoided .....

Ans. (a) carrying a passenger.
(b) easing off the throttle.
* (c) using the brakes.
(d) using the indicators.

Q.
AM0132

When descending a long steep hill you should .....

Ans. (a) engage a high gear at an early stage.
* (b) engage a low gear at an early stage.
(c) avoid using the front brake.
(d) avoid using the rear brake.

Q.
AM0133

When descending a steep and winding road, braking should .....

Ans. (a) be continuous throughout the decline, but using only the front brake.
(b) be periodic, whether on the straight or around bends.
* (c) be on the straight only.
(d) be continuous throughout the decline.

Q.   You should brake firmly only when .....
AM0134

Ans.   (a)   in a low gear.
         (b)   on a dry road.
         (c)   in a high gear.
    *   (d)   travelling in a straight line.

Q.   You should brake firmly only when .....
AM0135

Ans.   (a)   using the rear brake only.
         (b)   using front and rear brakes together simultaneously.
    *   (c)   on the straight.
         (d)   using the front brake only.

Q.   When you prepare to use both brakes, which of the
AM0136   following is correct .....

Ans.   (a)   use both at the same time.
         (b)   use the rear brake first.
    *   (c)   use the front brake first.

Q.   When applying both brakes on a good dry surface on
AM0137   a straight road, braking force should generally be .....

Ans.   (a)   even pressure on both brakes.
         (b)   slightly more pressure on the rear.
    *   (c)   slightly more pressure on the front.

Q.   When applying both brakes on a wet or slippery
AM0138   surface on a straight road, braking force should
         generally be at .....

Ans. *   (a)   even pressure on both brakes.
         (b)   slightly more pressure on the rear.
         (c)   slightly more pressure on the front.

Q. Which 4 of the following would affect the stopping
AM0139 distance?

Ans. * (a) The speed of the motorcycle.
    * (b) Road condition.
    * (c) Tyre condition.
       (d) The engine capacity.
    * (e) The degree of maintenance of the motorcycle.

Q. Having a sidecar on the motorcycle .....
AM0140

Ans.   (a) will reduce stopping distance.
     (b) has no effect on stopping distance.
     (c) will reduce stopping distance going uphill.
     (d) will reduce stopping distance going downhill.
  * (e) will increase stopping distance going downhill.

Q. What is the stopping distance on a good dry road
AM0141 when travelling at 80 km/h?

Ans.   (a) 15 metres.
     (b) 20 metres.
     (c) 25 metres.
  * (d) 55 metres.

Q. Which 3 of the following affect your stopping
AM0142 distance?

Ans. * (a) The condition of the brakes, suspension and tyres.
    * (b) How fast you are travelling.
    * (c) The gradient of the road.
      (d) Oil pressure.
      (e) Engine temperature.

Q. Which 2 of the following affect your stopping
AM0143 distance?

Ans. * (a) Your reaction time.
         * (b) The weather and road conditions.
         (c) Oil pressure.
         (d) Engine temperature.

STABILITY AND SKIDDING

Q. Which four of the following might affect the stability
AM0144 of your motorcycle on the road and cause you to
        loose control?

Ans. * (a) Water.
         * (b) Mud.
         * (c) Wet leaves.
         (d) Shadows.
         * (e) Loose gravel or dirt.

Q. Crossing road markings or train rails at an oblique
AM0145 angle may .....

Ans. (a) cause the brake to lock.
         (b) cause the wheel spokes to buckle.
         * (c) destabilise the motorcycle.
         (d) cause the gears to slip.

Q. A motorcyclist travelling at a given speed requires a clear line in order to be able to maintain that speed. Having to accelerate/decelerate or change direction in order to avoid a protruding danger .....

AM0146

Ans.
   (a) would cause the front tyre to deflate.
   (b) would always allow you to maintain the stability of the motorcycle.
   (c) may cause the gears to slip.
* (d) may cause you to lose control of the motorcycle.

Q. To reduce speed on a slippery road, you should .....

AM0147

Ans. * (a) close the throttle gradually.
   (b) open the throttle fully.
   (c) engage top gear.
   (d) apply the footbrake.

Q. Select 2 answers. By applying both brakes with greatest pressure on the front .....

AM0148

Ans.
   (a) the weight of the rider is equally distributed on the motorcycle.
* (b) the weight of the motorcycle and rider is thrust forward.
   (c) the weight of the motorcycle and rider is thrust backwards.
* (d) the front tyre is secured on the road giving better grip.

Q. Applying both brakes with greatest pressure on the rear may cause .....

AM0149

Ans.
   (a) the weight of the rider to be thrust forward.
   (b) the front tyre to be secured on the road giving better grip.
   (c) the weight of the motorcycle and rider to be thrust downwards, improving tyre grip.
* (d) the rear wheel to lock.

Q.
AM0150

Select 2 answers. If the accelerator jams while you are driving along, you should .....

Ans. * (a) engage a neutral gear.
   (b) engage a low gear.
   (c) apply rear brake to bring motorcycle to a halt.
 * (d) switch off the ignition.
   (e) apply front brake to bring motorcycle to a halt.

Q.
AM0151

Crossing road markings such as lines and directional arrows .....

Ans. (a) improves tyre grip and reduces stopping distance.
   (b) should only be done in a high gear.
 * (c) reduces tyre grip and increases stopping distance.
   (d) reduces tyre grip only in wet weather.

Q.
AM0152

You are crossing tram lines. You should be aware that .....

Ans. (a) an amber light will flash to warn of approaching trams.
   (b) there may be glare from the lines.
 * (c) the lines may be slippery, particularly when wet.
   (d) the lines may be of different width.
   (e) you may not cross while carrying a passenger.

Q.
AM0153

When crossing tram lines, you should be aware that .....

Ans. (a) you should sit further back on the seat.
   (b) the traction control system will only operate on the front wheel.
   (c) you should sit further forward.
 * (d) steering and braking may be affected.

Q.
AM0154

Select 3 answers. While riding along, you should not take a prolonged look down at the front wheel as this may .....

Ans.   *   (a)   reduce stability.
        *   (b)   cause you to inadvertently change direction.
        *   (c)   reduce your field of view.
            (d)   increase tyre wear.
            (e)   increase any vibration from the road.

Q.
AM0155

Which of the following would reduce the risk of skidding?

Ans.   *   (a)   Gentle acceleration.
            (b)   Smooth tyres.
            (c)   Excessive speed.
            (d)   Rough acceleration.
            (e)   Excessive or sudden braking.

Q.
AM0156

Which of the following would not cause skidding?

Ans.   (a)   Harsh acceleration.
            (b)   Banking the machine too far over when turning and cornering.
            (c)   Frame out of alignment.
        *   (d)   Applying brake pressure gradually.
            (e)   Wheels not in line.

Q.
AM0157

Select 3 answers. To avoid skidding, you should .....

Ans.   *   (a)   not use the front brakes when machine is banked over.
            (b)   increase use of the throttle on a bend.
        *   (c)   operate the clutch smoothly.
        *   (d)   take the machine around corners in a steady course.

Q.

AM0158

Select 4 answers. To avoid skidding you should .....

Ans. * (a) test tyres frequently for correct pressure.
  * (b) negotiate bends in a low gear.
  * (c) ensure luggage is securely fastened to prevent sway.
  * (d) take the machine around corners in a steady course.
  (e) block change down the gears, when on a bend.

Q.

AM0159

Your wheel skids when you accelerate in heavy rain. To regain control you should .....

Ans. * (a) ease off the throttle.
  (b) apply front brake and change to low gear.
  (c) change to a low gear.
  (d) apply both brakes.
  (e) only change to a low gear where the motorcycle has linked braking.

ALERT DRIVING, AND CONSIDERATION FOR ROAD USERS

AWARENESS BY OTHER DRIVERS

Q.
AM0160

Select 3 answers. Which of the following should a motorcyclist allow for as regards awareness by other drivers. They .....

Ans.
* (a) might not be expecting a motorcycle.
* (b) might be watching for cars or large vehicles.
   (c) will have full visibility and observation of you.
   (d) will be fully familiar with riding a motorcycle.
* (e) might underestimate your speed.

Q.
AM0161

Select 3 answers. Which of the following should a motorcyclist allow for as regards awareness by other drivers. Other vehicle drivers will .....

Ans.
* (a) not always know if you wish to avoid a manhole cover, or pothole.
   (b) always allow you the same space as their vehicle.
* (c) not always check their blind spots before changing lanes or turning.
* (d) when turning right, not always check for motorcyclists on their left.
   (e) check that you have sufficient space and time for your right of way.

Q.
AM0162

Select 3 answers. Which of the following should a motorcyclist allow for as regards awareness by other drivers. Other vehicle drivers .....

Ans.   * (a) may not anticipate you taking action in wind or rain.
      * (b) may not watch for you at junctions.
        (c) will take particular care and observation for motorcyclists.
      * (d) may not always see you tailing a truck or bus.
        (e) will expect you to appear suddenly from behind a large vehicle.

Q.
AM0163

Select 3 answers. Which of the following should a motorcyclist allow for as regards awareness by other drivers. Other drivers .....

Ans.   * (a) may not be aware of your presence.
        (b) will be aware of the skills of riding a motorcycle.
        (c) will avoid obstructing your line of sight.
      * (d) may not allow that you have a two wheel machine and may have to take evasive action which they need not take.
      * (e) may not expect you to appear suddenly from behind a large vehicle.

INCREASING AWARENESS OF YOUR PRESENCE

Q.
AM0164

Select 3 answers. Which of the following should you do to increase awareness of your presence?

Ans.   * (a) Follow a straight line as much as possible.
      * (b) Avoid a driver's blind spots.
        (c) Share a road lane and ride parallel to other traffic.
        (d) Stay behind large vehicles fitted with wide angle mirrors.
      * (e) Follow a predictable riding style.

Q.

AM0165

Select 3 answers. Which of the following should you do to increase awareness of your presence .....

Ans.
    (a) rev the engine to indicate your intention to overtake.
    (b) rev the engine when weaving between traffic.
* (c) ride where you can be seen and leave good distance behind the preceeding vehicle.
* (d) ride the machine in a continuous easy manner without harsh acceleration.
* (e) clearly signal your intentions in good time.

OBSERVATION/FIELD OF VIEW

Q.

AM0166

You are riding a motorcycle in heavy rain. What should you do to improve visibility?

Ans.
    (a) Increase speed.
* (b) Reduce speed.
    (c) Lift up the visor on your helmet.
    (d) Wear eye protection in addition to your helmet.

Q.

AM0167

While riding a motorcycle, you could ensure better visibility to other drivers by .....

Ans.
    (a) sitting up straight in the saddle.
    (b) occasionally weaving slightly from side to side.
* (c) wearing reflective or fluorescent material or a "Sam Browne" belt.
    (d) staying in the centre of your lane.

Q.
AM0168

While riding a motorcycle, you could ensure better visibility to other road users by .....

Ans. * (a) driving with dipped headlights on.
     (b) wearing dark-coloured clothing.
     (c) driving crouched over the steering.
     (d) driving without lights in day time.

Q.
AM0169

On average, you should take observations in your mirrors .....

Ans.   (a) every 2 minutes.
     (b) every minute.
     (c) every 90 seconds.
  * (d) every 10 seconds.
     (e) every 30 seconds.

Q.
AM0170

Select 4 answers. You should use your mirrors when .....

Ans. * (a) turning.
  * (b) before making a 'U'-turn.
  * (c) moving off.
     (d) changing gears.
  * (e) overtaking.

Q.
AM0171

Select 4 answers. Before making a 'U'-turn, you should .....

Ans. * (a) use your mirrors.
     (b) only give hand signals.
  * (c) ensure the road is clear in both directions.
  * (d) be sure the road is wide enough to complete this safely.
  * (e) look over your shoulder.

Q.
AM0172

Select 3 occasions on which you should check your blind spot for traffic.

Ans. * (a) Moving off.
* (b) Changing lane in town traffic.
* (c) Changing direction.
(d) Before using the brakes.
(e) Stopping.

Q.
AM0173

Select 3 answers. Observation of which of the following give you an indication that precautions might be taken .....

Ans. * (a) movement in reflections in shop windows.
(b) an alarm sounding in a parked car.
* (c) movement in shadows.
(d) the sound of music from a parked vehicle.
* (e) exhaust smoke coming from stationary vehicles.

Q.
AM0174

You are going around a bend on an unlit road at night with no apparent oncoming traffic. Which lights should you use?

Ans. (a) Position lamp.
(b) Dipped headlights.
* (c) Full beam headlights.

Q.
AM0175

You should use the full high beam headlights .....

Ans. (a) in fog.
(b) when there is good street lighting.
(c) when meeting oncoming traffic.
(d) if dazzled by oncoming traffic.
(e) when meeting another vehicle.
* (f) when driving on unlit roads, at night.

Q.
AM0176

While driving along a main road with many side roads, drivers emerging from side roads may not see you. Select 2 answers for what you should do.

Ans.
    (a) Rev your engine.
    (b) Increase your speed for overtaking.
    (c) Ride near the middle of the road.
* (d) Ride at a slow speed so as to be able to slow down/stop.
* (e) Look well ahead and anticipate.

Q.
AM0177

While you are riding along a driver has begun to emerge into your path from a side road. You should .....

Ans.
    (a) continue as normal.
* (b) be ready to slow down and stop.
    (c) sound the horn while continuing as normal.
    (d) beckon the driver on.
    (e) beckon the driver to stop.

GOOD JUDGEMENT AND PERCEPTION

AWARENESS

Q.
AM0178

How can a more powerful c.c. motorbike affect your sense of perception? It can induce you to .....

Ans.
    (a) drive slower than you realise.
* (b) drive faster than you realise.
    (c) think that you would be less likely to be affected by crosswinds.
    (d) think that you can overtake more often than you should.

Q.
AM0179

You are riding a motorcycle and you wish to change lanes. What should you do first?

Ans. * (a) Use your mirrors and look around where necessary before indicating and moving over.
(b) Use your indicators and move over.
(c) Use your indicators and give a hand signal where necessary before moving over.
(d) First accelerate then use your indicators and move over.

DRIVING RISK FACTORS RELATED TO VARIOUS ROAD CONDITIONS, IN PARTICULAR AS THEY CHANGE WITH THE WEATHER AND THE TIME OF DAY OR NIGHT

Q.
AM0180

What are the lighting requirements for a motor-cycle at night?

Ans. * (a) Headlight, red rear light, a number plate light and a red rear reflector.
(b) Brake-light and a headlight.
(c) Indicators, a brake-light and a headlight.
(d) Headlight, red rear light, and indicators.

Q.
AM0181

What lights must your motorcycle show when parked at night on an unlit road?

Ans. * (a) A white light to the front and red light to the rear.
(b) No lights are required.
(c) Dipped headlight and a red parking light to the rear.
(d) Only sidelights.

Q. How can strong winds affect a motorcyclist?

AM0182

Ans. (a) They have no effect provided the bike is driven slowly.
   (b) They have no effect provided the bike is driven in a high gear.
   (c) They can help the motorcyclist manoeuvre more easily.
 * (d) They can blow the motorcyclist off course.

Q. In fog, you should reduce speed and .....

AM0183

Ans. (a) use dipped headlights and follow the off side position.
   (b) use full headlights and follow the off side position.
 * (c) use dipped headlights and follow the central position.
   (d) use full headlights and follow the near side kerb.

Q. Select 2 answers. In hot weather if the tar surface is melting and soft .....

AM0184

Ans. (a) tyre grip is improved as more of the tyre is on the road.
   (b) stopping distances are unaffected.
 * (c) stopping distances are increased.
 * (d) the road may be slippery.

Q. Select 2 answers. In bright sunlight, visibility of which of the following might be impaired .....

AM0185

Ans. (a) full beam headlight.
   (b) dipped headlights.
 * (c) brake-light.
 * (d) indicators.
   (e) reflectors.

NECESSARY DOCUMENTS

DRIVING LICENCE AND LEARNER PERMIT MATTERS

Q.
AM0186
When may a Learner Permit motorcyclist carry a pillion passenger?

Ans.   (a) When the passenger holds a full motorcycle licence.
* (b) Never.
    (c) When the driver is over 25 years of age.
    (d) During daylight hours only.

Q.
AM0187
What is the maximum engine capacity that the holder of a category A1 licence may drive?

Ans.   (a) 150 c.c.
    (b) 100 c.c.
* (c) 125 c.c.
    (d) 175 c.c.

Q.
AM0188
What is the maximum engine capacity that the holder of a category M licence may drive?

Ans. * (a) 50 c.c.
    (b) 55 c.c.
    (c) 65 c.c.
    (d) 75 c.c.

Q.
AM0189

What is the maximum kilometre speed per hour motorcycle which a category M licence holder may drive?

Ans.
    (a) 65 km/h.
    (b) 55 km/h.
* (c) 45 km/h.
    (d) 35 km/h.

Q.
AM0190

May the holder of a category A, A1 or M Learner Permit or driving licence drive a tricycle or quadricycle?

Ans.
    (a) Yes.
* (b) No.
    (c) Yes, with a driving licence only.

Q.
AM0191

What is the maximum engine power that a motorcyclist with a category A licence for less than 2 years may drive?

Ans.
    (a) 11 kilowatts.
* (b) 25 kilowatts.
    (c) 35 kilowatts.
    (d) 40 kilowatts.

Q.
AM0192

For how many years is a category A licence holder restricted to driving motorcycles with a maximum engine power of 25 kilowatts?

Ans.
    (a) 1.
* (b) 2.
    (c) 4.
    (d) 3.

Q. A motorcyclist who wishes to drive a motorcycle with a power output greater than 11 kilowatts must hold which category licence?

AM0193

Ans.   (a) M.
      (b) A1.
  * (c) A.
      (d) W.

Q. What is the maximum engine power which a motorcyclist with a category A1 licence may drive?

AM0194

Ans. * (a) 11 kilowatts.
      (b) 15 kilowatts.
      (c) 25 kilowatts.
      (d) 35 kilowatts.

SAFETY FACTORS RELATING TO VEHICLE AND PERSONS CARRIED

CHILDREN DRIVING

Q. When should children be allowed to drive a motorcycle?

AM0195

Ans. * (a) Never.
      (b) When it is off the public road.
      (c) When it is being driven at very slow speeds.
      (d) When it is a motorcycle designed for a child.

CARRYING A PASSENGER ON A MOTORCYCLE

Q.

AM0196

How would you maintain your balance on a motorcycle while carrying a passenger?

Ans. * (a) Instruct the passenger to sit astride the machine and to lean over on bends in the same direction as yourself.
(b) Negotiate bends at a higher speed than normal.
(c) Lean forward more than normal.
(d) Lean backwards more than normal to improve your grip.

Q.

AM0197

You should maintain balance on the motorcycle when carrying a passenger by .....

Ans. (a) instructing the passenger to lean in the opposite direction to you on bends.
(b) ensuring that the passengers body weight is centred as much as possible over the rear wheel.
* (c) ensuring that the passenger sits astride the machine and leans in the same direction as you on bends.
(d) ensuring that the passenger maintains an upright position.

Q.

AM0198

When carrying a passenger on a motorcycle, you should ensure that the passenger wears .....

Ans. * (a) securely fastened helmet and appropriate personal protective equipment.
(b) leather boots.
(c) rain protection clothing.
(d) eye protection.

Q.
AM0199

When is it permissible for a passenger to sit sideways on a motorcycle?

Ans. * (a) Never.
(b) When the roads are wet.
(c) When strong side winds are blowing.
(d) When the passenger is elderly.

ENVIRONMENTAL MATTERS

SMOKE

Q.
AM0200

If you take the exhaust off your motorcycle, your engine .....

Ans.   (a) will overheat.
(b) oil will be contaminated.
* (c) noise and smoke pollution will increase.
(d) will perform at optimum levels.

GETTING OFF THE MOTORCYCLE

Q.
AM0201

What precautions should you take before getting off a motorcycle?

Ans.
    (a) Park the machine on its stand.
    (b) Lean the machine against a kerb.
* (c) Switch off the ignition.
    (d) Engage first gear.

Q.
AM0203

When a passenger is getting off your motorcycle, you should ensure that the .....

Ans.
    (a) motorcycle is always resting on its stand.
* (b) motorcycle is always stopped in a safe place.
    (c) passenger gets off from the right-hand side of the motorcycle.
    (d) passenger gets off from the left-hand side of the motorcycle.

OTHER

Q.

AM0204

Motorcycles on a motorway must .....

Ans.
   (a) only use left-hand lane.

   (b) display dipped headlights at all times.

   (c) not carry a pillion passenger aged less than 13 years of age.

* (d) have an engine capacity of 50 c.c. or more.

Q.

AM0205

You have just overtaken a large vehicle and you wish to move back to the left-hand lane. You should .....

Ans. * (a) check the left-hand mirror, signal and move back when it is safe to do so.

   (b) wait until the driver of the large vehicle signals to you to move back into the left-hand lane.

   (c) accelerate, signal and move back quickly.

   (d) signal left, and gradually move back.

CHAPTER 2

PART I

CATEGORY C and D

NECESSARY DOCUMENTS

Q.
CD0002

How frequently must your vehicle be submitted for a **Certificate of Roadworthiness test?**

Ans. * (a) Annually.
(b) Every 2 years.
(c) Every 3 years.
(d) Annually, if the vehicle is three years or older.

Q.
CD0003

What Learner Permit drivers in Categories C, C1, D and D1 are not required to be accompanied by the holder of a full licence?

Ans. * (a) None.
(b) Drivers aged 21 years or older.
(c) Holders of 2nd Learner Permit only.
(d) Drivers in C1 and D1.

Q.
CD0004

What is the maximum trailer weight which may be towed without holding an E licence category?

Ans. (a) 650 kg.
* (b) 750 kg.
(c) 550 kg.
(d) 450 kg.
(e) 1,250 kg.

DRIVING HOURS AND REST PERIODS

Q.
CD0006

What is the maximum permitted number of driving hours you may drive without taking a break?

Ans.
    (a) 3 hours.
    (b) 4 hours.
* (c) 4.5 hours.
    (d) 3.5 hours.

Q.
CD0007

What is the maximum number of hours you may drive in a given week?

Ans. * (a) 56 hours.
    (b) 46 hours.
    (c) 50 hours.
    (d) 40 hours.

Q.
CD0008

What is the maximum permitted number of driving hours in a fortnight?

Ans.
    (a) 70 hours.
    (b) 80 hours.
* (c) 90 hours.
    (d) 100 hours.

Q.
CD0009

The minimum break time that should be taken for each break during or following a driving period is .....

Ans. * (a) 15 minutes.
    (b) 30 minutes.
    (c) 45 minutes.
    (d) 20 minutes.

Q.
CD0010

What is the minimum break time, which must be taken following a 4.5 hour driving period?

Ans.
    (a) 30 mins.
* (b) 45 mins.
    (c) I hour.
    (d) 25 minutes.

Q.
CD0011

You have driven for 56 hours in the first week of a two-week period. What is the maximum number of hours you may drive in the second week?

Ans.
    (a) 44 hours.
* (b) 34 hours.
    (c) 54 hours.
    (d) 24 hours.

Q.
CD0012

On how many days of the working week may a driver drive for up to 10 hours?

Ans.
    (a) 3.
    (b) I.
* (c) 2.
    (d) 5.
    (e) 4.

Q.
CD0013

On how many days of the working week may you drive?

Ans.
    (a) 7.
* (b) 6.
    (c) 5.
    (d) 4.
    (e) As many as you like.

Q. On three days of the week, the minimum daily rest
CD0014 period may be reduced to .....

Ans. (a) 7 hours.
　　(b) 0 hours.
　　(c) 6 hours.
　　(d) 8 hours.
　* (e) 9 hours.

Q. The normal minimum weekly rest period is .....
CD0015

Ans. (a) 55 consecutive hours.
　* (b) 45 consecutive hours.
　　(c) 35 consecutive hours.
　　(d) 60 consecutive hours.
　　(e) 25 consecutive hours.

Q. When may you carry out other duties other than
CD0016 driving on your rest day?

Ans. (a) Only when vehicle is parked at the depot.
　　(b) Only when parked at a public bus park.
　　(c) On a category D1 vehicle only.
　* (d) Never.

Q. This tachograph symbol means .....
CD0017

Ans. (a) rest period.
　　(b) break period.
　* (c) driving period.
　　(d) stationary period for loading.

Q. This tachograph symbol means .....

CD0018

Ans. (a) rest period.
(b) break period.
(c) driving period.
* (d) periods when the driver is available to work.

Q. This tachograph symbol means .....

CD0019

Ans. (a) rest period.
* (b) other work i.e. work other than actual driving.
(c) driving period.
(d) stationary period for loading.

Q. This tachograph symbol means .....

CD0020

Ans. * (a) rest period.
(b) break period.
(c) driving period.
(d) stationary period for loading.

Q. When driving on a cross-border or international journey, the tachograph rules .....

CD0021

Ans. (a) vary between EU Member States.
(b) begin only when driving in the EU from the beginning of the week.
* (c) continue to apply.
(d) begin afresh at each border crossing.
(e) begin only on the first complete day spent in another EU Member State.

Q. CD0022 **Who is responsible for ensuring that a tachograph sheet is properly completed and inserted into the tachograph?**

Ans.
    (a) The owner of the vehicle.
    (b) The hire company.
* (c) The driver.
    (d) The transport manager.

Q. CD0023 **Which of the following information is recorded on a tachograph sheet?**

Ans.
    (a) Distance covered and average fuel consumption.
    (b) Fuel consumption and vehicle speed.
* (c) Driving time, vehicle speed and distance covered.
    (d) Journey destinations and vehicle speed.

Q. CD0024 **Which of the following information is recorded on a tachograph sheet?**

Ans.
    (a) Distance covered and average fuel consumption.
    (b) Fuel consumption and vehicle speed.
* (c) Rest periods.
    (d) Journey destinations and vehicle speed.

Q. CD0025 **Which used tachograph sheets must be retained by the driver?**

Ans.
    (a) The last 7 days on which you drove.
    (b) The last 14 days on which you drove.
* (c) The current day and those used by the driver for the 28 calendar days immediately preceding that day.
    (d) The last month on which you drove.

Q. CD0026 **When must a new tachograph sheet be placed in a tachograph?**

Ans. * (a) At the start of each working day.
    (b) At the start of each week.
    (c) Every 12 hours of each working day.
    (d) At the end of each working day.
    (e) Every 9 days.

Q. CD0027 **What time and day denote the beginning of a week for tachograph purposes?**

Ans.   (a) 0600 hours on Monday.
    (b) 0800 hours on Monday.
* (c) 00.00 hours on Monday.
    (d) 0700 hours on Monday.

Q. CD0028 **You drive two or more vehicles as part of your working day. What are the tachograph requirements?**

Ans.   (a) Use a different tachograph sheet only if the number of driving hours in the day exceeds 10.
* (b) Use the same tachograph sheet in each vehicle.
    (c) Use the same tachograph sheet only if the vehicles are of similar dimensions.
    (d) Use a different tachograph sheet for each vehicle.

Q. Another driver will use your vehicle during the day
CD0029 after you have first driven it. You should .....

Ans. (a) leave your tachograph sheet in place only if you will again
be driving that day.
(b) use a fresh tachograph sheet only for a period when the
vehicle is being driven outside the country.
(c) leave one tachograph sheet inserted in the tachograph
for use per day.
(d) remove your tachograph sheet and use a fresh sheet
when you resume driving later that day.
* (e) remove your tachograph sheet for the period of your
absence and insert it again only when you are driving the
vehicle.

Q. What is the danger in not complying with break
CD0030 period requirements?

Ans. * (a) The driver could become tired while driving.
(b) The driver could become distracted.
(c) The driver could become too comfortable.
(d) The driver could become dehydrated.

Q. A driver's rest period may be taken in a parked
CD0031 vehicle if .....

Ans. (a) the vehicle is parked in a designated rest area.
(b) there are no passengers on board.
(c) the windows of the vehicle are left open.
* (d) it is fitted with a bunk.

Q.

CD0032

What can a bus or truck driver do to stay alert on a long journey?

Ans.

    (a) Listen attentively to the radio.

    (b) Turn up the temperature in the driver compartment.

    (c) Take a stimulant.

* (d) Wind down the window and reduce the temperature in the driver compartment.

Q.

CD0033

As a professional driver working long journeys, you should be aware that .....

Ans.

    (a) your driving experience will compensate for fatigue.

    (b) tiredness will not affect you if you have taken caffeine drinks.

    (c) you should only drink hot refreshments in order to counter fatigue.

* (d) fatigue may affect your alertness and ability to react.

Q.

CD0180

Another driver will use your vehicle fitted with digital tachograph during the day after you have driven it. You should .....

Ans.

    (a) leave your driver's card in slot one of the digital tachograph unit.

* (b) remove your driver's card from the digital tachograph unit and insert it again only when you are driving another vehicle.

    (c) remove your driver card and hand it to the new driver.

Q. Who is responsible that a driver card is properly
CD0181 inserted into the digital tachograph unit?

Ans.   (a) The owner of the vehicle.
      (b) The Transport Manager.
* (c) The driver of the vehicle.

Q. Which of the following information is recorded on a
CD0182 driver's card?

Ans.   (a) Average fuel consumption.
* (b) Driving time, vehicle speed and distance covered.
      (c) Destinations and speed.
      (d) Days of the week and distance covered.

Q. When must you use your driver's card?
CD0183

Ans.   (a) At the beginning of the week.
* (b) At the beginning of each working day.
      (c) At the end of each working day.
      (d) At the beginning of each daily or weekly rest period.

Q. Select 2 answers. Which of the following driver
CD0184 records must be produced by a driver to an
enforcement officer at a roadside inspection?

Ans.   (a) Company digital cards.
      (b) Digital Tachograph workshop card.
* (c) Any manual record and printout made during that day.
* (d) Any manual record used by the driver for the 28
          calendar days immediately preceding that day.
      (e) Any manual record used by any driver in the vehicle for
          the 28 days immediately preceding that day.

Q.
CD0185

Select 2 answers. Which of the following driver records must be produced by a driver to an enforcement officer at a roadside inspection?

Ans. * (a) The driver's driver card.
     (b) Digital workshop cards.
     (c) Any analogue charts used by any driver in the vehicle for the 28 days immediately preceding that day.
   * (d) Any analogue charts for days which the driver drove a vehicle fitted with an analogue recording equipment in the preceding 28 calendar days.

Q.
CD0186

You drive two or more vehicles fitted with digital tachograph as part of your working day, one of these vehicles covers a period which is exempt and "out of scope" from drivers' hours and tachograph requirements. You should .....

Ans. (a) remove the driver card from the vehicle unit when undertaking out of scope activities.
   * (b) use the mode switch to "other work" activities.
     (c) remove the card from slot one and insert the card into slot two.
     (d) do nothing.

Q.
CD0187

Which one of the following is true?

Ans. (a) A driver's driver card may be used by another person.
   * (b) A driver card is personal to the driver issued with the card and is not transferable.
     (c) A driver card is the same as a driving licence.
     (d) A driver card may only be used on a vehicle listed on the driver card.

Q.
CD0188

Identify the pictogram below which shows the driving mode.

Ans. * (a)

      (b)

      (c)

      (d)

Q.
CD0189

When working away from a vehicle and the card is not inserted in the tachograph, you should .....

Ans. * (a) manually enter times and activities in the tachograph.
      (b) do nothing.
      (c) advise your employer orally of your activities.

JOURNEY PLANNING

Q.
CD0034

Select 4 answers. When estimating your journey times, you should allow extra time for .....

Ans. * (a) driving during the 'rush-hour' traffic.
     * (b) stoppage due to road works.
     * (c) driving in the vicinity of major sports events.
       (d) delay due to overheated exhausts.
     * (e) driving during adverse weather conditions.

Q.
CD0035

Select 4 answers. When estimating your journey times, you should allow extra time for .....

Ans. * (a) delays due to traffic accidents.
* (b) road works taking place.
* (c) mandatory rest breaks.
* (d) minor repairs to the vehicle.
(e) the clock on your dashboard may show the incorrect time.

Q.
CD0036

Select 3 answers. Which of these should influence the route which you plan to take?

Ans. * (a) The length of the vehicle.
* (b) The weight restriction of the vehicle.
(c) The number of gears on the vehicle.
* (d) The height of the vehicle.
(e) The number of axles on the vehicle.

Q.
CD0037

Select 3 answers. Which of these should influence the route you plan to take?

Ans. * (a) Humpback bridge.
* (b) The vehicle's ground clearance.
(c) The vehicle's air suspension.
* (d) Any road ramps.

Q.
CD0038

You come to a bridge, which has a weight limit, which is lower than that of your vehicle. You should .....

Ans. * (a) turn around and find an alternative route.
(b) switch off the engine and coast across to avoid vibrating the bridge.
(c) drive over it at low speed.
(d) drive over it at high speed.

VEHICLE WEIGHTS AND DIMENSIONS

Q.   **The maximum permitted weight of the vehicle .....**
CD0039

Ans.   (a)   refers to the unladen weight of the vehicle.

     *   (b)   refers to the weight of the vehicle plus the weight of the load which may be carried.

       (c)   refers to the unladen weight of the vehicle plus the weight of the fuel.

       (d)   refers to the weight of the load which may be carried.

Q.   **What does design gross vehicle weight mean?**
CD0040

Ans.   *   (a)   Vehicle weight plus maximum load weight which it is designed to carry.

       (b)   The maximum load weight less the vehicle weight.

       (c)   The maximum weight for the licence category.

       (d)   Unladen weight of the vehicle.

Q.   **Details of the unladen weight of a vehicle .....**
CD0041

Ans.   (a)   are only required to be shown on the motor tax disk.

       (b)   are only required to be displayed on vehicles over 10,000 kg g.v.w.

       (c)   are only required to be displayed on vehicles when unladen.

       (d)   are only required to be displayed on vehicles when laden.

     *   (e)   should be displayed on the left side rear of the vehicle.

Q.   **What is the maximum permitted rear-load overhang**
CD0042   **that does not require a red flag or marker?**

Ans.   (a)   0.5 metre.
    *   (b)   1 metre.
       (c)   1.5 metres.
       (d)   2.5 metres

Q.   **What is the maximum permitted rear-load**
CD0043   **overhang with a red flag?**

Ans.   (a)   1 metre.
       (b)   1.5 metres.
       (c)   2.5 metres.
    *   (d)   3 metres.

Q.   **A rear load overhang in excess of which length is**
CD0044   **required to have a red flag or marker?**

Ans. *   (a)   1 metre.
       (b)   1.5 metres.
       (c)   2 metres.
       (d)   3 metres.

Q.   **When is a red flag a sufficient marker for a rear-load**
CD0045   **overhang that exceeds one metre?**

Ans.   (a)   At all times.
    *   (b)   Only during the day.
       (c)   When glass or fragile material is overhanging.
       (d)   Only at night.

Q.

CD0046

What is the maximum permitted side-load overhang in millimetres?

Ans. * (a) 300.
(b) 400.
(c) 600.
(d) 700.

Q.

CD0047

The maximum permitted length of an articulated vehicle is .....

Ans. (a) 15.5 metres.
* (b) 16.5 metres.
(c) 17.5 metres.
(d) 19.5 metres.
(e) 20.5 metres.

BRAKING SYSTEMS

Q.

CD0058

What does a speed limiter do?

Ans. (a) Maintains the vehicle at a constant speed.
(b) Prevents the engine from over-revving.
* (c) Prevents the vehicle from exceeding a pre-set speed.
(d) Indicates when vehicle is exceeding maximum permitted speed.

Q.

CD0059

What does an engine governor do?

Ans. (a) Maintains the vehicle at a constant speed.
* (b) Prevents the engine from over-revving.
(c) Prevents the vehicle from exceeding a pre-set speed.
(d) Indicates when vehicle is exceeding maximum permitted speed.

Q.
CD0060

Select 2 answers. Speed can be reduced without using the footbrake by .....

Ans.

(a) applying the diff-lock.

* (b) engaging the retarder, if fitted.

(c) pressing the clutch pedal.

(d) shifting gears upwards.

* (e) lifting your foot off the accelerator.

Q.
CD0061

Given similar road conditions and vehicle speeds, what braking distances will a truck or bus/minibus need compared to a car?

Ans. * (a) Longer distances.

(b) Shorter distances.

(c) The same.

Q.
CD0062

In an air-brake system, what would be the first indication of low air pressure .....

Ans. * (a) a warning light coming on or a buzzer sounding in the cab.

(b) the footbrake pedal being hard.

(c) the vehicle will not move until the air tanks have been drained.

(d) a loud rumbling noise from the compressor.

Q.
CD0063

After moderate use of the brakes, you notice that the air-gauges are not returning to normal. You should .....

Ans.

(a) lubricate the air-brake compressor.

(b) drain the air tanks.

(c) check the tyre pressures.

(d) check that the exhaust brake is disengaged.

* (e) proceed with caution and stop if the buzzer sounds.

Q. If the air-brake gauges are reading low, this indicates
CD0064 that .....

Ans. * (a) there is an air leak in the braking system.
　　　 (b) brake-pads are worn down and need replacing.
　　　 (c) the anti-lock braking system is worn and needs replacing.
　　　 (d) there is an air leak in the exhaust brake system.

TECHNICAL MATTERS, WITH A BEARING ON ROAD SAFETY

Q. If you notice that a wheel nut is missing, you should
CD0069 balance the wheel by .....

Ans. (a) reducing the torque on the
　　　 remaining nuts.
　　　 (b) increasing the torque on the
　　　 remaining nuts.
　　　 (c) reducing the torque on the
　　　 two adjacent nuts.
　　* (d) having the nut replaced before
　　　 driving.

Q. What does this symbol mean?
CD0070

Ans. (a) Accelerator pedal jammed.
　　　 (b) Faulty footbrake.
　　　 (c) Trailer not properly connected.
　　* (d) Electrical cut-off switch.

Q.
CD0071

What does a load-sensing valve do?

Ans.
    (a) Warns the driver when a gearshift is required.
    (b) Warns the driver when the vehicle is overloaded.
* (c) Adjusts the brake pressure which is applied at the wheels.
    (d) Warns the driver of an uneven load distribution.

Q.
CD0072

'Road-friendly' suspension .....

Ans. * (a) reduces the impact of a vehicle's weight on the road.
    (b) increases the impact of a vehicle's weight on the road.
    (c) allows vehicles to exceed the weight restrictions on bridges.
    (d) allow the vehicles to carry a longer load than normal.

Q.
CD0073

An indication of a defect in the power assisted steering system is that it would .....

Ans.
    (a) cause the front tyres to lose pressure.
    (b) cause the steering to lock up.
    (c) make the steering seem light and easy to turn
* (d) make the steering seem heavy and stiff to turn.

Q.
CD0075

What would indicate that you have a problem with the power steering?

Ans. * (a) Inability to easily turn the steering wheel.
    (b) Steering loose.
    (c) Low air-pressure gauge.
    (d) Noisy transmission system.

Q. CD0076   **Which of the following need <u>not</u> be inspected daily for a truck or bus, which is in constant use?**

Ans.
     (a) Mirror condition and setting.
     (b) Lights/lenses front and rear.
     (c) Tyre condition.
     (d) Windscreen wipers.
 * (e) Brake-lining.
     (f) Oil and water levels.

Q. CD0077   **A truck or bus, which is in constant use, should be completely visually inspected .....**

Ans.
     (a) weekly.
     (b) after every 5,000 kilometres.
     (c) monthly.
 * (d) daily.
     (e) twice yearly.

Q. CD0078   **Why is it dangerous to drive with the vehicle not in gear?**

Ans.
     (a) It affects the steering.
 * (b) It reduces the brake assistance available.
     (c) It causes an over supply of air available for use by the brakes.
     (d) It places a minimal amount of drag on the brakes.

Q. CD0079   **What is the purpose of a diff-lock?**

Ans.
     (a) It improves the security of the vehicle by ensuring that the wheels cannot be stolen.
     (b) It holds the selected gear to improve traction on steep slopes.
 * (c) It locks up the differential on soft ground.
     (d) It slows the engine speed without applying the brakes.

Q. You should use a diff-lock on your truck .....

CD0080

Ans. * (a) when driving onto soft ground.
     (b) when block changing the gears.
     (c) when driving on a steep gradient.
     (d) when the vehicle load exceeds 10,000 kg.
     (e) to secure the cab when parking.

Q. You should use a diff-lock on your truck .....

CD0081

Ans. * (a) when driving on snow or ice.
     (b) when block changing the gears.
     (c) when driving on a steep gradient.
     (d) when the vehicle load exceeds 10,000 kg.
     (e) to secure the cab when parking.

Q. Having used the diff-lock to move off on a slippery surface, you should disengage when .....

CD0082

Ans. * (a) the truck is underway.
     (b) the engine has reached normal operating temperature.
     (c) the vehicle is unloaded only.
     (d) the drive axle has warmed.

Q. What effect can wet weather have on your vehicle's exterior mirrors?

CD0083

Ans. (a) It can keep them clean.
     (b) It has no effect.
     (c) It can cause a short circuit in electrically heated mirrors.
  * (d) It can distort your rear vision.

Q. Your driving mirror(s) should reflect .....

CD0085

Ans. * (a) as much as possible of the road that is not in your line of vision.
    (b) the passenger area of the vehicle.
    (c) the area behind the vehicle.
    (d) the area to each side of the vehicle.

Q. Spray suppression equipment should be fitted to your vehicle to .....

CD0086

Ans. * (a) reduce the amount of water which is sprayed up by the speed of the wheels.
    (b) improve tyre traction in the wet.
    (c) reduce the build up of mud on the undercarriage of the vehicle.
    (d) reduce spray levels from the windscreen washer.

Q. The function of the transmission system in a truck or bus is to .....

CD0088

Ans. (a) send and receive radio messages.
    * (b) transmit power from engine to the wheels.
    (c) match speed of engine to speed on the road.
    (d) disengage the drive to the wheels.

AIR TURBULENCE

Q.
CD0093

Select 4 answers. Air turbulence caused by the fast speed of high-sided vehicles would have most effect on .....

Ans. * (a) pedestrians walking at the side of the road.
   (b) minibuses.
   * (c) motorcyclists.
   (d) trailers in tow.
   * (e) cyclists.
   * (f) cars towing a caravan.

Q.
CD0094

What negative effect can your vehicle's slipstream have when overtaking a motorcyclist?

Ans. * (a) The motorcyclist can be blown off course.
   (b) The motorcyclist can drive at a faster speed.
   (c) The motorcyclist can be deafened by the wind noise.
   (d) The motorcyclist could be drawn to your vehicle.

Q.
CD0095

What negative effect could your vehicle's slipstream have on a cyclist?

Ans. * (a) It can affect the cyclist's stability.
   (b) It has no effect provided you keep within the speed limit.
   (c) It can draw the cyclist towards your vehicle.
   (d) It can push the cyclist toward oncoming traffic.

Q.
CD0096

Dust or debris displaced from the road by your vehicle could .....

Ans.   (a) block the exhaust.
     (b) cause the brake's air-lines to collapse.
   * (c) discomfort pedestrians or cyclists and affect their visibility.
     (d) cause the brake's air-lines to expand.

Q.
CD0097

What should you be aware of when driving past pedestrians at speed?

Ans. * (a) They can be affected by your vehicle's slipstream.
     (b) They will hear the noise of your vehicle and keep in.
     (c) The wing mirrors on your vehicle are always high enough to avoid hitting them.
     (d) You should pass pedestrians as quickly as possible to minimise the time they are exposed to the slipstream.

WEATHER RELATED MATTERS

Q.
CD0099

Select 2 answers. What should you do when you intend to start out on a long journey in bad weather conditions?

Ans. * (a) Enquire as to the weather and road conditions at your destination.
   * (b) Check the weather forecast for information about road and weather conditions relating to your journey.
     (c) Reduce tyre pressures to ensure better grip on the roads.
     (d) Increase tyre pressure to ensure better grip on the road.

Q.
CD0100

Select 2 answers. What should you do when you intend to start out on a long journey in bad weather conditions?

Ans. * (a) Check the weather forecast for information about road and weather conditions relating to your journey.
(b) Reduce tyre pressures to ensure better grip on the roads.
(c) Increase tyre pressure to ensure better grip on the road.
* (d) Top up the windscreen washer.

Q.
CD0101

When driving a diesel engine vehicle in cold weather, you should ensure that .....

Ans. * (a) winter grade fuel is being used.
(b) the fuel filter is drained.
(c) the fuel level in the tank does not drop below quarter full.
(d) engine is started a minimum of 10 minutes prior to driving.

Q.
CD0102

Select 2 answers. When driving in heavy rain, you should .....

Ans. (a) engage the diff-lock mechanism.
(b) switch your windscreen wipers onto high and drive at normal speed.
* (c) drive at a lower speed to allow for reduced visibility and increased braking distance.
(d) turn off the diff-lock mechanism.
* (e) use your windscreen wipers.

Q. How should a descent be negotiated in snow or
CD0103 frosty weather?

Ans. (a) Engage a higher gear than normal in order to avoid
wheel-spin.
(b) Always keep close to the left and use short sharp brake
applications to keep the speed down.
* (c) Engage a lower gear, and use gentle braking applications
to keep the speed down.
(d) Keep the clutch depressed and use gentle braking.

Q. What precautions would you take to avoid mud or
CD0104 spray from other vehicles when overtaking?

Ans. (a) Increase speed in order to reduce the time spent in
danger area.
(b) Drive close to the other vehicle in order to make use of
its slipstream.
* (c) Use your vehicle's wipers and windscreen washer
system.

Q. Select 2 answers. What should you do when
CD0105 overtaking a large vehicle that is throwing up spray?

Ans. * (a) Turn your windscreen wipers on and use the windscreen washer system.
(b) Increase speed in order to reduce the time spent in the
danger area while using the windscreen wipers.
* (c) Move out earlier than normal and give extra clearance.
(d) Overtake in an exaggerated loop and use the windscreen
washer system.

DRIVING LARGE OR HIGH-SIDED VEHICLES

Q.
CD0106
What effect can strong winds have on a high-sided vehicle?

Ans. * (a) It can make it more liable to overturn.
      (b) It could improve stability.
      (c) It could affect the braking and suspension mechanisms.
      (d) The vehicle could jack-knife.

Q.
CD0107
What should you avoid when driving a high-sided vehicle in strong winds?

Ans.   (a) Road tunnels.
      (b) Steep hills.
  * (c) Suspension bridges.
      (d) Humpbacked bridges.

Q.
CD0108
Which is the most stable in windy conditions?

Ans.   (a) A high-sided vehicle without a load.
      (b) A high-sided vehicle with an uneven load.
  * (c) A fully loaded high-sided vehicle driving at a reduced speed.
      (d) A lightly laden high-sided vehicle driving at a reduced speed.

Q.
CD0109
A large vehicle can have an intimidating effect on other road users because of .....

Ans.   (a) the size of the large wiper blades.
      (b) the number of gears it possesses.
      (c) the number of lights it possesses.
  * (d) the size and sound of the vehicle.

Q. You are using a different vehicle, that you are not
CD0110 familiar with driving. You should .....

Ans. * (a) drive initially with extra care and at lower speed than normal.
  (b) drive at your normal speed and become accustomed to its features over time.
  (c) avoid any long journeys until you are more familiar with the vehicle.
  (d) drive faster than normal in order to assess its capability.

Q. You are driving a vehicle with unfamiliar features.
CD0112 You should be aware that .....

Ans. (a) there may be different requirements as regards driving hours and rest periods.
  (b) the height, weight, length and width of the vehicle has to be declared on the vehicle's insurance disc.
  (c) the height, weight, length and width of the vehicle has to be declared on the vehicle's motor tax disc.
  * (d) the height, weight, length and width or the controls layout may be different to those of the vehicle you are used to driving.

Q. What effect can strong winds have on a light
CD0113 high-sided vehicle? They can .....

Ans. * (a) lessen stability.
  (b) improve stability.
  (c) reduce loading capacity.
  (d) increase loading capacity.

Q. CD0114

Select 2 answers. You are driving a long vehicle and you wish to turn left into a narrow road. You should .....

Ans. * (a) drive partly past the entrance to the junction before commencing the turn.

(b) use your GPS route tracking system to guide you round the turn.

(c) keep close to the left as you approach the turn in order to give yourself more room on the right as you enter the narrow road.

* (d) be aware that cyclists may come on your inside if you move to the right to make room to turn left.

Q. CD0115

You are driving a long vehicle and you wish to turn left into a narrow road. You should .....

Ans. (a) ensure that only the rear left-hand wheels mount the kerb.

* (b) take sufficient space on the approach to allow the turn to be made without mounting the kerb.

(c) signal to any driver emerging from your left to reverse and give you space.

(d) signal to any driver emerging from your right to reverse and give you space.

Q. CD0116

Why do you sometimes move to the right before making a left-hand turn?

Ans. * (a) To ensure that the inside rear wheels clear the corner.

(b) To prevent following traffic from overtaking in a dangerous manner.

(c) To allow following drivers to see what you are doing.

(d) To prevent fuel rocking in the fuel tank on the turn.

Q.
CD0120

You are driving a large truck or bus on a road, which has overhanging trees on the left. You should .....

Ans. * (a) drive in the normal position, but avoid hitting low overhanging branches.
(b) drive on the centre of the road.
(c) ignore the branches as the force of your vehicle will brush them aside.
(d) drive close to the left.

Q.
CD0121

Select 3 answers. You drive a low loader type vehicle. Which of the following should you allow for?

Ans. * (a) Narrow bridge.
* (b) Humpback bridge.
(c) Underground cables.
(d) Steep gradients.
* (e) Overhead cables.

Q.
CD0122

You are driving a rigid type truck car transporter. When the vehicle turns .....

Ans. * (a) the front overhang follows a wider course than the cab.
(b) the front overhang follows the line of the cab.
(c) the front overhang follows a shorter course than the cab.
(d) the hydraulic lifting system will prevent the vehicle from overturning.

Q.
CD0123

When driving an articulated type car transporter, you should be aware when turning that the front overhang .....

Ans.
    (a) follows the line of the cab.
* (b) follows a wider line than that of the cab.
    (c) follows a shorter line than the cab when turning right only.
    (d) follows a shorter line than the cab.

Q.
CD0124

Select 3 answers. When driving a car transporter you should plan ahead for .....

Ans.
    (a) culverts.
* (b) low bridges.
* (c) overhanging trees.
    (d) wind effect.
* (e) overhead cables.

Q.
CD0126

What precaution should you take when driving around a roundabout to avoid roll-over?

Ans. * (a) Reduce speed.
    (b) Increase speed.
    (c) Brake sharply.
    (d) Stay to the centre.

Q.
CD0128

What should you be aware of when driving a vehicle with a low body over a steep humpback bridge?

Ans. * (a) Ground clearance.
    (b) Tyre pressures.
    (c) Tail-swing.
    (d) Crosswinds.

Q. When planning a route what aspects of your vehicle
CD0129 should influence the route you take?

Ans. * (a) The length, width, weight and height of the vehicle.
(b) The type of transmission on the vehicle.
(c) The maximum speed of vehicle.
(d) Whether the vehicle has cruise control.

Q. When entering a loading bay or refuelling depot
CD0130 you should be aware of the .....

Ans. (a) weight of the vehicle.
(b) average fuel consumption of the vehicle.
* (c) height, width and length of the vehicle.
(d) ground clearance.

Q. A driver of a vehicle with a high centre of gravity
CD0131 should be aware that .....

Ans. * (a) the vehicle is more likely to roll over on a bend.
(b) the vehicle is more stable than a similar vehicle with a low centre of gravity.
(c) fuel consumption is higher than a vehicle with a low centre of gravity.
(d) the vehicle moves slower than a similar vehicle with a lower centre of gravity.

Q. You are driving up a steep hill and there is a 'slow
CD0133 lane' on the left. You should .....

Ans. (a) straddle the lanes.
* (b) drive in the slow lane.
(c) drive in the outer lane if your vehicle is unladen.
(d) drive only in the slow lane when towing a trailer.

Q.
CD0134

You are going straight ahead at a 'mini-roundabout' up ahead where your vehicle will have restricted space for manoeuvre. You should .....

Ans.

(a) ensure that your wheels straddle the centre of the roundabout.

(b) ensure that your wheels do not straddle the centre of the roundabout.

* (c) treat it as a normal roundabout as best your vehicle enables you to do.

(d) disregard it, as your vehicle will always have space to clear the roundabout.

Q.
CD0135

Your large bus or truck is being overtaken by a motorcyclist in windy weather. You should be aware that on passing your vehicle .....

Ans.

(a) the wind turbulence will make the motorcycle more stable.

(b) the motorcycle may spray leaves from the ground into your field of view.

* (c) the wind turbulence will make the motorcycle less stable.

(d) the wind turbulence will not affect the stability of the motorcycle.

Q.
CD0136

Select 4 answers. You wish to overtake another large vehicle. You should consider .....

Ans. * (a) the speed of the vehicle being overtaken.

(b) the height of the vehicle being overtaken.

* (c) the width and length of your vehicle.

* (d) the width and length of the vehicle being overtaken.

* (e) the speed of oncoming traffic.

Q.
CD0137

Select 3 answers. You wish to overtake another large vehicle. You should consider .....

Ans. * (a) the speed of following traffic.
(b) the number of axles on your vehicle.
(c) the height of your vehicle.
* (d) the width and condition of the road.
* (e) the weight, load distribution and speed of your vehicle.

Q.
CD0138

You have just overtaken another large vehicle and you wish to move back to the left-hand lane. You should .....

Ans. * (a) check the left-hand mirror, signal and move back when it is safe to do so.
(b) wait until the driver of the large vehicle signals to you to move back into the left-hand lane.
(c) accelerate, signal and move back quickly.
(d) signal left, and gradually move back.

Q.
CD0139

When driving your truck or bus in a convoy, you should .....

Ans. (a) use the cruise control system, if available.
(b) drive closer than normal to the left-hand side of the road.
(c) drive closer than normal to the right-hand side, to see ahead.
* (d) allow space for the vehicle in front to stop suddenly and safely, and for cars to overtake your vehicle safely.

RESTRICTED VISION

Q. CD0140

What effect can sunlight have on grimy windows?

Ans.
    (a) It can enhance visibility.
* (b) It can create a mirror effect and reduce visibility.
    (c) It can eliminate a heavy build-up of condensation on the windows.
    (d) It can reduce glare on the windows.

Q. CD0141

When driving straight ahead you may ensure visibility to the side and rear of the vehicle by .....

Ans.
    (a) using your interior mirror and looking out the side window.
* (b) making full use of exterior mirrors.
    (c) putting your head out the driver's window and looking behind.
    (d) using your interior rear-view mirror.

Q. CD0143

How can a high mounted cab affect your ability to see other road users?

Ans.
    (a) It can make it easier to see pedestrians and cyclists to the side of your vehicle.
* (b) It can make it more difficult to see pedestrians and cyclists close up.
    (c) It can reduce long range visibility making it more difficult to drive in wet weather.
    (d) It can reduce long range visibility making it easier to see other road users.

Q.   **Your wing mirrors have been covered by a film of**
CD0144   **mud and dust. You should .....**

Ans.   (a) angle them towards the front for a distance in order to clean them.

      (b) drive on as normal, as driving in the slipstream of other traffic will clean them eventually.

*   (c) clean them before continuing.

SAFETY OF VEHICLE LOADING AND PERSONS CARRIED

Q.   **When delivering or collecting passengers or goods**
CD0145   **you should .....**

Ans.   (a) drive up on the footpath in order to minimise obstruction to other traffic.

      (b) park on a corner provided the hazard warning lights are switched on.

*   (c) avoid causing obstruction to other road users.

      (d) not stay parked for more than a few minutes.

Q.   **How can overloading affect your vehicle?**
CD0146

Ans.   (a) The accelerator can slip, rendering the vehicle immobile.

*   (b) Its stability could be affected.

      (c) The air filter can become clogged.

      (d) The load-sensing valve can become jammed.

GETTING OUT FROM THE VEHICLE

Q.
CD0149
What precautions should you take to secure the vehicle before getting out of it? Ensure that .....

Ans.   (a) there is an adequate supply of air in the air-tanks.
    (b) the turbo-charger has cooled down.
* (c) the handbrake is on and the ignition is switched off.
    (d) the exhaust brake is applied, that the ignition is switched off, and that a low gear is engaged.

Q.
CD0150
What precautions should you take before getting out of the vehicle?

Ans.   (a) Leave the engine running with the parking brake 'on'.
    (b) Switch off the engine and make sure the gear is in neutral.
* (c) Switch off the engine and apply the handbrake.

Q.
CD0152
What precaution should you take when allowing passengers to get out of your bus or minibus?

Ans. * (a) Ensure that they get out of the side away from the centre of the road.
    (b) Ensure that there is no oncoming traffic.
    (c) Ask them to get out as quickly as possible.
    (d) Watch for traffic in your rear-view mirrors and advise them when to get out.

DRIVING IN TUNNELS

Q.
CD0153
You intend to drive through a tunnel. You should .....

Ans. * (a) check that the height of your vehicle is less than the signed limit.
      (b) stop regularly to inspect the load.
      (c) carry the minimum amount of fuel in case of fire.
      (d) drive in a lower gear than normal to reduce exhaust pollution.
      (e) drive close to the vehicle in front to reduce congestion.

Q.
CD0154
You intend to drive through a tunnel. You should .....

Ans.   (a) carry extra fuel.
    * (b) check the tunnel height before starting your journey.
      (c) check for a weight limit.
      (d) disengage the global positioning system.
      (e) check the tunnel height as you approach it.

Q.
CD0156
Select 2 answers. Before entering a tunnel, you should .....

Ans.   (a) register at the first tunnel station.
      (b) wear sunglasses, if available, to prevent glare from the lights.
    * (c) take off your sunglasses.
    * (d) keep a safe distance.
      (e) drive compact to the vehicle in front.

Q. When driving through a tunnel, you should .....

CD0157

Ans.
    (a) drive close to the central dividing line.
* (b) maintain a safer distance from the vehicle in front.
    (c) monitor the exhaust filtering system to your vehicle.
    (d) drive with full headlights switched on.
    (e) reduce the tyre pressures to improve grip.

Q. In a tunnel if there is unexpected traffic congestion, you should .....

CD0158

Ans.
    (a) keep compact to the vehicle in front.
    (b) leave your vehicle.
    (c) keep a greater distance from the vehicle in front.
* (d) switch on your hazard warning lights.
    (e) stop at the nearest emergency exit.

Q. When halted by stationary traffic in a tunnel, you should .....

CD0159

Ans.
    (a) select a low gear, and keep the engine ticking over.
    (b) switch on your fog lights.
* (c) switch off the engine.
    (d) only give hand signals.

Q. Select 3 answers. In a tunnel, in the event of a breakdown or accident, you should .....

CD0160

Ans.
    (a) beckon other traffic to overtake.
* (b) switch on your hazard warning lights.
    (c) not use a warning triangle.
* (d) move the vehicle to a lay-by or hard shoulder, if possible, to make room for overtaking traffic.
* (e) call for help from an emergency station.

Q.
CD0161

If your vehicle breaks down in a tunnel, you should .....

Ans.
    (a) hitch a lift to the nearest service area and get help.
    (b) flag down a passing motorist and ask for help.
    (c) wait in the vehicle until help arrives.
    (d) walk to the end of the tunnel and call the police.
* (e) use the emergency telephone to call for help.

Q.
CD0162

Select 2 answers. In a tunnel, in the event of a breakdown or accident, you should .....

Ans. * (a) call for help from an emergency station.
    (b) reverse the vehicle, if necessary, to make room for overtaking traffic.
    (c) beckon other traffic to overtake.
* (d) switch on your hazard warning lights.

Q.
CD0163

While driving in a tunnel your vehicle goes on fire. You should .....

Ans.
    (a) drive to the nearest emergency station.
    (b) drive to the nearest emergency exit.
    (c) wait for the tunnel traffic radio to announce procedure.
    (d) drive to nearest tunnel lay-by.
* (e) leave the vehicle and follow the emergency escape route lights.

TAKING EMERGENCY/CORRECTIVE ACTION

Q.
CD0165

You are driving along in a truck or bus without anti-lock brakes and get a front wheel skid while braking. You should .....

Ans. * (a) release the footbrake.
      (b) turn the steering gently left or right.
      (c) push in the clutch and take your foot off the accelerator.
      (d) apply the footbrake strongly.

ACCIDENTS

Q.
CD0166

How should following traffic be warned in the event of an accident?

Ans. * (a) Place the red warning triangle on the road a short distance back from your vehicle.
      (b) Switch on the vehicle's left-hand indicator.
      (c) Have a passenger or passer-by wave them down.
      (d) Place the red reflectorised triangle on the road at the right back-end of the vehicle.

Q.
CD0167

When should you use the emergency red warning triangle?

Ans.   (a) When loading or unloading your vehicle.
      (b) When reversing on a main road.
  * (c) When an accident or breakdown occurs.
      (d) When loading or unloading your vehicle at night on an unlit road.

ENVIRONMENTAL MATTERS

Q.
CD0168
What should you do to avoid excessive exhaust pollution from your vehicle?

Ans.
   (a) Drive at higher speeds than normal in order to reduce the time spent on the road.
   (b) Use a fuel additive to increase the fuel octane rating.
* (c) Have your vehicle serviced regularly.
   (d) Keep your engine clean and make sure its fluid levels are checked regularly.

Q.
CD0169
Fuel efficiency is improved by .....

Ans.
   (a) accelerating hard up through the gears to reach the desired speed as quickly as possible.
   (b) driving the vehicle in lower gear for as long as possible before changing up.
* (c) using gentle acceleration and making gear changes as recommended by the manufacturer's specification.
   (d) maintaining high average speed.

Q.
CD0170
To reduce exhaust pollution when driving, you should .....

Ans.
   (a) use ultra-high sulphur diesel.
* (b) ensure that the engine is serviced regularly.
   (c) ensure that in damp or very cold weather the engine is covered by a weather sheet insulation.
   (d) ensure that the air-conditioning is used throughout long journeys.

OTHER MATTERS

Q.
CD0171

Select 2 answers. To keep alert when driving a truck at night you should .....

Ans.
    (a) keep the cab warm and comfortable.
    (b) eat a heavy meal in advance.
* (c) keep plenty of cool air circulating in the cab.
    (d) keep plenty of warm air circulating in the cab.
    (e) maintain a high speed so as to finish early.
* (f) take rest periods, preferably walking in fresh air.

Q.
CD0173

You are driving on a slip-road, about to join a motorway. You should .....

Ans.
    (a) stop on the hard shoulder until a gap arises in the traffic which is on the motorway.
    (b) drive along the hard shoulder for a distance until a gap in the traffic allows you to merge.
* (c) try to match your speed to the traffic on the motorway and merge into it gradually as a gap arises.
    (d) use the size of your vehicle to compel other drivers to give way to you.

Q.
CD0174

You are driving up a steep hill and there is a 'slow lane' on the left. You should .....

Ans.
    (a) drive only in the slow lane when towing a trailer.
    (b) drive in the outer lane if your vehicle is unladen.
    (c) straddle the lanes.
* (d) drive in the slow lane.

Q.
CD0175

At a junction with green traffic lights in your favour, elderly people are crossing. You should .....

Ans. * (a) allow them to cross in their own time.
(b) proceed if you can edge your way through.
(c) tell them to be careful and wave them across.
(d) beckon them to return to the side.

Q.
CD0176

Select 3 answers. At road junctions you should take particular care for which of the following most vulnerable road users?

Ans. (a) Tractor drivers.
* (b) Pedestrians.
* (c) Motorcyclists.
* (d) Cyclists.
(e) Car drivers.

Q.
CD0177

Select 3 answers. At traffic lights you should take particular care for which of the following coming up on your left?

Ans. (a) Cars.
* (b) Pedestrians.
* (c) Motorcyclists.
* (d) Cyclists.
(e) Minibuses or vans.

Q. At a pelican crossing or traffic lights pedestrians are crossing after the traffic light facing you shows green. You should .....

CD0178

Ans.
    (a) move off slowly.
    (b) beckon them along as quickly as they can.
    (c) sound your horn as a warning and proceed with care.
 * (d) wait patiently and let them cross at ease.
    (e) rev your engine to encourage them to hurry along.

CHAPTER 2

PART II

CATEGORY C

NECESSARY DOCUMENTS

Q.
C0001
To drive a vehicle with a maximum design gross vehicle weight of 7,500 kgs, you must hold a licence in .....

Ans. (a) Category W.
      (b) Category A1.
* (c) Category C1 or C.
      (d) Category D1 or W.

Q.
C0002
What is the maximum design gross vehicle weight which the holder of a category C1 licence may drive?

Ans. (a) 6,500 kg.
* (b) 7,500 kg.
      (c) 8,500 kg.
      (d) 9,500 kg.

Q.
C0003
In order to obtain an EC (articulated truck) driving licence, a driver must first obtain a licence in category .....

Ans. (a) C1.
* (b) C.
      (c) D.
      (d) EC1.

Q.
C0004

In order to obtain an **EC1 (light rigid truck and trailer)** driving licence, a driver must first obtain a licence in category .....

Ans.

    (a) ED1.

    (b) ED.

*   (c) C1.

    (d) A.

Q.
C0005

In order to obtain an **EC (articulated truck)** driving licence, a driver must be at least what age?

Ans.

    (a) 17 years.

*   (b) 18 years.

    (c) 19 years.

    (d) 21 years.

Q.
C0006

In order to obtain an **EC1 (light rigid truck)** driving licence, a driver must be at least .....

Ans.

    (a) 21 years of age.

    (b) 19 years of age.

    (c) 17 years of age.

*   (d) 18 years of age.

Q.
C0007

Is the holder of a category **C1** licence entitled to tow a trailer?

Ans. *

    (a) Yes, up to 750 kg. gross vehicle weight.

    (b) Yes, up to 1,000 kg. gross vehicle weight.

    (c) No.

    (d) Yes, up to 850 kg. gross vehicle weight.

Q. Is the holder of a category C Learner Permit
entitled to tow a trailer when driving a category
C vehicle?

C0008

Ans. * (a) No.
(b) Yes, provided the unladen weight of the trailer does not exceed the weight of the truck.
(c) Yes, provided the trailer does not exceed 1250 kg. gross vehicle weight.
(d) Yes, provided the trailer is not brought on a motorway.
(e) Yes, provided the trailer does not exceed 750 kg. gross vehicle weight.

Q. Is the holder of a category C driving licence
entitled to tow a trailer when driving a category
C vehicle?

C0009

Ans. (a) Yes, provided the unladen weight of the trailer does not exceed the weight of the truck.
* (b) Yes, provided the trailer does not exceed 750 kg. gross vehicle weight.
(c) Yes, provided the trailer is not brought on a motorway.
(d) Yes, provided the trailer does not exceed 1000 kg. gross vehicle weight.
(e) Yes, provided the trailer does not exceed 1250 kg. gross vehicle weight.

Q. What is the maximum number of passengers that
can be carried by the holder of a category C or C1
licence?

C0010

Ans. (a) 10.
(b) 6.
* (c) 8.
(d) 7.

Q. The plated weight of a vehicle is .....

C0012

Ans. * (a) the gross laden maximum weight at which it is allowed to be driven.

(b) the unladen weight of the vehicle excluding fuel, tools and accessories.

(c) the gross vehicle weight of the vehicle less the unladen weight.

Q. This information sign displayed on your vehicle indicates .....

C0013

Ans. (a) the international freight number.

* (b) the type of material carried.

(c) haulage licence number.

(d) the gross vehicle weight.

SPEED LIMIT

Q. The maximum permitted speed of a truck is .....

C0014

Ans. (a) 60 km/h.

* (b) 80 km/h.

(c) 90 km/h.

(d) 100 km/h.

Q. The maximum permitted speed of a truck on a motorway is .....

C0015

Ans. * (a) 80 km/h.

(b) 90 km/h.

(c) 100 km/h.

(d) 120 km/h.

VEHICLE WEIGHTS AND DIMENSIONS

Q.
C0016

Your articulated truck weighs 44 tonnes g.v.w. It must have .....

Ans. * (a) anti-lock brakes, air suspension and 6 axles.
      (b) 16 forward gear ratios, and speed limiters.
      (c) 16 forward gear ratios, air suspension, and speed limiters.
      (d) 16 forward gear ratios and anti-lock brakes.
      (e) anti-lock brakes, air suspension, and 12 forward gears.

Q.
C0017

What is the maximum permitted laden weight in tonnes of an **EC** articulated truck on **6 axles** with conventional (non air) suspension?

Ans. (a) 36.
      (b) 38.
  * (c) 40.
      (d) 42.
      (e) 44.

Q.
C0018

What is the maximum permitted laden weight in tonnes of a **4 axle rigid truck** with conventional (non air) suspension?

Ans. (a) 25.
  * (b) 30.
      (c) 35.
      (d) 40.

Q.
C0019

What is the maximum permitted laden weight in tonnes of a 4 axle rigid truck with road friendly (air) suspension?

Ans.
    (a) 28.
* (b) 32.
    (c) 36.
    (d) 40.

Q.
C0020

What is the maximum permitted laden weight in tonnes of a 3 axle rigid truck with conventional (non air) suspension?

Ans. * (a) 25.
      (b) 28.
      (c) 30.
      (d) 32.

Q.
C0021

What is the maximum permitted laden weight in tonnes of a 2 axle rigid truck with conventional suspension?

Ans. * (a) 18.
      (b) 20.
      (c) 22.
      (d) 24.

BRAKING SYSTEMS

Q.
C0024

What is the maximum road speed that can be attained by a truck with a speed limiter?

Ans.
    (a) 60 km/h.
    (b) 80 km/h.
* (c) 90 km/h.
    (d) 100 km/h.

Q.
C0025

What is the design gross vehicle weight above which new trucks must be fitted with speed limiter?

Ans.
    (a) 2,000 kg.
    (b) 3,000 kg.
* (c) 3,500 kg.
    (d) 4,500 kg.

Q.
C0026

Trailers over which laden weight are required to be fitted with a braking system?

Ans.
    (a) Trailers which exceed 1,350 kg. in laden weight.
    (b) Trailers which exceed 1,000 kg. in laden weight.
* (c) Trailers which exceed 750 kg. in laden weight.
    (d) Trailers which exceed 1,250 kg. in laden weight.

Q.
C0027

Trailers over which laden weight are required to be fitted with a braking system?

Ans.
    (a) 1/4 the laden weight of the drawing vehicle.
    (b) 2/3 the laden weight of the drawing vehicle.
* (c) 1/2 the laden weight of the drawing vehicle.
    (d) 1/3 the laden weight of the drawing vehicle.

TECHNICAL MATTERS, WITH A BEARING ON ROAD SAFETY

Q. A warning buzzer in the cab usually indicates .....

C0028

Ans.   (a) the lights have been left switched on.
    * (b) low air pressure in the braking system.
      (c) low fuel level.
      (d) low level of radiator fluid.

Q. The airlines at the rear of an uncoupled tractor unit
C0029 should .....

Ans.   (a) be let hang loose at the rear
          of the cab.
      (b) be connected together.
    * (c) be properly secured on hooks.
      (d) have their taps turned on.

Q. Why should the fifth wheel drawing plate on an
C0030 articulated truck be sufficiently greased?

Ans.   (a) To improve fuel efficiency.
      (b) To reduce tyre wear.
      (c) To cushion the weight of the
          trailer.
    * (d) To reduce wear.

Q. After driving over rough or broken ground you
C0031 should check that .....

Ans. * (a) stones are not jammed between the rear double-wheels.
      (b) the air intakes are not blocked.
      (c) the engine temperature is normal.
      (d) the fuel gauge is not stuck.

Q. A 'range change' gearbox allows the driver to .....

C0032

Ans.
    (a) choose between manual and semi-automatic transmission.
    (b) pre-select a gear for a particular purpose.
    (c) select different speeds for the rear wheels.
* (d) select a series of either high or low ratio gears depending on the load being carried and/or the terrain.

Q. A two-speed axle .....

C0033

Ans. *
    (a) doubles the number of gear ratios available to a driver.
    (b) holds the drive-axle at a particular speed when the vehicle is heavily laden.
    (c) allows the driving wheels at the rear of the truck to rotate at different speeds.
    (d) doubles the braking ability available to the driver.

Q. An 'unloader valve' .....

C0034

Ans.
    (a) operates the tailboard platform to facilitate unloading.
* (b) releases excess air pressure in the braking system.
    (c) permits tipper bodies to be raised or lowered.
    (d) releases excess oil pressure from the tipper body system.

SAFETY OF VEHICLE LOADING

Q.
C0035
Select 2 answers. Which of the following should you consider for load distribution?

Ans. * (a) That individual axle weights are not exceeded.
* (b) That gross vehicle weight is not exceeded.
(c) That any part of the load to be first removed is at the rear.
(d) That any part of the load to be first removed is at the front.

Q.
C0036
Select 2 answers. Which of the following should you ensure when part of the load has been removed?

Ans. (a) That the remaining load is moved to the rear.
(b) That the gross vehicle weight is not reduced.
* (c) That none of the axles have become overloaded because of transfer of weight.
* (d) That the remaining load is evenly distributed.
(e) Whether any of the load is over the cab unit.

Q.
C0037
Select 2 answers. Loads should .....

Ans. * (a) not cause danger or nuisance to other road users.
(b) not be more than 5 metres in width.
(c) be distributed so that no part is over the tractor unit.
* (d) not cause the front axle weight to exceed the rear axle weight.

Q.
C0039

How might an unevenly distributed load affect a truck?

Ans.
    (a) Overall fuel consumption is improved.
* (b) The truck's stability is adversely affected.
    (c) Gears are more difficult to change.
    (d) Acceleration is reduced.

Q.
C0040

What effect does sharp braking have on a loosely secured load?

Ans.
    (a) The load tends to go to the rear of the vehicle.
    (b) The load scatters to all sides of the vehicle.
    (c) The load remains stable.
* (d) The load tends to go to the front of the vehicle.

Q.
C0041

What effect does increasing the load have on your vehicle's braking ability?

Ans. * (a) It increases the normal stopping distance required.
    (b) It reduces the normal stopping distance required.
    (c) It has no effect provided the brakes are in good condition.
    (d) It has no effect provided the shock absorbers are in good condition.

Q.
C0042

How does air-suspension affect a vehicle's carrying capacity compared to conventional suspension?

Ans. * (a) It allows extra weight to be carried.
    (b) It requires that less weight be carried.
    (c) It allows you to distribute the load unevenly.
    (d) It makes no difference.

Q. **What additional precautions should be taken when transporting bulk liquid?**

C0043

Ans. * (a) The tanks should be sectioned off.
      (b) Tyre pressures should be increased.
      (c) Short sharp braking movements should be used to bring the vehicle to a halt.
      (d) Tyre pressure should be reduced.

Q. **How should a load of loose dusty material be carried?**

C0044

Ans. * (a) It should be covered with a tarpaulin or sheeting.
      (b) It should remain uncovered.
      (c) It should be dampened down with a water-hose.
      (d) It should be covered with a net.

Q. **When carrying hazardous materials, you should ensure that .....**

C0045

Ans. (a) you drive only at night in built up areas.
      (b) you have a telephone in the vehicle.
  * (c) you comply with the regulations on the conveyance of dangerous substances by road.
      (d) you have permission from the Garda Síochána for the load.

Q. **When carrying out an inspection under a raised tipper body. You should ensure that .....**

C0046

Ans. (a) the body is raised to its full extent.
      (b) the hydraulic oil reservoir is full.
  * (c) the body is supported by props.
      (d) the engine is running so as to prevent the body from collapsing.

Q.
C0047

What should you be aware of when tipping a load from your vehicle?

Ans. * (a) Overhead cables, or power-lines.
(b) That the tipping mechanism is engaged before opening the tail gate.
(c) That you should drive forward for a distance in order to ensure complete discharge of the load.
(d) That the body is fully raised before opening the tail gate.

Q.
C0050

The maximum weight, which an axle is designed to carry .....

Ans. * (a) may not be exceeded.
(b) may be exceeded on journeys of less than 80 kilometres from the depot or base.
(c) may be exceeded when heavy-duty suspension is added.
(d) may be exceeded when extra or wider wheels are added.

Q.
C0051

A lifting axle .....

Ans. (a) is coupled to a power take-off unit which operates an accessory such as a crane or winch.
* (b) may be raised or lowered depending on the load being carried.
(c) is adjustable for different road types.

Q.
C0053

When braking to bring an articulated tanker vehicle to a stop on a straight road, the liquid load may .....

Ans. * (a) push the vehicle forward.
(b) push the vehicle to the side.
(c) make the trailer wheels bounce.
(d) make the trailer wheels skid.

Q. If driving a tanker where the tank is not divided into
C0054 compartments and which is half full, when coming to
a stop you should .....

Ans. * (a) ease off the footbrake.
    (b) avoid using the footbrake.
    (c) pump the footbrake.
    (d) use the parking brake.

Q. Ropes are unsuitable to tie down a load of girders
C0055 because they .....

Ans. (a) are hard to tie.
    (b) will loosen when wet.
    (c) will loosen when dry.
* (d) wear and snap.

Q. A truck carrying loose sand should be covered to .....
C0056

Ans. (a) prevent the sand from entering the fuel.
    (b) prevent the sand from entering the air intake.
* (c) prevent the sand from blowing away.
    (d) improve stability.

Q. Jack-knifing of an articulated truck is more likely to
C0058 occur when the trailer is .....

Ans. (a) loaded at the front.
* (b) loaded at the rear.
    (c) unloaded.
    (d) fully loaded.

Q. It is important to distribute the weight evenly over the axles when loading to .....

C0059

Ans.   (a) facilitate easy unloading.
         (b) facilitate easy loading.
         (c) make it easier to cover.
    * (d) ensure maximum stability.

Q. You are loading an **ISO** cargo container. Which of the following is true?

C0060

Ans.   (a) Its own weight will secure it.
         (b) The twist locks must be open.
    * (c) The twist locks must be secured.
         (d) The container should be tied in place.

Q. Who is responsible if you drive an overloaded truck?

C0061

Ans.   (a) The transport manager.
    * (b) Both the driver, and the owner.
         (c) The owner only.
         (d) The driver only.

Q. Who is responsible for making sure that a trucks load is secure during your journey?

C0062

Ans.   (a) The transport manager.
    * (b) The driver.
         (c) The warehouse loader.
         (d) The driver's helper.

Q.
C0064

You must make an urgent delivery of a container, but you notice that some of the twist-locks, or container securing devices, are broken. You should .....

Ans. (a) drive at a reduced speed with a red flag to the rear of the vehicle.
(b) adjust the diff-lock to secure the container.
* (c) not drive until the twist-locks have been repaired or replaced.
(d) adjust the load-sensing valve on the truck.
(e) use ropes or straps to secure the container.

Q.
C0065

Twist locks should be used to secure .....

Ans. (a) the wheels when parking on a hill.
(b) the steering when parking.
* (c) a steel cargo container onto the vehicle or trailer.
(d) the plate for securing the trailer to the tractor unit.

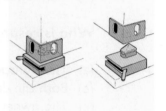

Q.
C0066

Steel girders should be loaded so as to .....

Ans. (a) be protected from the elements.
(b) place most of the weight over the front axles.
(c) place most of the weight over the rear axles.
(d) ensure they are not protruding at the rear of the vehicle.
* (e) ensure the weight is distributed evenly on the vehicle.

Q.
C0067

When carrying a load of steel girders, you should .....

Ans.
    (a) ensure that your vehicle is equipped with amber flashing warning lights.
    (b) stack them on their edges.
* (c) secure them with strong chains or similar devices.
    (d) stack them in a pyramid in the centre of the vehicle body.

Q.
C0068

When carrying a load of steel scaffolding poles, you should .....

Ans.
    (a) secure the bottom poles, and stack the rest on top.
    (b) secure them firmly with ropes.
* (c) secure them firmly with strong chains or similar devices.
    (d) secure them firmly with elastic ties.

Q.
C0069

When cornering with a load of steel girders, the momentum will tend to .....

Ans.
    (a) push the vehicle into the bend.
* (b) push the vehicle away from the bend.
    (c) keep the vehicle stable on the road.
    (d) help to reduce the vehicle speed.
    (e) be stabilised by the vehicle's power steering.

Q.
C0070

Your load of steel girders comes loose as you drive along. You should .....

Ans.
    (a) ring the Gardaí to warn other drivers.
* (b) stop in a safe place and have the load re-secured.
    (c) switch on headlights to warn other drivers.
    (d) drive more slowly to your destination.
    (e) increase speed to shorten the journey time.

Q.
C0071

An ISO cargo container on a vehicle should be secured to the vehicle with .....

Ans.

   (a) wooden stays and chocks.
   (b) chains.
   (c) ropes.
   (d) leather straps.
* (e) twist locks.

Q.
C0072

Select 2 answers. Before reversing into this loading bay, you should .....

Ans. * (a) check for presence of other people.
     (b) ensure the trailer brake is on.
  * (c) make sure the cargo doors are open.
     (d) make sure the cargo doors are closed.

Q.
C0073

Before using a tail lift, you should ensure that .....

Ans.

   (a) the wheels are chocked.
   (b) the handbrake is off.
   (c) the engine is running.
* (d) the ground is level.

Q.
C0074

When using a tail lift, you should ensure that .....

Ans.

   (a) there is a helper present.
* (b) there are no pedestrians or vehicles present.
   (c) the engine is running.
   (d) the diff-lock is engaged.

Q.
C0075

When using a tail lift, it is recommended that which of the following be fitted to the lift?

Ans.
    (a) Green flashing beacons.
    (b) Red flashing beacons.
 * (c) High visibility markers.
    (d) Amber flashing beacons.

Q.
C0078

When driving a truck with hazardous goods/ substances who is responsible for ensuring that a hazchem sign is displayed?

Ans.
    (a) The fleet manager.
    (b) The owner.
    (c) The loader.
 * (d) The driver.

Q.
C0081

What is the maximum permitted distance between a drawing vehicle and a trailer?

Ans.
    (a) 1 metre.
    (b) 2 metres.
    (c) 3 metres.
    (d) 4 metres.
 * (e) 4.5 metres.

Q.
C0082

A warning device, or a flag, must be attached to a drawbar when the distance between the towing vehicle and trailer exceeds .....

Ans.
    (a) 5.5 metres.
    (b) 3.5 metres.
    (c) 2.5 metres.
 * (d) 1.5 metres.
    (e) 4.5 metres.

VEHICLE SAFETY EQUIPMENT

Q.
C0083

What colour rear markings must be fitted to a category C type vehicle?

Ans. * (a) Red fluorescent and red reflectorised stripes.
(b) Black and amber reflectorised stripes.
(c) Red and amber reflectorised stripes.
(d) Black and red reflectorised stripes.

Q.
C0084

What is the purpose of rear under-run barriers?

Ans. * (a) To prevent cars or light goods vehicles from going under the body of the vehicle from the rear.
(b) To facilitate access to the side and rear doors.
(c) To prevent the theft of the spare wheel and tools.
(d) To stabilise the rear of the vehicle when loaded.

GETTING OUT FROM THE VEHICLE

Q.
C0085

How should a driver get out of a truck cab?

Ans. (a) Jump clearly to the ground.
(b) Use the steps and hand-rails provided while facing away from the cab.
* (c) Use the steps and hand-rails provided while facing towards the cab.

ENVIRONMENTAL MATTERS

Q.
C0086

Select 3 answers. When leaving a construction site or quarry, you should ensure that .....

Ans.   (a)   the retarder is engaged.
 *   (b)   the wheels and mudguards are not covered with mud and debris.
 *   (c)   the tailboard is secured.
 *   (d)   no stones are lodged between the twin-wheels.
       (e)   the diff-lock is engaged.

OTHER MATTERS

Q.
C0087

The hard shoulder of a motorway may be used when .....

Ans.   (a)   stopping the vehicle so the driver can rest.
       (b)   stopping to receive a call on a mobile phone.
       (c)   overtaking on the left.
       (d)   parking in order to transfer cargo to a smaller truck or van.
 *   (e)   stopping in an emergency or breakdown.
       (f)   a learner truck driver is under instruction on motorway driving.

Q.
C0088

You are late with a delivery and there is a bus lane on the left, just up ahead. During the hours indicated you may .....

Ans.
    (a) drive in it if you intend to turn left up ahead.
    (b) drive in it if your delivery is to be made just up ahead.
* (c) not drive in it.
    (d) use it for a short distance.

Q.
C0089

Select 2 answers. What should you be aware of when mounting a tanker .....

Ans. * (a) slipping off.
    (b) that the tank is empty before you mount.
    (c) that you wear stud capped boots.
* (d) overhead cables.

CHAPTER 2

PART III

CATEGORY D

NECESSARY DOCUMENTS

Q.
D0001

In order to obtain an **ED (large coach and trailer)** driving licence, a driver must first obtain a licence in category .....

Ans.
    (a) ED1.
* (b) D.
    (c) EC.
    (d) D1.

Q.
D0002

In order to obtain an **ED1 (minibus and trailer)** driving licence, a driver must first obtain a licence in category .....

Ans.
    (a) EC1.
* (b) D1.
    (c) EC.
    (d) A.

Q.
D0003

Is the holder of a category **D or D1 Learner Permit** allowed to carry passengers for hire or reward while driving a bus?

Ans.
    (a) Yes.
* (b) No.
    (c) Yes during the second or subsequent Learner Permit.
    (d) Yes, when there are 8 or fewer passengers.

Q.

D0005

You hold a category D1 driving licence and hold a category D Learner Permit. You are taking driving lessons to obtain a category D licence. Must you display 'L' plates on the bus or coach?

Ans.

(a) Not while being accompanied by a qualified driver holding a category D licence.

(b) No, provided the bus is fitted with an exhaust brake.

* (c) Yes.

(d) Yes, if driving on a motorway.

(e) No, provided the bus is fitted with speed limiters.

Q.

D0006

You hold a full D1 licence and you are taking driving lessons in order to obtain a full D licence, must you be accompanied by the holder of a full category D Licence?

Ans. * (a) Yes.

(b) No, provided your insurance company has been notified.

(c) No, provided you do not carry passengers for reward.

(d) No, provided you are operating on a scheduled service and you don't travel more than 50 km from your base.

Q.

D0007

You hold a full category D licence which is restricted to automatic transmission (code 78). May you drive a conventional manual bus or coach with that licence?

Ans.

(a) Yes, provided you do not carry passengers for reward.

* (b) No.

(c) Yes, provided you are operating on a scheduled service and you do not go more than 50 km from your base.

(d) Yes, provided you do not carry more than 8 passengers.

Q. **A Public Service Vehicle licence is required .....**

D0008

Ans. * (a) when driving a vehicle which is carrying passengers for reward.
      (b) only if driving a school bus.
      (c) only if driving a taxi or hackney-cab.
      (d) only if driving a vehicle with passenger accommodation for more than eight persons.

Q. **A Road Passenger Certificate must be held by .....**

D0009

Ans. (a) a bus or coach driver for a vehicle with passenger capacity for more than 16 persons.
    * (b) a person or firm with a business involved in the transporting by road of persons for reward.
      (c) a sports club or charity involved in transporting by road persons other than for reward.
      (d) a bus driver.

SPEED LIMIT

Q. **The maximum permitted speed on a motorway of a single-deck bus or minibus (having passenger accommodation for more than 8 persons) which is not designed to carry standing passengers is .....**

D0060

Ans. (a) 65 km/h.
      (b) 70 km/h.
      (c) 80 km/h.
    * (d) 100 km/h.
      (e) 120 km/h.

Q.

D0061

The maximum permitted speed on a dual-carriageway of a single-deck bus or minibus (having passenger accommodation for more than 8 persons) which is not designed to carry standing passengers is .....

Ans.
- (a) 55 km/h.
- (b) 60 km/h.
- (c) 70 km/h.
- (d) 80 km/h.
- * (e) 100 km/h.

Q.

D0062

The maximum permitted speed on a national primary road of a single-deck bus or minibus (having passenger accommodation for more than 8 persons) which is not designed to carry standing passengers is .....

Ans.
- (a) 55 km/h.
- (b) 60 km/h.
- (c) 70 km/h.
- * (d) 80 km/h.
- (e) 100 km/h.

Q.

D0063

The maximum permitted speed on a motorway of a double-deck bus or minibus (having passenger accommodation for more than 8 persons) which is not designed to carry standing passengers is .....

Ans.
- (a) 65 km/h.
- (b) 70 km/h.
- (c) 75 km/h.
- (d) 80 km/h.
- * (e) 100 km/h.

Q.
D0064

The maximum permitted speed on a dual-carriage way of a double-deck bus or minibus (having passenger accommodation for more than 8 persons) which is not designed to carry standing passengers is .....

Ans.
    (a) 55 km/h.
    (b) 60 km/h.
    (c) 80 km/h.
* (d) 100 km/h.
    (e) 110 km/h.

Q.
D0065

The maximum permitted speed on a national primary road of a double-deck bus or minibus (having passenger accommodation for more than 8 persons) which is not designed to carry standing passengers is .....

Ans.
    (a) 50 km/h.
    (b) 55 km/h.
    (c) 65 km/h.
* (d) 80 km/h.
    (e) 100 km/h.

Q.
D0066

The maximum permitted speed on a motorway of a single-deck bus or minibus (having passenger accommodation for more than 8 persons) which is designed to carry standing passengers is .....

Ans. * (a) 65 km/h.
    (b) 70 km/h.
    (c) 80 km/h.
    (d) 100 km/h.
    (e) 120 km/h.

Q.

D0067

The maximum permitted speed on a dual-carriageway of a single-deck bus or minibus (having passenger accommodation for more than 8 persons) which is designed to carry standing passengers is .....

Ans.

    (a) 55 km/h.

    (b) 60 km/h.

* (c) 65 km/h.

    (d) 80 km/h.

    (e) 100 km/h.

Q.

D0068

The maximum permitted speed on a national primary road of a single-deck bus or minibus (having passenger accommodation for more than 8 persons) which is designed to carry standing passengers is .....

Ans.

    (a) 60 km/h.

* (b) 65 km/h.

    (c) 70 km/h.

    (d) 80 km/h.

    (e) 100 km/h.

Q.

D0069

The maximum permitted speed on a motorway of a double-deck bus or minibus (having passenger accommodation for more than 8 persons) which is designed to carry standing passengers is .....

Ans. * (a) 65 km/h.

    (b) 70 km/h.

    (c) 75 km/h.

    (d) 80 km/h.

    (e) 100 km/h.

Q. The maximum permitted speed on a dual-carriageway of a double-deck bus or minibus (having passenger accommodation for more than 8 persons) which is designed to carry standing passengers is .....

D0070

Ans.
    (a) 55 km/h.
    (b) 60 km/h.
* (c) 65 km/h.
    (d) 75 km/h.
    (e) 80 km/h.

Q. The maximum permitted speed on a national primary road of a double-deck bus or minibus (having passenger accommodation for more than 8 persons) which is designed to carry standing passengers is .....

D0071

Ans.
    (a) 50 km/h.
    (b) 55 km/h.
* (c) 65 km/h.
    (d) 80 km/h.
    (e) 85 km/h.

VEHICLE WEIGHTS AND DIMENSIONS

Q. The maximum permitted weight in tonnes of a two-axled bus is .....

D0016

Ans.
    (a) 16.
    (b) 17.
* (c) 18.
    (d) 19.

Q.
D0017

What is the maximum permitted width of a bus?

Ans.   (a) 2.20 metres.
       (b) 1.59 metres.
    * (c) 2.55 metres.
       (d) 2.81 metres.

Q.
D0018

What is the maximum permitted height of a double-deck bus?

Ans. * (a) 4.57 metres.
       (b) 5.57 metres.
       (c) 6.57 metres.
       (d) 6.00 metres.

BRAKING SYSTEMS

Q.
D0019

What is the maximum speed governor setting for buses?

Ans. * (a) 100 km/h.
       (b) 120 km/h.
       (c) 80 km/h.
       (d) 75 km/h.

Q.
D0020

What is the minimum gross vehicle weight above which buses must be fitted with a speed governor?

Ans.   (a) 8,000 kg.
       (b) 9,000 kg.
    * (c) 10,000 kg.
       (d) 12,000 kg.

Q.   **What buses are required to have a speed limiter**
D0021   **fitted?**

Ans.   (a)   Double-deck buses only.
     (b)   Buses with more than 16 passenger seats and a g.v.w. of
           more than 10,000 kg.
  *   (c)   Buses with more than 8 passenger seats.
     (d)   Accordion/bendi buses only.

WEATHER RELATED MATTERS

Q.   **What effect can strong crosswinds have on a**
D0022   **double-deck bus?**

Ans.   *   (a)   It makes it more liable to turn over.
     (b)   It reduces braking time.
     (c)   It increases braking time.
     (d)   It increases fuel efficiency.

CARRYING PASSENGERS

Q.   **How many passengers may you carry on your bus?**
D0023

Ans.   *   (a)   As many as your PSV licence allows you.
     (b)   As many as there are seats available.
     (c)   As many as can fit in without a crush.
     (d)   As many as there are seats available, plus three standing.

Q.
D0024

What is the maximum number of adult passengers which a D1 licence entitles you to carry in your minibus?

Ans.
    (a) 14.
*   (b) 16.
    (c) 18.
    (d) 12.

Q.
D0026

When driving your bus your responsibility is .....

Ans.
    (a) keeping to a set timetable.
*   (b) the safety and comfort of your passengers.
    (c) that the destination notice is visible.
    (d) to ensure that cruise control is only operated in built up areas.

Q.
D0027

You are about to move off after picking up some passengers. You should check .....

Ans.
    (a) the right-hand mirror.
*   (b) both wing mirrors.
    (c) the left-hand mirror and interior mirror.
    (d) the left-hand mirror.

Q.
D0028

What effect could overloading with passengers or goods have on a vehicle?

Ans.
    (a) It does not have any effect provided you drive slowly.
*   (b) It can lessen the vehicle's road-holding ability.
    (c) It can reduce the vehicle's tyre pressure.
    (d) It can improve the vehicle's road-holding ability.

Q.
D0029

When carrying children, when should the passenger doors be locked?

Ans. * (a) When a child might open a door while the bus is moving.
(b) Never, as easy entry and exit from the bus or minibus is essential for safety.
(c) Only when there are not enough seat-belts for passengers.
(d) Only when there is not an adult attendant on the bus.

Q.
D0030

You are the driver of a double-deck bus. How would you monitor passengers on the top deck? By .....

Ans. (a) asking someone to watch over them.
(b) checking upstairs when parked at bus stops.
(c) listening for sounds upstairs.
* (d) frequent use of the internal mirrors and camera, if fitted.

Q.
D0031

While driving, the internal mirrors on a double-deck bus are used for watching for .....

Ans. (a) traffic on your right-hand side.
(b) any overtaking traffic.
* (c) passengers using the stairs.
(d) cyclists coming on your left-hand side.

Q.
D0032

Select 4 answers. For safety and comfort of your passengers you should .....

Ans. * (a) brake gently.
* (b) plan well ahead.
* (c) stop close to the kerb.
(d) stop away from the kerb.
* (e) accelerate smoothly.
(f) always drive with the air vents open.

Q.
D0033

Select 2 answers. On which of the following occasions would passengers most likely be thrown about. When the bus is .....

Ans.
     (a) reversing slowly.
     (b) turning right.
  * (c) braking severely.
  * (d) cornering harshly.
     (e) changing lane.
     (f) overtaking.

Q.
D0034

Select 2 answers. You should show care to your passengers by which of the following .....

Ans.
     (a) not speaking when collecting fares.
  * (b) allowing them time to get seated.
     (c) reaching destinations on time.
  * (d) not exceeding the permitted number of passengers.
     (e) driving with skylight only partly opened.

Q.
D0035

Select 4 answers. You should accelerate smoothly in order to .....

Ans. * (a) reduce wear on the engine.
  * (b) reduce wear on the tyres.
     (c) reduce wear on the gears.
  * (d) improve fuel consumption.
  * (e) improve passenger comfort.
     (f) reduce wear on the clutch.

Q.
D0036

When may you carry a passenger on the trailer of a bus?

Ans.
     (a) When the bus has no more than 16 passenger seats.
     (b) Only when you hold a category ED licence.
  * (c) Never.
     (d) Only when there are fixed passenger seats in the trailer.

SAFETY OF VEHICLE LOADING

Q.
D0037

Where should passengers' luggage be stowed?

Ans.
    (a) In the passageway.
    (b) Behind the seats.
 * (c) In the luggage compartment and hand luggage in the overhead rack.
    (d) Under the seats.

VEHICLE SAFETY EQUIPMENT

Q.
D0038

What safety equipment must be carried on your bus or minibus?

Ans. * (a) Fire extinguisher and first aid kit.
     (b) Fire extinguisher, fan, and public address system.
     (c) First aid kit and public address system.
     (d) First aid kit and safety flares.

GETTING OUT FROM THE VEHICLE

Q.
D0039

Your bus has a driver's door on the offside. You should exit the cab by .....

Ans.
    (a) jumping gently to the ground.
    (b) climbing down facing outwards.
 * (c) climbing down facing inwards.
    (d) climbing down forward using the door as support.

Q. When should the passengers' door be opened on
D0040 your bus or minibus?

Ans. (a) When travelling in a built up area at low speeds.
(b) When within 15 metres of a bus stop.
* (c) Only when stopped at a place which is safe for
passengers to get out.
(d) In bad weather when visibility is poor and you need to
check for traffic coming from behind.

Q. You are a school bus driver advising children about
D0041 alighting from your bus. You should advise them .....

Ans. (a) not to talk while getting from the bus.
* (b) to stay well in off the road until the bus has moved away.
(c) to only cross from the rear of the bus.
(d) to only cross in front of the bus so that you can observe
them crossing.

Q. What should you do when you wish to stop to allow
D0042 passengers to get off your bus?

Ans. (a) Stop as close as possible to a junction.
* (b) Stop where they will not be in danger from other traffic.
(c) Pull up on the footpath.
(d) Stop as close as possible to their destination.

Q. Select 2 answers. When driving, you should be aware
D0043 that .....

Ans. (a) emergency doors, on the upper deck must be locked.
(b) the passenger doors on an articulated compartment
must be locked.
* (c) the passenger doors should never be locked.
* (d) the emergency door should never be locked.
(e) the emergency doors should be locked to prevent exit
between scheduled route stops.

Q.

D0044

Select 2 answers. Your bus has been involved in an accident where fuel has spilled on to the road, and nobody is injured, you should firstly .....

Ans.

    (a) dilute the fuel on the road with water before disembarking the passengers.

* (b) get the passengers to a safe area as quickly as possible.

* (c) warn passengers not to smoke.

    (d) wipe up the fuel on the road before disembarking the passengers.

Q.

D0045

Your bus is broken down in the middle of the road following a crash. There are no injuries. What should you do?

Ans.

    (a) Ask your passengers to remain seated until help arrives.

    (b) Ask your passengers to make a dash to the roadside.

* (c) Guide each passenger individually to the roadside.

    (d) Have all the passengers disembark in a group.

Q.

D0046

What should you do first if your bus or minibus is disabled in a crash where there are no injuries?

Ans. * (a) Guide your passengers to safety.

    (b) Ask your passengers to remain in their seats.

    (c) Ensure the gears are left in neutral except on a hill.

    (d) Ensure all doors are locked.

    (e) Place a red warning triangle on the road.

Q.

D0047

Your bus or coach is involved in a collision on a motorway, you should .....

Ans. * (a) ask the passengers to remain in their seats unless there is a risk of fire.

(b) ask the passengers to leave their seats and then move the bus to the hard shoulder.

(c) move the bus to the hard shoulder and then ask the passengers to leave their seats.

(d) ask the passengers to give any injured persons something to drink.

Q.

D0048

Your vehicle has broken down on an automatic railway level crossing. What should you do first?

Ans. * (a) Phone the signal operator so that trains can be stopped.

(b) Walk along the track to give warning to any approaching trains.

(c) Try to push the vehicle clear of the crossing as soon as possible.

(d) Turn on the warning bells at the crossing.

Q.
D0049

In this situation, when entering the minor road you should .....

Ans.

    (a) approach tight on the left-hand side, mounting the kerb if necessary.

    (b) ensure the bus does not cross the central dividing line of the minor road.

    (c) ensure the bus does not cross the central dividing line of the main road.

  * (d) take adequate space to avoid mounting the kerb.

Q.
D0050

Select 2 answers. Driving smoothly should .....

Ans. * (a) reduce tyre wear.

    * (b) preserve the condition of your bus, thus reducing maintenance costs.

    (c) reduce the number of occasions you need to change the anti-waxing agent.

    (d) increase the risk of skidding.

    (e) increase fuel consumption.

Q.
D0051

Which of the following would you check for in your left-hand side mirror?

Ans.   (a) That the driver's door is closed properly.

    * (b) For vehicles coming up on the left.

    (c) If passengers are standing.

    (d) That the left-side indicator is working.

Q. D0052

Select 2 answers. When leaving the cab of your bus, which of the following is important? That .....

Ans. * (a) the parking brake is on.
* (b) you watch for any approaching traffic.
(c) the emergency door is open.
(d) the engine is left running.

Q. D0053

Select 2 answers. When leaving the cab of your bus, which of the following is important? That .....

Ans. (a) the public address radio is on.
(b) the retarder brake is on.
* (c) you operate the electrical master switch.
* (d) the engine is switched off.

Q. D0054

Select 3 answers. When driving through a bus station you should .....

Ans. (a) turn off the public address system
* (b) drive in low speed.
* (c) watch out for people leaving or boarding other buses.
* (d) use your mirrors more than normal.
(e) not sound the horn.
(f) turn on the public address system.

Q. D0055

Select 2 answers. You should use your hazard warning lights .....

Ans. * (a) to warn drivers of an unexpected hazard which they may not be able to see.
(b) when driving on a contra-flow bus lane.
(c) when driving in a with-flow bus lane.
* (d) when you have broken down.

Q.
D0056

Air suspension systems fitted to a bus gives .....

Ans.
    (a) reduced fuel consumption.
    (b) uneven tyre wear.
    (c) faster acceleration.
* (d) a comfortable ride for passengers.

Q.
D0057

Compared to a bus with air suspension, a bus with spring leaf suspension gives .....

Ans.
    (a) a more comfortable ride for passengers.
* (b) a less comfortable ride for passengers.
    (c) better road holding.
    (d) better tyre wear.

Q.
D0058

The hard shoulder of a motorway may be used for .....

Ans.
    (a) letting passengers on a long journey stretch their legs in a short walk.
    (b) overtaking on the left.
* (c) stopping in an emergency.
    (d) picking up or setting down passengers.
    (e) stopping the vehicle so the driver can rest.

Q.
D0059

Select 4 answers. Which of the following should you be aware of before moving off?

Ans. * (a) The effect of any sudden moving of the bus.
      * (b) Persons attempting to get on the bus.
      * (c) Persons attempting to get off the bus.
         (d) That all passengers have a bus pass.
      * (e) Standing passengers upstairs.
         (f) That all mobile phones are turned off.

NOTES

NOTES

NOTES